TREES OF
PENNSYLVANIA
AND THE NORTHEAST

TREES OF PENNSYLVANIA

AND THE NORTHEAST

Charles Fergus

illustrations by Amelia Hansen

STACKPOLE
BOOKS

Copyright © 2002 by Charles Fergus
Illustrations copyright © 2002 by Amelia Hansen

Published by
STACKPOLE BOOKS
5067 Ritter Road
Mechanicsburg, PA 17055
www.stackpolebooks.com

Printed in the United States

10 9 8 7 6 5 4 3 2 1

First edition

Cover design by Wendy Reynolds
Cover photographs by the author

Library of Congress Cataloging-in-Publication Data

Fergus, Charles.
    Trees of Pennsylvania and the Northeast / Charles Fergus ; illustrations by
  Amelia Hansen.— 1st ed.
       p.   cm.
  Includes bibliographical references (p.).
  ISBN 0-8117-2092-6
    1. Trees—Pennsylvania—Identification.   2. Trees—Northeastern States—
Identification.   I. Title.

QK 183 .F47   2002
582.16'09748—dc21
                                  2002021747

CONTENTS

ODD OTHERS

COMMON INTRODUCED TREES

ACKNOWLEDGMENTS

I thank Jim Finley, associate professor in the School of Forest Resources at Penn State, for supplying me with much pertinent information and for reviewing the manuscript of this book. Jim is a good friend and a perceptive and knowledgeable observer of trees and the eastern woods.

Thanks are also due Nancy Marie Brown, Kim Steiner, Jack Schultz, Don Davis, John Skelly, Gary Moorman, Larry McCormick, Kathy Fescemyer, Tom Hall, Jean Fike, Chris Klinedinst Firestone, Ed Dix, Steve Wacker, Mike Kusko, Jim Connor, Butch Davey, Maurice Hobaugh, Jeff Stuffle, Kerry Britton, Olga Alvarado, John Kunsman, Dale Gericke, Phil Sollman, and Nick Bolgiano.

This book is dedicated to the memory of Vaughen T. Smith, who appreciated trees and crafted wonderful things from their wood; and to my father, C. Leonard Fergus, who helped awaken in me a love of trees.

C. F.

I couldn't have finished the illustrations for this book without help. My greatest environmental teacher and guide is John Eastman, whose generous donation of time, energy, wisdom, and friendship enabled me to find trees that I never would have found on my own. Thanks also to Tom Mohill, who more than once cheerfully helped me track down some elusive tree inside the Kalamazoo Nature Center's arboretum. Thanks go to Monica Ann Evans, whose dedication has elevated the arboretum to a place of true scientific value. And thanks go to my husband, Paul, who kept me well fed throughout the project.

A. H.

INTRODUCTION

The importance of trees in Pennsylvania is implicit in the state's name: *Pennsylvania* is Latin for Penn's Woods, the woods of William Penn, the Quaker who founded his New World colony here in 1681. King Charles II bestowed the name upon granting Penn his royal charter. At that time, a primeval forest covered the landscape of Pennsylvania, unbroken save for a few natural openings—bogs and fens, grasslands bordering rivers, and tracts denuded by lightning-sparked fires—as well as patches that Native Americans had cleared for agriculture or had burned off to provide forage for the animals they hunted, including deer. Over the next two centuries, English and European immigrants and their descendants cut down essentially all of the old-growth trees, taking and using their wood and other products and clearing the land to create farms. By 1900, more than two hundred thousand farms and nineteen million acres of farmland had opened more than two-thirds of Pennsylvania to the sun.

In a small book written by an elderly and now-deceased neighbor of mine, there is printed a photograph of our local area. The view was taken around 1900 from the uplift of land known as the Allegheny Front, which forms the western boundary of Bald Eagle Valley. The photograph shows acre after acre of fields, stitched with long stake-and-rider fences. Today most of those fields have vanished beneath trees—including many that I observed and studied in researching this book.

As the twenty-first century opens, seven and a half million acres of Pennsylvania remain as farmland. Much of the rest of the state, including a great deal of marginally fertile land that never yielded much in the way of crops, has reverted to trees. Not necessarily tall, majestic specimens like those that greeted Europeans when they arrived, but members of a younger forest, a new forest, one that is in a state of flux, responding to influences of microscopic pathogens, insect pests, air pollution, rising global temperatures, a huge deer herd, and an expanding, ever more urbanized human population.

Trees, and the forests and copses and woodlots that they form, serve many functions. They limit soil erosion and protect watersheds by soaking up rainfall. They allow other organisms to live, because they release oxygen as a by-product of photosynthesis. They provide shelter for many kinds of wildlife. They help stabilize the earth's climate by absorbing carbon dioxide, a gas produced naturally and by humans burning fossil fuels. They yield wood, which we turn into a plethora of products, including fuel, paper, lumber for building our homes, and items as diverse as clothespins and fine furniture.

Pennsylvania is a meeting place for tree species that exist mainly in the South and northern trees whose ranges extend south into the Keystone State. Our 108 species represent a truly diverse sylvan flora. Today some authorities recognize five broad forest communities in Pennsylvania (see the map on page xii).

Trees can be separated into two general categories: needle-leaved and broad-leaved. The needle-leaved species, which number only 12 of the 108 natives, are the older, less highly evolved group. They include fir, hemlock, spruces, tamarack, pines, and cedars. Their needlelike foliage performs the same function as do the leaves of the broad-leaved species: capture sunlight and then use it, in combination with water and nutrients picked up by the roots, to create carbohydrates, which fuel the tree's growth and reproduction. The needle-leaved trees are sometimes called conifers, because they bear their seeds in woody cones. (Some of the broad-leaved species also present their seeds in cones or conelike structures.) Often people call the needle-leaved trees evergreens, as they hold on to their verdant needles for more than one growing season, although one of the needle-bearing species, tamarack, sheds its needles each fall, right along with the broad-leaved trees.

The broad-leaved species evolved later than the needle-leaved trees. Instead of needles, broad-leaved trees possess leaves: flattened blades of different shapes and sizes, depending on the individual tree and the species. Photosynthesis takes place just below the surface of the leaves. Broad-leaved trees shed their foliage in autumn; if they did not, snow and ice would build up on the leaves, tearing them off and damaging the twigs and branches that bear them. Broad-leaved trees are also known as deciduous, referring to the periodic shedding or falling off of the foliage.

From the time I was a child, I have stood in awe of trees—and not just the huge, impressive ones, but also the multitudinous scraggly types and sprawling sorts and gangly saplings, trees that branch low and trees that tower high. I find trees beautiful, intricate, and reassuring. They are plants, to be certain, but sometimes they seem to have minds of their own; clearly they have strategies—embedded in their genes, if not the product of an intellect—to help them survive and prosper.

Trees are vibrantly alive. They cannot pick up their roots and wander, but they travel through the dispersal of their seeds. They move in the wind. Their leaves flutter or whisper or sing, their branches sway, their trunks groan and creak, their nuts thud the ground. They are steadfast, yet remarkably changeable. An exciting aspect of trees is how different they appear at different times of the year. Trees are a key part of how I perceive nature and sense its ongoing cycle.

In spring, their swollen buds promise that winter's austerity is at an end. Trees put forth flowers, including some that are quite beautiful, if rarely observed, high in the branches—flowers that develop into fruits and nuts of the utmost importance to many wild animals.

Summer's foliage covers up the frameworks of the deciduous trees, a forgivable event since the leaves are so young and soft-appearing and verdant, full of promise, perfect in shape and appearance. The leaves cast shade during the heat of full summer—shade that refreshes the woodland walker, shade that is essential to nesting birds, amphibians dwelling in moist nooks, trout finning in chill streams. The leaves of late summer have become tattered, pinholed, skeletonized, used by life; they remind us that time is limited and must come to an end for every living thing.

The leaves change color in autumn; they shut down their energy-producing process, photosynthesis, as the days grow shorter and light becomes more limited. As their green chlorophyll deteriorates, hidden pigments in the leaves are unmasked, and the forest becomes a kaleidoscope of bright colors set against the abiding green of the needle-leaved trees. The deciduous leaves come flurrying down. On the forest floor, they deteriorate and release elements essential for plant and animal growth. Nuts fall, changing the behavior and patterns of movement of wildlife.

I think I like trees best of all in winter, when their shapes stand out boldly along city streets, above harvested fields, and against the snowy forest floor. The forces and exigencies that affect a tree, and the lifestyle that it follows, can be seen in the shape and stature and soundness of its trunk, in its fruit, limbs, and twigs. Each tree, no matter how twisted or stunted, presents a fundamental and honest beauty.

Forest Communities of Pennsylvania

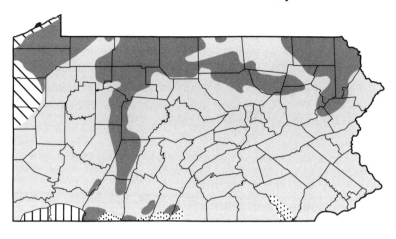

▢ **Appalachian Oak Forest**

▨ **Northern Hardwood Forest**

◩ **Beech and Maple Forest**

▦ **Oak, Hickory, and Pine Forest**

▥ **Mixed Mesophytic Forest**

Forest scientists recognize five major forest communities in Pennsylvania. The map above and the text below are adapted from "Natural Vegetation," by Frederick H. Utech, in *The Atlas of Pennsylvania,* published in 1989 by Temple University Press, Philadelphia. In addition to the trees listed as dominant or common, many other species occur in the different communities.

Appalachian Oak Forest. Dominated by oaks, including white oak *(Quercus alba),* northern red oak *(Quercus rubra),* and chestnut oak *(Quercus montana).* Other common trees are black birch *(Betula lenta),* black-gum *(Nyssa sylvatica),* red maple *(Acer rubrum),* hickories *(Carya* species), tuliptree *(Liriodendron tulipifera),* and white pine *(Pinus strobus).* This forest type cloaks much of the Appalachian Mountain chain from Pennsylvania southward.

Northern Hardwood Forest. This woodland type is sometimes referred to as the beech/birch/maple forest. Common species include sugar maple *(Acer saccharum)*, yellow birch *(Betula alleghaniensis)*, American beech *(Fagus grandifolia)*, eastern hemlock *(Tsuga canadensis)*, white ash *(Fraxinus americana)*, northern red oak *(Quercus rubra)*, black cherry *(Prunus serotina)*, American basswood *(Tilia americana)*, and white pine *(Pinus strobus)*. The northern hardwoods stretch from the Great Lakes states across northern Pennsylvania and through much of New England, with scattered outposts in the southern Appalachians.

Beech and Maple Forest. Sugar maple *(Acer saccharum)* and American beech *(Fagus grandifolia)* are dominant, with black walnut *(Juglans nigra)*, tuliptree *(Liriodendron tulipifera)*, and American basswood *(Tilia americana)* also common. This forest type occurs from Michigan and Indiana east to New York.

Oak, Hickory, and Pine Forest. Dominant trees includes hickories *(Carya* species), Virginia pine *(Pinus virginiana)*, pitch pine *(Pinus rigida)*, white oak *(Quercus alba)*, chestnut oak *(Quercus montana)*, and scarlet oak *(Quercus coccinea)*. This southeastern forest community reaches its northern limit in Pennsylvania.

Mixed Mesophytic Forest. "Mesophytic" refers to a plant growing in an environment that receives a moderate amount of moisture. Some of the many dominant tree species in this forest community are sugar maple *(Accer saccharum)*, yellow buckeye *(Aesculus octandra)*, American beech *(Fagus grandifolia)*, tuliptree *(Liriodendron tulipfera)*, white oak *(Quercus alba)*, northern red oak *(Quercus rubra)*, and American basswood *(Tilia americana)*. This community achieves its best development in West Virginia, Ohio, Kentucky, and Tennessee, as well as Pennsylvania.

NEEDLE-LEAVED TREES

BALSAM FIR

Balsam comes from the ancient Greek *balsamon,* referring to a Middle Eastern shrub from which myrrh, an ingredient in perfume and incense, is obtained. A North American evergreen tree, balsam fir *(Abies balsamea)* earned its name from the fragrance of its needles—an essence that Donald Culross Peattie, in *A Natural History of Trees,* terms "the dearest odor in Nature."

I went looking for balsam fir on a cool July morning at Algerine Swamp Natural Area in Lycoming County, northern Pennsylvania. Hermit thrushes sang from hidden perches, and a ruffed grouse flew up on stuttering wings from the huckleberry shrubs at my feet. I passed through a damp, shady woods just south of the swamp; mosses covered the ground, and dozens of *Boletus* mushrooms gleamed maroon and gold against the viridian carpet. A pleasant, spicy smell entered my consciousness; I realized I'd been getting whiffs of it for some time.

The trees stood all around me. The knee- and waist-high seedlings were strongly cone-shaped. Branches circled each trunk, jutting out laterally from the main stem at nearly right angles. So regular and symmetrical were the tiered boughs that the small trees looked almost artificial. Their limbs held up gleaming, dark green needles; when I stripped off a few and crushed them between my fingers, their fragrance filled the air. In the past, loggers and woodsmen stuffed their pillows with sprays of balsam and made their beds on balsam boughs. For me, the scent evoked memories of campsites on the shores of Minnesota lakes, of laughing cries of loons, of waves lapping against a canoe's hull.

Although common farther north, balsam fir is rare in Pennsylvania. It is the only fir species native to the Northeast. It occurs from northern Labrador, Quebec, and Ontario south through much of New England to

A young balsam fir has a strongly conical shape, with branches extending from the main stem at nearly right angles.

the mountains of Virginia and West Virginia; westward, *Abies balsamea* ranges to northern Alberta.

Balsam fir needles are about 3/4 inch long, flattened, and arranged in a pair of opposing rows that at first glance appear to fringe the twigs. In fact, the needles spiral around the twigs, a characteristic easily discerned through a magnifying lens. You can tell balsam fir from the superficially similar hemlock by the fir's classic steeple shape and the whorled arrangement of its branches (hemlock is more irregular in shape and branch pattern); by the needles attached directly to the twig (hemlock needles stand off on small, woody knobs); and by the 2- to 4-inch cones carried upright in the fir's crown (hemlock's diminutive cones dangle at the branch tips).

As an evergreen, balsam fir holds on to its leaves year-round and thus is able to photosynthesize whenever the sun shines. The balsam fir's thin needles, its conical shape, and its single trunk protect against snow buildup and winter damage.

Each spring, a balsam fir grows vertically from its uppermost leading bud. At the same time, side buds send out whorls of three to six branches, and branches already growing lower on the trunk expand and push farther outward; count the tiers of branches, and you will know the tree's age. Its tapering shape helps a fir shed snow, much as an umbrella sheds rain. When snow starts to cling and build up, the boughs sag downward, resting on those of the next layer below. The cone gradually collapses on itself like a half-closed umbrella, the strong, springy branches bending inward toward the trunk and offering less surface area where snow can accumulate. Should the wind start to blow, the snow may cascade down and the branches rise again.

Balsam fir is a small- to medium-size tree. It generally reaches a height of 30 to 50 feet and occasionally makes 75 feet. The largest balsam fir known in the United States occupies a yard near a house on the outskirts of Fairfield, in Adams County, Pennsylvania. When last measured in 1997, the tree stood 104 feet tall; it was 151 inches in circumference (the arm spread of an average adult male human is about 72 inches) and had a 48.5-foot crown spread. The forester who measured it told me he believed the tree was about sixty years old.

In more natural settings, balsam fir grows in cool swamps and bogs in northern Pennsylvania, and along the edges of these wetlands. At Algerine Swamp, after stumbling onto the balsam fir seedlings, I located the probable parent trees, mixed in with black spruce, eastern hemlock, white pine, and pitch pine. The varied tribe of conifers stood on the mat of sphagnum moss that covered the open, sunny swamp. In New England and Canada, balsam fir often grows on drier sites with quaking aspen, white spruce, and paper birch.

Using a hand lens, I studied the bark of one of the balsam firs. It was light brown, fairly smooth, and stippled with tiny blisters. I punctured one of the blisters with a sharp twig and dabbed up a bit of the intensely fragrant resin. The Penobscot Indians of Maine applied this sticky substance as a plaster onto burns, cuts, and sores, and the loggers who worked in the Maine woods noticed and followed suit. Until recently, the resin found application as a waterproof cement for mounting cover slips over thin-sectioned specimens on microscope slides and for cementing lenses into optical instruments.

Balsam firs put out male and female flowers on the same tree. The female flowers are slightly higher in the crown, where they are not as likely to be pollinated by the tree's own male flowers. Pollinated female flowers develop into seed cones with a fairly cylindrical shape. The immature cones have a violet or purplish tint. A tree produces cones annually, with a large crop appearing every two to four years. Small, winged seeds fall from the cones in autumn, winter, and the following spring; they germinate from late May to early July. Balsam fir seedlings are shade-tolerant and can grow in the understory beneath mature trees. The root system forms a shallow, spreading mat.

Aphids, midge larvae, and caterpillars feed on and parasitize balsam fir. A major pest is the spruce budworm, a caterpillar that eats the needles of spruces and firs. In some areas, it has killed many trees. Porcupines, snowshoe hares, moose, and deer nibble on various parts of balsam fir; small rodents and songbirds eat the seeds; yellow-bellied sapsuckers chisel feeding wells in the bark; and grouse, especially spruce and sharp-tailed grouse in northern areas, nip off and eat the needles. Solitary vireos, yellow-rumped warblers, and evening grosbeaks frequently nest in balsam firs.

The wood of *Abies balsamea* is light in weight, at 26 pounds per cubic foot, pale, limber, and soft; in contact with the ground, it rots rapidly. People use it for paneling, boxes for transporting foods such as fish (the wood does not impart any taste or odor), crates, barrels, and other products that do not require much structural strength. In Canada, particularly, balsam fir goes into paper pulp, although the species yields less pulp per cord than denser softwoods such as spruce.

The same conical shape that helps a fir resist snow and ice also gladdens the human heart. Balsam fir is a popular Christmas tree: pretty, fragrant, inclined to hold on to its needles. At a neglected tree farm near our home, we usually select and cut down a leggy balsam fir, then take home the top 12 or so feet. After enjoying its sylvan presence in our living room for the better part of a month, we prop up the tree outside near our bird feeder. Chickadees and juncos shelter from winter's cold and wind amid the dense boughs, as they do in the boreal forest.

HEMLOCK

Pennsylvania is graced with many old-growth hemlock stands, remnants of the original forest that covered much of the Northeast before Europeans arrived. The commonwealth also has countless younger groves of these graceful conifers, as well as individual hemlock trees scattered throughout the hardwood forests that today dominate in Penn's Woods. The hemlock is so prominent in our woodlands that it has been named the state tree.

The eastern hemlock *(Tsuga canadensis)* is sometimes called Canada hemlock or spruce pine. It ranges from Nova Scotia west across southern Quebec and Ontario to Michigan, Wisconsin, and Minnesota; through New England and New York; statewide in Pennsylvania, with the greatest densities in the northern counties; and in high, cool settings in the Appalachians as far south as Georgia and Alabama. Outlying populations exist in Ohio and Indiana. A close relative, the Carolina hemlock, *Tsuga caroliniana,* occurs in the mountains from West Virginia to western South Carolina and northern Georgia. Botanists recognize around ten hemlock species in North America and Asia, including four on this continent. Hemlocks do not occur naturally in Europe at this time, but fossils show that they once grew there.

Hemlocks thrive in cool, moist woodlands, and in ravines and along the banks of streams and creeks. They grow more frequently on north-facing than on south-facing slopes. Usually they show up singly or in scattered local groupings rather than in extensive pure stands. In summer, a grove of hemlocks is a dim, humid place, full of blue-green shade, a refuge from heat and glare. In winter, the same grove is a green island in a forest otherwise gone drab and gray.

Most hemlocks are roughly cone-shaped. If it grows in the open, a hemlock's crown will be full and dense, with layers of branches descending to within a few feet of the ground. In a crowded stand, an individual tree will have a trunk free of lateral branches for many feet and a crown that is short and narrow. The slender outer branches are flexible, protection against breakage during winter storms.

The needles are borne on tiny, thread-thin stems, which attach to short, woody, peglike structures, called sterigmata, studding the sides of the twigs. The needles are not pointed like those of a pine or spruce. Hemlock needles are blunt or round-ended, thin, flattened, and 1/3 to 2/3 inch long. At first glance, they appear to be arranged in twin sprays, one lining each side of the twig, but actually they spiral around the twig. An inconspicuous, often sparse third row of needles grows on top of the twig, angling forward toward the twig's tip. Seen from the side or above, hemlock foliage is a dark blue-green; viewed from below, it looks silvery. The needles account for this bicolored aspect: they are dark green on top and pale below. The pale aspect comes from a chalky white line on either side of the central rib. The white line is a series of stomates, openings that allow gas exchange between the needle and the atmosphere. A needle conducts photosynthesis for about three years before dying and falling off.

Hemlock bark is grayish brown to reddish brown, rough and hard, with long, vertical furrows separating broad, scaly ridges. On a mature tree, the bark is almost an inch thick and may constitute up to 20 percent of the tree's total volume. The inner bark is a bright cinnamon red.

A hemlock has shallow, spreading roots; close to the trunk, the roots' upper surfaces, cloaked with ruddy bark, may stand aboveground. The roots snake past or straddle rocks, then angle down into the earth. Shade-loving trees, hemlocks flourish in the deep woods. With their shallow root systems, they are less vulnerable to toppling during storms when they stand ranked with other trees; however, they remain susceptible to ground fires and drought. Search about in a hemlock grove, and you may find "stilt-rooted" trees, which sprouted in moss on top of a boulder or on an old log or stump, then sent their roots down around that perch to reach mineral soil. A stilt-rooted hemlock is particularly apt to be pushed over by strong wind.

Hemlock flowers appear in April and May. Male and female flowers emerge on the same branch or on different branches in the same tree. The male flowers are about 1/4 inch long, rounded, and yellow; female flowers are twice that size, oblong, and pale green. Wind carries pollen from the male to the female flowers; the latter develop into seed cones by autumn. The cones look like little footballs, dangling below the tips of the branchlets. The overlapping cone scales readily absorb moisture from the air and dry out again just as rapidly. When the weather is dry and windy, the scales part, letting the breeze free the small, lightweight (roughly 187,000 per pound) seeds, two of which line each scale. A 20-mile-an-hour wind can carry the winged seeds more than 4,000 feet. Most seeds fall during autumn and winter, soon after the cones mature. Stands of full-grown hemlocks yield good seed crops every two or three years, and an individual tree can continue producing cones for 450 or more years.

The seeds fall to the ground and germinate. Seedlings take root in moist, well-decomposed litter; in moss capping soil, wood, and rocks; and in rotted wood on top of a decomposing stump or a "nurse log," often that of another hemlock. Hemlocks growing in straight lines show where a nurse log once lay. Drought means death for small hemlocks, and full, open sunlight can dry out the soil around the seedlings' roots, killing them. They do better in partial or even full shade. Once established, a hemlock receiving full sunlight may extend its height by 18 inches a year, whereas a seedling deeply shaded in the forest understory may take forty to sixty years to reach a height of 6 feet.

When scientists studied hemlocks in an old-growth stand at Heart's Content Scenic Area, Warren County, Pennsylvania, they found saplings 2 to 3 inches in diameter at breast height that were two hundred years old—waiting in the shade beneath ancient, but ultimately mortal, giants. A tree with a diameter of just over 10 inches was 359 years old; nearby dominant trees were the same age but stood much taller and were 24 to 36 inches in diameter. (It can be difficult to determine the true age of a hemlock, because saplings under severe suppression in the understory may not form a growth ring each year.) When an opening occurs in a hemlock grove, as when a mature tree succumbs to insect pests, drought, root damage, or a combination of such factors, smaller trees respond by growing rapidly toward the light. With time, formerly suppressed hemlocks can become dominant trees themselves, claiming their share of the canopy.

Hemlock seedlings in the understory beneath hardwood trees grow slowly. But if no serious disruption—fire, logging, insect plague—hits the stand, the hemlocks inevitably become taller than the broad-leaved trees, most of which are finally shaded out. (One exception is the shade-tolerant American beech.) Ecologists say that such a stand has reached the climax stage: an assemblage of trees that cannot be invaded or replaced by other species requiring more light to establish themselves.

Most hemlocks live 150 to 200 years, although many become much older. The oldest recorded age is 988 years, a tree with a diameter of 84 inches and a total height of 160 feet. The current Pennsylvania state record, as recognized by the Pennsylvania Forestry Association, stands in Cook Forest State Park, Clarion County. It is 125 feet tall and 193 inches around the trunk. The national record hemlock, in Great Smoky Mountains National Park, Tennessee, is 165 feet tall and has a 202-inch circumference.

Needles, old cones, and fallen twigs carpet the ground beneath a stand of hemlocks. The soil is fairly dry and highly acidic from the accumulated litter. Few herbaceous plants survive on this inhospitable substrate and in the dim light; among them are rattlesnake plantain, wood sorrel, wild sarsaparilla, Canada mayflower, teaberry, starflower, New York fern, and Indian cucumber-root. Hardwood trees mixing with hemlocks in their typical habitats include yellow birch, black birch, sugar maple, red maple, American beech, tuliptree, black-gum, and various oaks. White pines mingle their pale green needles with the hemlocks' darker foliage. Underground fungi can be abundant, sending up their fruiting bodies—mushrooms—after periods of wet weather, particularly in late summer and early fall. Two common fungi are the honey mushroom, *Armillaria mellea,* and *Ganoderma tsugae,* a tough, woody, shelflike conk, its upper surface a gleaming mahogany color. The species name *tsugae* emphasizes the fungus's frequent association with *Tsuga canadensis,* the eastern hemlock.

More than twenty-four types of insects feed on hemlocks, including moth caterpillars and wood-boring beetles. The hemlock woolly adelgid is a new and potentially devastating pest. It is about the size of one of the aphids that cluster on the stems of tomato plants. The insect appeared on the West Coast of North America in the early 1900s, perhaps on trees or shrubs imported from Asia. Western hemlock species showed some resistance to the adelgid, but eastern hemlocks have not fared as well: the adelgids are destroying hemlocks, or acting in concert with other environmental factors to cause the death of hemlocks from New England to Virginia. Adelgids have been found in thirty-two of Pennsylvania's sixty-seven counties, mainly in the northeastern, southeastern, and south-central parts of the state.

Adelgid nymphs feed by sucking sap from hemlock twigs. Millions of nymphs can infest a single tree. Their feeding causes needles to die and fall off prematurely. When adelgids invade trees already stressed by drought, mortality can be high. Some trees seem able to hang on and survive an adelgid infestation, which may be relieved when winter temperatures freeze the insects or rains wash them away. Entomologists are searching in Asia for parasites and predators to fight the adelgid, but no one knows if these potential natural controls will halt the invasion, or which or how many of our hemlocks are doomed to perish.

The dense evergreen crowns of hemlocks provide nesting cover for many birds, including the veery, golden-crowned kinglet, several warbler species (the colorful Blackburnian warbler is also known as the hemlock warbler), dark-eyed junco, pine siskin, and sharp-shinned hawk. Their deep shade keeps streams cool even on hot summer days; cold-water aquatic life, from insect larvae to trout, requires such chill waters. Other wild animals, such as the small-footed bat, depend on cool, shady habitats. This rare species often hibernates in caves and mine shafts in hemlock forests.

Yellow-bellied sapsuckers drill rows of holes in hemlock bark and feed on the sap that oozes into the excavations. Red squirrels and other rodents consume large quantities of hemlock seeds, as do birds such as the black-capped chickadee, red and white-winged crossbills, and pine siskin. In winter, hemlocks offer shelter to ruffed grouse, wild turkeys, and perching birds. When snow is deep, deer may congregate in hemlock groves; the trees hold great loads

In winter, porcupines nibble on twigs and branch sprays in hemlocks; after the cuttings fall to the ground, deer feed on them.

of snow on their dense boughs, so that the snow on the ground is not nearly as deep as beneath pines or bare-branched hardwoods. The deer browse on hemlock foliage and twigs within reach. Porcupines climb into the crowns of hemlocks and stay there for days, nipping off foliage and eating bark. I often find sprays of needles and branchlets lying beneath hemlocks; deer tracks in the snow show where the whitetails have eaten the porcupine's leavings.

No one seems able to explain why the hemlock, a tall and stately tree, should bear the name of a poisonous Old World plant (Socrates was invited to cause his own death by drinking a draught of poison hemlock, a relative of parsley). Native Americans of several tribes prepared a drink from hemlock needles and inner bark to treat illnesses such as colds and diarrhea. They also ground up the inner bark and used it as flour.

Rich in tannic acid, hemlock bark can be used to cure leather, to which it imparts a reddish tint. In the late 1800s and early 1900s, loggers felled countless hemlocks, spudded off the bark—it came off in huge sheets in spring—and sold it to the leather-tanning industry. Sometimes the dead, naked trunks, called "peelers," were left to rot.

Hemlock wood is coarse-grained and brittle, inferior to pine for most, though not all, building purposes. The knots are hard and can dull or chip steel saw blades. People have used hemlock lumber for beams, shingles, laths, railroad ties, crating, and pulp. A few years ago, I built a small barn and asked a local sawyer to cut us some pine for siding. He shook his head. "Use hemlock instead," he suggested. "It holds nails better than pine and lasts a lot longer. All the old barns here in the valley have hemlock siding."

Stands of old-growth hemlock have been preserved in Pennsylvania, many of them designated as state forest natural areas. A 118-acre grove at Alan Seeger Natural Area, Huntingdon County, has huge trees that are more than five hundred years old; seventy years ago a forester described the stand as "the finest example of virgin hemlock on streambed alluvium in Pennsylvania." Sweet Root Natural Area in Bedford County includes eighty acres of old-growth hemlock, still standing as of the summer of 2000 but killed by the hemlock woolly adelgid. Other state forest natural areas with old-growth hemlocks include the Hemlocks, Perry County; Detweiler Run, Huntingdon County; Snyder-Middleswarth, Snyder County; Jakey Hollow, Columbia County; Bark Cabin, Lycoming County; Forrest H. Dutlinger, Clinton County; Joyce Kilmer, Union County; Mt. Logan, Clinton County; and Anders Run, Warren County. People wishing to visit the natural areas can consult my book *Natural Pennsylvania: Exploring the State Forest Natural Areas* for accounts of and directions to those special places.

SPRUCES

Two spruces are native to Pennsylvania: black spruce, *Picea mariana,* and red spruce, *Picea rubens.* Neither is common in the Keystone State. Spruces are essentially northern trees. These evergreens bear short, stiff, sharp-pointed needles that grow all the way around the twigs like the bristles on a stout, cylindrical brush—or, as the writer Hal Borland observes in *A Countryman's Woods,* "like the hair on the tail of an angry cat." In contrast, pines set forth their needles in bundles, the number of needles per bundle varying among species, and hemlocks and firs have rows of needles fringing their twigs. Individual spruce needles appear square when viewed in cross section. The needles are seated on small, woody knobs called sterigmata; the knobs remain after the needles drop, giving the twigs a rough, bumpy appearance.

White spruce, *Picea glauca,* ranges from eastern Canada and northern New England west to Alaska; although not native to Pennsylvania, it has been planted in the state, including on state forest and state game lands. Two other spruces have been widely planted as ornamental and forest trees: blue spruce, *Picea pungens,* and Norway spruce, *Picea abies.* (See Common Introduced Trees for information on these non-native species.)

Black Spruce *(Picea mariana).* A dense stand of black spruce occupies the north border of the bog at Bear Meadows Natural Area in southern Centre County. Over the years, the trees' straight trunks have shed, or self-pruned, their lower branches. Their dark, bushy tops knit together 20 to 30 feet up, merging with the crowns of eastern hemlocks and balsam firs. The evergreens' differently shaped needles mesh to intercept virtually all of the sunlight, so that the ground beneath this sylvan ceiling is a tenebrous place even on a bright day. Rooted in the muck and saturated sphagnum moss are hemlock seedlings and head-high great rhododendron shrubs with leathery evergreen leaves. Entering the cool, shaded grove, you feel you have wandered into a swamp much farther north, in New England or Canada.

Black spruce gets its name from the dark hue of its foliage. The needles are about 1/4 to 1/3 inch long and remain on the tree for seven to ten years. Crushed, they give off a clean, resin-scented fragrance. The twigs are covered with tiny hairs: strip off the needles and use a hand lens to verify this characteristic.

Picea mariana has a large range, from Labrador west to Alaska, from the northern limit of tree growth, where black spruce is but a creeping shrub, south to Wisconsin and Michigan, and pockets in north-central and northeastern Pennsylvania. Black spruce is the dominant tree in the muskeg bogs of Canada, and up north it also colonizes dry habitats away from standing water. Another name for the species is bog spruce, and in Pennsylvania, *Picea mariana* grows almost exclusively in bogs: cold, poorly drained sites with acidic water and meager soil. The range map for black spruce in *Atlas of United States Trees,* developed by the U.S. Forest Service, implies that the species reaches its southern limit at or near Bear Meadows bog in Centre County.

An excellent habitat in which to view black spruce is a kettlehole bog, a feature of formerly glaciated regions, including northern Pennsylvania. Such wetlands came into being as the last ice age ended around ten thousand years ago, when glaciers that had invaded from the north began to

*Tamarack (left) and black spruce (right) thrive in acidic bogs,
growing on top of floating mats of sphagnum moss.*

melt. Huge pieces of ice broke off from the retreating masses and became
stranded; the weight of the ice chunks kept the land beneath them from
rebounding as the glaciers withdrew. As the ice fragments melted, the ket-
tle-shaped depressions they had caused filled up with water.

In a typical kettlehole bog, over time plants begin to encroach on the
open water, starting from the pond's edges. A floating mat of sedges and
mosses, especially sphagnum mosses, covers the pond like a jar lid. As years pass
and organic detritus builds up, the mat becomes thicker and more compacted.
Seeds of trees and shrubs blow onto the surface or are deposited there by animals. Venture out onto a quaking bog, as these sites are called, and it will feel
as if you are walking across a giant water bed. Trees jutting up from the sphagnum substrate—red maple, black-gum, balsam fir, white pine, and pitch pine,
as well as black spruce—may actually sway back and forth as you slog past.

On an open bog mat, black spruce typically develops into a spindly tree
with a triangular plume of dark bluish green foliage gathered at the top of
the trunk. Such trees are not tall, usually around 30 feet. Some rise no
higher than a human's head: when its roots do not contact mineral soil, a
tree grows very slowly indeed. On better, drier sites, black spruce may
reach 100 feet in height, with a trunk 3 feet in diameter. In New York in
the late 1800s, foresters with magnifying glasses counted the annual growth
rings on stumps of logged-off black spruces. "In many cases it [was] impos-

sible to count these rings, or 'grains' as the woodsmen term them, with the naked eye," according to an account in *The Adirondack Black Spruce,* by William F. Fox, published in 1895. The foresters found that the average 12-inch-diameter black spruce was 128 years old; the average 24-incher was 195. One 29-inch stump had 321 annual rings.

In a bog setting, a spruce's roots usually do not probe deeper than a foot or two into the saturated substrate. They fan out near the surface, making a big footprint rather like a snowshoe that protects the tree from being blown over by wind. Some roots become shaped like I-beams, strengthening their support. As a spruce grows taller and becomes heavier, it may sink down into the bog; or water levels may rise when beavers dam a stream, or as decayed sphagnum builds up in the form of peat on the bottom of the pond. In such instances, a half-submerged spruce may send roots radiating out from its trunk, which in turn put down rootlets and send up shoots. Or the tree may layer, its lowest branches rooting and sending up shoots where they touch the bog surface. The shoots become trees. After several years, the taller parent—perhaps wind-toppled by this time, or with a snapped-off trunk— is surrounded by a ring of younger, shorter, genetically identical offspring.

Black spruces flower in May. Each tree produces both male and female blossoms. Wind-borne pollen from the males fertilizes the female reproductive structures. On a given tree, female flowers chemically recognize and usually reject pollen from the tree's own male flowers, assuring the cross-pollination that promotes genetic variation within a species.

The fertilized female flower, cylindrical and about $1/8$ inch long, develops into a woody cone, grayish brown and $1/2$ to $11/2$ inches long. A spruce sets cones mainly in its upper branches. The cones, which dangle beneath the twigs, release their seeds during winter. They drop off the following spring, or they remain on the branches for several years, gradually releasing seeds. The cones of some black spruces are semiserotinous, partly cemented shut with pitch. If a fire burns a stand of black spruce, the pitch melts and the cones shed copious seeds, which fall onto a charred and open seedbed, where they germinate readily. (For a more detailed discussion of this fire-survival strategy, known as cone serotiny, see Pitch Pine.)

Although it thrives best in full sunlight, black spruce is moderately shade-tolerant: its seeds will germinate and its seedlings will grow in the shade cast by larger trees. Two common north-country competitors—balsam fir, which is native to Pennsylvania, and northern white-cedar, planted in the state—are even more shade-tolerant than black spruce and may thrive beneath a black spruce stand.

The red crossbill uses its offset mandibles to pry apart the scales of black spruce cones, then extracts the seeds with its tongue.

Red squirrels clip off black spruce cones; they strip out the small, winged seeds and eat them on the spot or store them for future consumption. Squirrels can remove up to 90 percent of the cones in a stand. Crossbills are birds that compete directly with red squirrels for spruce kernels. Research by wildlife biologists suggests that a crossbill needs to eat a spruce kernel about every seven seconds, all day long during daylight hours, to survive a typical northern winter. In New England and Canada, spruce grouse home in on black spruce and other conifers. The birds—a darker, boreal version of our ruffed grouse—shelter in the evergreens in winter and eat the needles and buds. Deer and moose browse on spruce if other, more nutritious plants are not available, and use stands of the trees as resting or escape cover.

Sharp-shinned hawks, Cooper's hawks, and northern goshawks hide their nests in spruces. Wood-warblers and flycatchers nest and feed in stands of spruces; the different species exploit separate niches in the stand, or even in a single tree, to avoid competing directly for limited resources. One warbler species may nest far out on a conifer's limbs, while another builds its nest close to the trunk. One type of flycatcher may hunt for insects high in the crown, and another, related species patrols the lower branches. In the far north, black-backed woodpeckers, boreal chickadees, and gray jays favor spruce-fir woodlands.

Spruce budworm, the caterpillar stage of a woodland moth, is a major pest of *Picea* species. Budworms often build up their population in a nearby balsam fir stand, then shift to eating the needles of black spruce after denuding the firs. An intriguing parasite of black spruce is the eastern dwarf mistletoe. Seeds of this plant are deposited on a tree branch in a bird dropping; after a seed germinates, it sends out a modified root that penetrates the host's bark, forming a connection through which the mistletoe draws water and nutrients. The injury and invasion weaken and stunt the tree and sometimes cause it to grow distorted bushy clumps known as witches' brooms. Crinkly looking beard lichens often festoon the dead lower branches of a black spruce. The lichens are not parasites, but simply use the tree as a perch.

The wood of black spruce is pale and fairly heavy for a softwood: 33 pounds per cubic foot, dry weight. Carpenters use it for house construction, siding, and boat building; the best knot-free grades are in demand for the sounding boards of pianos. According to *The Adirondack Black Spruce,* in bygone days the bark was peeled from standing trees "by woodsmen, guides or sportsmen, who use it for covering the roof or sides of their shanties." Black spruce makes a poor firewood, snapping and spraying sparks from an open fireplace. Today its chief use is for paper pulp. Black spruce is Canada's foremost pulp species, and each year millions of cubic feet of the wood are ground up and processed into paper.

Native Americans steeped black spruce needles in hot water to make a tea rich in vitamin C. They used the resin and poultices made from the tree's inner bark to treat sores and inflammations, and concocted a drink from the inner bark that relieved aches and pains. Until it was replaced by chicle, the coagulated juice of a tropical plant, black spruce resin was collected and enjoyed as chewing gum. In the 1800s New England lumbermen brewed "spruce beer" from black spruce sap.

Pennsylvanians can familiarize themselves with black spruce in the bogs that dot the state's glaciated northern tier. Many such wetlands have been set aside as state forest natural areas, including Spruce Swamp, Lackawanna County; Bruce Lake, Pike County; Little Mud Pond Swamp, Pike County; Algerine Swamp, Lycoming County; and Tamarack Swamp, Clinton County.

Red Spruce *(Picea rubens).* In the past, some taxonomists considered red spruce to be a variety of black spruce, but today the two are classified as separate species. The needles of red spruce are marginally longer than those of black spruce; some twigs of red spruce are hairy and some are not, whereas those of black spruce are invariably hairy; and the cones of red spruce are larger, at $1^1/4$ to $1^5/8$ inches long, more of a reddish brown color, and glossier. When crushed, the scent of red spruce needles tickles the nose like that of orange rind.

Red spruce has a more limited range than black spruce: from southern Canada through the mountains of New England to New York, New Jersey, and Pennsylvania, and in the high Appalachians as far south as North Carolina and Tennessee. Red spruce achieves its greatest growth in the southern Appalachians, where the air is more humid and rainfall more abundant than in other parts of its range. Today the largest known red spruce stands in North Carolina, in Great Smoky Mountains National Park; it towers 123 feet into the air, is 169 inches in circumference, and has a 39-foot crown spread. At one time, such trees were plentiful. But logging in the southern Appalachians in the late 1800s and early 1900s reduced an estimated one and a half million acres of old-growth red spruce to scattered fringes and isolated patches.

In the Appalachians, red spruce often grows side by side with Fraser fir, a southern version of balsam fir. Plain-seeing mountain folk called the fir she-balsam, because the resin-filled blisters beneath the tree's bark reminded them of breasts; red spruce, which lacks the blisters, became he-balsam.

An uncommon tree in Pennsylvania, red spruce grows on cool, moist slopes and mountain summits, well-drained uplands, and the edges of streams and swamps. It occurs mainly in the northern part of the state. Red spruce likes to keep its toes dry, as the foresters say; I have seen it in the Poconos, growing near bogs but on slightly higher, drier ground than black spruce.

The Pennsylvania Natural Diversity Inventory represents a partnership between the state Bureau of Forestry, the Nature Conservancy, and the

Western Pennsylvania Conservancy. The project's purpose is to collect data on the state's rarest and most significant ecological features. Jean Fike, an ecologist working on the inventory, has written *Terrestrial and Palustrine Plant Communities of Pennsylvania,* which classifies and describes plant communities native to the state. Fike cites one example of a "Red Spruce Rocky Summit" woodland type, in Wyoming County in northeastern Pennsylvania at an elevation of 2,200 feet. On this stony, north-facing prominence, red spruce mixes with gray birch, pitch pine, red pine, eastern white pine, eastern hemlock, and red maple. Wind and ice have battered and pruned the smallish, stunted spruces, rooted in pockets of soil that have built up in cracks in the bedrock.

The pale-colored wood of red spruce weighs 28 pounds per cubic foot. Modern loggers market it along with black spruce and white spruce for use as paper pulp. The wood is soft and can be worked easily with tools. Thanks to air pockets in its structure, red spruce is resonant; boards of the highest quality, with no knots and a uniform grain texture, are crafted into fiddles, guitars, mandolins, organ pipes, and piano sounding-boards.

In the Appalachians, acid rain caused by air pollution may be harming red spruces. Hub Vogelman, a scientist at the University of Vermont, first suggested acid rain as a cause of mortality among spruces on Camel's Hump, a peak in the Green Mountains. Between 1965 and 1990, nearly three-quarters of the red spruces in Vogelman's study area died. Follow-up research suggests that an insect pest feeding on tree rootlets may also be responsible for some or perhaps most of the dead spruces on Camel's Hump and elsewhere.

TAMARACK

Tamarack *(Larix laricina),* also called American larch, is the only needle-leaved tree in the Northeast that drops all its foliage before winter. Other deciduous conifers include the baldcypress of the South and three genera of Asian trees.

For three seasons of the year, the swamp-dwelling tamarack is a colorful tree. In late April and early May, just before and as it begins renewing its foliage, tamarack puts forth small female flowers that are purplish red with green tips. The female flowers are fertilized by wind-blown pollen from even smaller, golden-yellow male flowers.

It takes up to six weeks for a tamarack to don its full complement of needles. The needles are about an inch long, soft and flexible, sprouting

Tamarack needles stand in delicate sprays along the twigs and
branches. The oval seed cones are 1/2 to 3/4 inch long.

from buds at the ends of short, lateral spurs on the branches and twigs. Most
of the needles stand in little tufts and fountain-shaped sprays. At first, they
are a tender green-gold. As summer strengthens, they take on a frosty blue-
green hue. And in autumn, they change to a soft, glowing gold. In October and November, the needles let go their hold and sift down to carpet the
ground beneath the bare-branched trees.

Tamaracks don't simply appear bare: they look dead, through and through.
On a recent winter foray to Tamarack Swamp Natural Area in Clinton
County, I hiked out onto the frozen bog amid hundreds of skeletal tamaracks. The trees' crowns were pyramids of warty twigs that seemed to hover
insubstantially above the reddish brown trunks. With their foliage absent, I
could study the trees' shapes: strongly conical, with upright trunks and
straight, slender branches. The top branches angled slightly upward, and the
lower branches paralleled the ground.

Some of the trees were covered with cones—shiny, pale brown ovals
about 3/4 inch long. They looked like hemlock cones, except that the tamaracks carried their cones upright on the surfaces of their twigs, rather than
dangling them, hemlock-fashion, at the branch ends. The cones develop
from female flowers fertilized in spring. Their scales start to open from late
August to mid-September, and they release their seeds during the next several months. The spent cones may hang on the tree for up to five years.

In a good year, a large, healthy tamarack may bear twenty thousand
cones containing three hundred thousand seeds. A typical stand may produce as many as five million germinable seeds in a bumper year. Tamaracks
put out at least some cones each year, with prolific crops every three to six
years. In most settings, trees reproduce through their seeds, but in swamps
in the northern part of the species' range, tamaracks may layer—root and
send up vegetative sprouts wherever their lower branches touch the ground.

At maturity, tamaracks are generally 50 to 75 feet tall and 14 to 20 inches in diameter at breast height. A few trees may achieve a height of 115 feet and a diameter of 40 inches. *Larix laricina* has one of the largest ranges of all North America conifers. It occurs from northern Canada—at the very northern limit of tree growth, where a tamarack may resemble a shrub more than a tree—south to New Jersey, Pennsylvania, and Ohio. Tamaracks range across the Great Lakes states and west to Alaska. In the Northeast, tamaracks usually grow in wetlands, although in New England, some trees ascend cool, north-facing slopes. In British Columbia and Alaska, tamaracks often form extensive pure stands. They require full sunlight and make their best growth in moist but well-drained loamy soil along streams, lakes, and swamps.

In Pennsylvania, look for tamaracks in the northern half of the state, mainly on the fringes of sphagnum bogs. The trees have also been planted in many areas. A tamarack seedling may take root on top of a sphagnum tussock. *Larix laricina* grows slowly in the bog environment; it may take a tree 250 years to achieve a trunk diameter of 20 inches. On the best sites, in direct sunlight, tamaracks shoot up quickly: 1 1/2 to 2 feet per year for the first twenty or thirty years, with growth slowing sharply when the crowns of neighboring trees knit together or after individuals reach age forty to fifty. A tamarack must remain part of the forest canopy to survive.

Even when fully leafed out, tamaracks, with their sparse foliage, allow light to filter through to the ground. A dense understory of shrubs and herbs often grows beneath the trees, including leatherleaf, creeping snowberry, common winterberry, spirea, sweetgale, poison sumac, and several species of blueberry and huckleberry. In Pennsylvania, tamaracks sometimes form mixed stands with black spruce, red spruce, balsam fir, white pine, and hemlock. Gray birch, yellow birch, red maple, black-gum, quaking aspen, and black ash are deciduous trees that often grow with or near tamaracks.

Young tamaracks often grow on hummocks of sphagnum moss in bogs.

Of the thousands of seeds produced by a tamarack, half may be eaten by mice, voles, and shrews. Red squirrels cut down cone-bearing branchlets and stash the cones for future eating. Red crossbills perch in the trees and use their specially adapted mandibles to pry the cone scales apart; the birds lift out the exposed seeds with their tongues. Porcupines gnaw on the bark, and snow-shoe hares eat bark and the growing tips of seedlings. Ruffed, sharp-tailed, and spruce grouse feed on buds and needles. A tamarack grove, especially one with other conifers and hardwoods mixed in, offers a range of feeding and nesting habitats for many birds, particularly flycatchers and wood-warblers.

Native Americans used various parts of the tamarack as medicine and for rope, twine, caulking, and arrow shafts. John Josselyn, a naturalist and historian of the Massachusetts Bay Colony, wrote during the seventeenth century: "The Turpentine that issueth from the Larch Tree is singularly good to heal wounds and to draw out malice . . . of any Ach by rubbing the place therewith."

Tamarack wood is heavy for a conifer—around 35 pounds per square foot—and makes a good fuelwood. Taking advantage of its rot resistance, carpenters have used it for house sills and boats. The wood does not split readily, making it a good choice for ladders, boxes, posts, poles, mine timbers, and railroad ties. In Alaska, young tamarack stems are fashioned into dogsled runners, boat ribs, and fish traps. The transparent glassine windows through which your name and address appear on bill-bearing envelopes are made from tamarack pulp.

More intriguing than the varied and ingenious human applications is the question of why the tamarack sheds its needles. Why does this tree, practically alone among the conifers, go to the expense of jettisoning all the needles that it grew only six months earlier? Deciduous broad-leaved trees drop their leaves to prevent damaging snow and ice buildup and to conserve water during winter, when frozen ground prevents water from reaching tree roots. Conifers, by the shape and placement of their boughs, avoid winter damage. They need not shed their needles to conserve water, because the needles are already adapted to retain the precious fluid.

As he explains in his book *The Trees in My Forest,* the ecologist Bernd Heinrich analyzed the relative limb strength of various conifers. The limbs of eastern white pine are weak compared with those of spruce and fir, but the pine grows its limbs thicker in compensation—and, as an added safeguard, sheds about half of its needles each autumn, so that winter's snow and ice will not build up excessively on the remaining foliage. Writes Heinrich: "If tamarack limbs could accumulate as much ice and snow as spruce and fir limbs do, they would regularly be snapped off the tree. This rarely happens. Being deciduous, tamaracks can apparently afford to have weaker limbs." Heinrich stops his analysis there, leaving me to wonder how—or if—tamaracks benefit from having weaker limbs.

I contacted Kim Steiner, a forestry professor at Penn State University. Steiner admitted that he, too, had wondered why tamaracks shed their needles. He told me of the three Asian coniferous genera that also drop their needles in winter. Millions of years ago, according to the fossil record, those or similar trees grew at high latitudes—north of the Arctic Circle, where no trees presently survive—during a time when the poles were not frozen and the earth was much warmer than it is today. In winter, balmy though it may have been, the polar night was dark and long. It did the trees no good to hang on to their needles, spending energy keeping those tissues alive at a time when the leaves could return nothing to the plant because darkness prevented them from conducting photosynthesis.

Paleobotanists have suggested that those far-northern trees evolved to shed their useless foliage as the days shortened in autumn, and then grow new needles when the sun reappeared and strengthened in spring. Later, as the climate cooled, the trees retreated south—in the case of the tamarack, not very far south—and retained the leaf-shedding trait.

WHITE PINE

On a hot, still evening in July, I was hiking on the Susquehannock Trail in the Hammersley Wild Area in northern Pennsylvania's Potter County. I trudged uphill, thinking about the long grade down the other side of the mountain, the last leg of the walk that would lead to the truck and, finally, to supper.

The smell stopped me in my tracks. Clean, bright, and resinous, it overcame all other senses: the scent of pine needles baking in the sun. Four white pines stood about 10 yards off the trail. Their trunks, a dark purple-gray, rose thick and straight. Scattered across the forest floor around the trees were broad, grayish green, jagged-topped stumps—all that remained of the primeval forest, the old-growth white pines that loggers had taken from this site a century earlier. Were the four sentinels rising before me descendants of those earlier giants? If so, they were well on their way to becoming giants themselves, their feathery crowns overtopping the boughs of nearby oaks and maples, rich green against the washed-out sky.

The eastern white pine *(Pinus strobus)* is named for its pale wood, light but strong in proportion to its weight, straight-grained, easy to work, and useful in many applications. White pine was the most highly sought-after tree when logging overspread the Northeast between the 1700s and the early 1900s. *Pinus strobus* ranges from Newfoundland west to Manitoba and south to Iowa, northern Illinois, central Indiana, eastern Ohio, Pennsylvania, and, in the Appalachian Mountains, as far as Georgia. In New England and New York, white pines grow mainly at elevations from sea level to 1,500 feet; in Pennsylvania, from 500 to 2,000 feet; and in the southern Appalachians, between 1,200 and 3,500 feet. White pine is the largest pine species east of the Rocky Mountains.

Pinus strobus is common statewide in Pennsylvania. It usually grows in mixed stands with other trees, both conifers and hardwoods. People have also planted it widely for reforestation purposes and as an ornamental. In *Pennsylvania Trees,* published in 1928, Joseph Illick notes that white pine was most abundant in the mountainous parts of the state, where it once formed heavy stands. It is "found sparingly in the southwest and southeast," he writes, "where it is usually limited to cool ravines and north slopes."

White pine makes its best growth on fertile, moist, well-drained soil. It also arises from dry, sandy soil, rocky slopes, and stream banks. It favors slightly damper settings than red pine, which is a companion over much of its range, although not so often in Pennsylvania, where red pine, a more northerly species, is rare. White pines stand alongside pitch pines and black spruce in wet sphagnum bogs in northern Pennsylvania. On exposed ridgetops, such as the spine of Mt. Logan Natural Area in Clinton County, white pines grow gnarled and bent; the wind keens through the boughs of those tenacious specimens.

In full sunlight, the crown of *Pinus strobus* forms a broad, irregular triangle. Usually the tree keeps its branches most of the way to the ground. The trunk tapers upward; sometimes the crown forks into two or more uprights. The multiple tiers of branches snub up at the tips. The twigs themselves finger skyward from the branches, the needles in bright green clusters underscored by the horizontal black lines of the limbs. A woods-grown white pine, in competition with surrounding trees, shoots up straight and tall, with little taper to its trunk, few lateral branches (the lower ones die and "self-prune," or fall off over time), and a small, conical crown. It is the woods pine that gladdens the lumberman's heart.

Remember "five" to identify this conifer. It is our only pine to hold its needles in bundles of five. Usually it sends out five side buds clustered

Hemlock (left) has a looser, more irregular pattern of limbs than white pine (right) whose horizontal boughs often turn up at their ends.

around a central bud. The side buds become the branches that surround the trunk in a whorled pattern, with one whorl for each year the tree has been alive, although the lowest whorls may be shed through self-pruning. The distance between the whorls shows how much vertical growth the tree added in a given year.

The needles are 2 to 5 inches long, slender and springy, light green to bluish green. Snip one in half and look at it in cross section with a magnifying lens. The form is triangular, the edges toothed. The straight rows of tiny pale dots lining two sides of the needle are breathing pores. Needles remain on the tree for a year and a half—two growing seasons—before turning brown and falling off in autumn. A pine sheds about half of its needles each fall.

On a young tree, the bark is smooth. It becomes rough over the years, divided into broad, scaly ridges by long, shallow fissures. The overall dark shade of the bark, which often has a purplish tinge, may be streaked by whitish gum or resin seeping down from wounds or where branches were snapped off by storms. A white pine usually sends forth three to five large roots, which spread outward and sink downward. There is no taproot, but its lateral roots make the tree tolerably wind-firm.

White pines grow rapidly, increasing in height an average of 16 inches per year. When fully mature, a tree may tower up to 200 or even 220 feet, but most are cut before they achieve such a stature, and a 100-foot pine in today's forests must be considered a very large specimen. Old-growth white pines can have trunks 6 feet in diameter, although 3 to 4 feet is more usual. Individual trees live 200 years and may reach and exceed 450 years.

Male and female flowers blossom on the same tree. The female flowers are bright pink, with purple-rimmed scales; they emerge high in the tree's crown. The male flowers are yellow, oval, and about 1/3 inch long, clustered at the base of the new growth of needles at the stem's end. In spring, around May in Pennsylvania, the male flowers release their pollen, and the wind spreads it far and wide. The yellow pollen is so abundant that it sometimes makes a haze in the air and forms a skin on the surfaces of ponds, lakes, and river backwaters.

Female cones need two years to mature, so for much of the year, a tree will carry two sizes of cones. At first green in color and tightly sealed with resin, the cones ripen to a tan or light reddish brown. Mature cones are 5 to 10 inches long, cylindrical, curving, and borne on the end of a 1/2-inch woody stalk. The cone scales do not have prickles. Cones, usually shed in winter and spring, are most often found on the ground with the thin, rounded scales opened wide, showing that the seeds have been discharged.

White pine seeds are 1/4 inch long, dark brown, and fitted with a thin, 1/2-inch, asymmetrical wing. Wind can carry them up to 700 feet in open areas. An old pine left in a pasture to give shade for livestock will spread its seeds—and its progeny—across the land; in this way does abandoned farmland become woods again. White pines as young as five to ten years can bear cones. Trees begin setting out good numbers of cones when they reach twenty to thirty years. A mature tree produces an average of two hundred to three hundred cones yearly. Bumper seed crops usually issue forth every three to five years, with a few seeds produced during intervening years.

Like those of many other pines, the seeds of *Pinus strobus* sprout prolifically on ground that has been cleared by fire. Seedlings also prosper on land disturbed by logging. Botanists classify *Pinus strobus* as a "gap-phase species," which means it will germinate in the shade cast by the forest canopy but will grow to maturity only if overstory trees die and fall, creating a gap in the canopy that lets sunlight reach the ground. White pine is considered more shade-tolerant than the aspens, red oak, red maple, gray birch, and black spruce, and less shade-tolerant than yellow birch, eastern hemlock, American beech, sugar maple, and balsam fir.

A white pine seedling grows slowly at first. Ten years may pass before it stands 5 feet tall, even in full sunlight. After that, growth takes off, and trees can be 60 feet high and have a 2-foot trunk diameter in only thirty years. A pine extends upward and outward from buds known as candles because of their cylindrical form. These growth structures are fragile: a bird landing on one can snap it, changing the tree's future form. A white pine achieves all of its lengthening and produces its next year's growth buds in about a month, from early June to around the first of July.

Several diseases and pests plague eastern white pine. The white pine weevil, a beetle, lays its eggs in the growing buds. The larvae feed on the new tissue and kill the leading shoot. Side buds then compete to replace the leader, and the tree ends up with several stems or, if attacked repeatedly, a deformed, bushy crown; such a specimen is known as a "cabbage pine." The weevil only attacks trees growing in direct sunlight. White pine blister rust is a fungus that apparently came from Europe on nursery stock. It invades the inner bark, causing cankers that can girdle branches or trunk and lead to death. To control the rust, foresters grub out currant and gooseberry shrubs, hosts in which the fungus spends part of its life cycle, within a quarter mile of pines.

Early explorers reported vast "veins" of pines growing through much of what is now Pennsylvania and New York. It is possible that those huge, pure, aboriginal stands had filled in areas devastated by hurricanes or great forest fires. According to Donald Culross Peattie in *A Natural History of Trees,* white pine yielded "the most generally useful wood our country has ever possessed." From it people fashioned house paneling and trim, doors, window sashes, furniture, shingles, matches, covered bridges, ships' figureheads, and the masts and spars of clipper ships. In colonial times, three blows of an axe etched "the King's Broad Arrow" onto the trunks of the tallest, straightest white pines, reserving them for the Royal Navy; colonists' resentment of this practice fueled anti-British sentiment that ultimately led to the Revolutionary War.

White pine wood weighs about 25 pounds per cubic foot, air-dried. It is widely used for lumber and paper pulp. As a construction material, it saws easily, resists splitting, and holds paint well. It's handsome wood: the pine paneling I put up in our bedroom has aged to a rich golden yellow, contrasting prettily with the dark, ruddy knots.

Hawks, owls, ravens, crows, blue jays, grackles, and a host of perching birds—mourning doves, flycatchers, grosbeaks, finches, and warblers—hide their nests in the thick, green boughs of white pines. Black-capped chickadees, white- and red-breasted nuthatches, pine and evening grosbeaks, pine siskins, and red and white-winged crossbills eat the seeds, as do mice, voles, chipmunks, and squirrels. Red squirrels often cut down cones, then dismantle them starting from the bottom up. In *Mammals of the Eastern United States,* John Whitaker and William Hamilton note that red squirrels bury the green cones of pines "in damp earth, for if they were allowed to dry, the seeds would quickly be wind-scattered and lost." Writes the naturalist John Eastman in *The Book of Forest and Thicket,* "A red squirrel can strip an average-size cone (about forty-five seeds) in two minutes." I have watched red squirrels carry mushrooms—the red-and-white fruiting bodies of *Russula emetica*—into white pines and hang them in branch crotches for storing.

Porcupines, squirrels, and snowshoe hares eat the bark. I've tried to transplant seedlings to my wooded acres, but unless I fence them securely, deer browse them off during winter. Eastman reports frequently finding raccoon dung on the ground beneath large white pines; the raccoons "often use pines as daytime resting areas," he writes, "leaving scats on the ground before they climb."

I can think of two specialized uses for the white pine. The fallen cones, impregnated with resin, make great campfire starters. Even at the advanced age of fifty, and knowing I'll pay for it later with sore arms and gum-blackened palms, I sometimes feel the irresistible need to climb limb above limb in an open-grown pine—my favorite stands along a hiking path at Black Moshannon State Park in Centre County—until, swaying in the crown, heart thumping, smelling fragrant needles, listening to the wind as it combs through the boughs, I can look out over meadow and bog and touch and be touched by the sky.

PITCH PINE

In our woods, I found a pine knot half buried in the leaves. Over a foot long, it had a fish's shape: curving, sleek, tapered at one end and blunt at the other; it even sported a finlike projection in the middle. Gray, weathered wood skinned the knot, and black char marks bespoke a fire that must have swept across the mountain long before we owned our plot. With my pocketknife, I scraped at the surface, exposing wood that gleamed a rich golden brown. Dense and rock-hard, it resisted the knife blade. It had a sweet, pungent smell like the dust chewed out of a two-by-four when a saw cuts it. The knot was a branch stub from a pitch pine, a type of tree that does not now grow on our land.

Pitch pine *(Pinus rigida)* occurs in scattered sites statewide across Pennsylvania. The species ranges from southern Maine to northern Georgia and from the Atlantic coast west to southern Ohio and eastern Kentucky and Tennessee. Pitch pine is the most abundant conifer on Cape Cod, Massachusetts; on New York's Long Island; and in the New Jersey Pine Barrens. Pennsylvania lies at the heart of the species' range. According to Pennsylvania state forester Joseph Illick and assistant research forester John Aughanbaugh, in a bulletin on *Pinus rigida* published in 1930, "Pitch pine reaches its best development in Pennsylvania."

Continue Illick and Aughanbaugh: "It flourishes under adverse conditions. It will grow on almost any kind of soil and under all sorts of moisture conditions." Pitch pine prospers in acidic soils, sandy soils, gravelly soils, and soils that are almost nonexistent, as on rocky ridges. It even grows on soil derived from the breakdown of serpentine rock, laden with heavy metals that are toxic to many plants. In northern Pennsylvania, pitch pine stands in chilly upland bogs, rooted shallowly atop beds of floating sphagnum moss. According to Illick and Aughanbaugh, pitch pine "almost never occurs naturally on limestone soils [but] will make good growth when planted thereon." Seldom is pitch pine found on heavy clay soils. In hilly areas, it usually grows on the warmer, drier slopes, those facing south or west.

To see some pitch pines, I drove to an area known as the Barrens, about 5 miles west of State College in Centre County. There, pitch pines rise above thickets of bear oak and amid copses of bigtooth aspen. Snow covered the ground, and the deciduous trees were bare. The pines stood out sharply, mature specimens 50 feet in height, with trunks more than a foot in diameter. As I gazed at the shapes of the pines scattered across the undulating landscape, each one seemed distinctive, giving the impression of a tribe of rough, rugged, weatherbeaten individuals.

The pines' foliage varied from a deep forest green to a bright yellowish green, often with different tints on the same tree. The needles had a coarse look to them; they were borne on thick, twisted branches. The branches formed wide, roughly pyramidal crowns sprinkled with dead boughs and often with one or more living gnarled limbs jutting out at an odd angle. Dark cones peppered the trees' crowns. On the trunks, interconnecting fissures broke the bark into irregular plates and flat-topped ridges. The plates and

Pitch pine has a rough, scraggly aspect.

ridges were reddish brown, the fissures dark brown verging on black, a color that gives the pitch pine an alternate common name: black pine.

On one of the trees, a bough drooped to within a few feet of the ground; I shouldered my way to it through the bear oaks. The pine's needles were 4 inches long. In *Pinus rigida,* needle length varies from 3 to 6 inches; next to red pine, pitch pine has the longest needles of Pennsylvania's conifers. The twisted, stiff needles were held in bundles of three; the bundles emerged all along the warty, yellowish brown twigs.

A half-opened cone presented a roundish shape. Most pitch pine cones are 1 to 3 inches in length. This one was about 2 inches long and 2 inches in diameter. A sturdy, curving prickle armed each woody scale. The seed-bearing cones can hang on for a long time in pitch pine, up to ten or more years.

The gravel road along which I'd parked was once the bed of a railroad that serviced an iron ore mining town, Scotia, built by the industrialist Andrew Carnegie in the nineteenth century; the settlement dwindled and had vanished by the mid-1920s. The pitch pines along the road were the lingering silvic expression of the lumbering and mining that had dominated the Barrens for more than a century: in particular, the forest fires caused by charcoal-making operations and by the wood-burning locomotives that huffed and puffed along the rail line. Logging and charcoaling began in the area in the early 1800s. According to an elderly farmer whose land abuts the Barrens to the north, the last big fire raced across the tract in the late 1930s.

A fire-adapted species, pitch pine benefits from blazes that kill competing hardwoods such as oaks and maples. Pitch pine bark is thick: on mature trees, a full 2 inches thick a foot above the ground. The bark insulates and protects the trunk against fire damage. If a conflagration blows up into a full-fledged crown fire, with flames leaping from tree to tree and turning each into a blazing pyre, a pitch pine may yet be able to survive. The tree's trunk and branches are studded with dormant buds, so that even if all the needles burn off, the tree can swiftly send out a new crop. Most other needle-bearing trees die if they lose their foliage all at once. If burned too badly, or if sawed down, a pitch pine—especially a young, vigorous tree 8 inches or less in diameter—will usually resprout, pushing up new shoots from a zone known as the root collar, where the stem and the root system merge. Even large pitch pines up to eighty years old can send out these basal sprouts.

Pitch pines in dry places, such as sandy coastal-plain forests that are repeatedly swept by fire, produce what scientists term serotinous cones. Using binoculars, I could see what I thought were serotinous cones in the tops of some of the trees in the Barrens. Resin tightly seals the scales of these cones. The cones do not release seeds unless extreme heat melts the resin. Serotinous cones are a pitch pine's ace-in-the-hole: should a fire become severe enough to kill the tree, its cones will open and scatter seeds. The seeds fall on ground newly scoured of hardwood saplings and grass, a perfect habitat for pines.

Pitch pine carries two seeds behind each scale on its cones. The seeds are oval, winged, and 3/4 inch long. Illick and Aughanbaugh saw fit to count the number in a pound of seeds: sixty-five thousand, on average. The wind shakes the seeds from the cones and may carry them 100 feet or farther from the parent tree.

Many pitch pines have both serotinous and nonserotinous cones. The nonserotinous cones open and distribute their seeds mainly in winter. Squirrels, grouse, quail, and smaller birds eat the seeds. Wildlife also use the trees in other ways. Nick Bolgiano, a veteran birder, tells me that male golden-winged warblers often perch in the tops of pitch pines in the Barrens, where they sing to proclaim territories and attract mates. After mating, the female warblers nest on the ground among the bear oaks. The golden-winged warbler is becoming rare in the Northeast, and the Barrens is one of the premier sites remaining for the species in Pennsylvania. Bolgiano also finds many pine warblers and chipping sparrows nesting in the pitch pines.

Pitch pines sprout readily on burned-over land; on clear-cut tracts where the soil has been broken up and ground-cover plants disturbed; and on abandoned fields. If fires keep sweeping those lands clear, the pitch pines will persist and may become dominant. *Pinus rigida* is the least shade-tolerant of the eastern pines. If hardwoods overtop them, pitch pines may linger; however, their seedlings will not sprout on a shaded forest floor or where leaf duff accumulates too thickly for their tiny rootlets to penetrate. White-tailed deer browse pitch pine seedlings, nipping off buds and twigs. Because we have suppressed fire in our forests for many decades and allowed the deer population to burgeon, today eastern forests offer much less habitat to pitch pines than they did a century in the past.

In 1930, Illick and Aughanbaugh reported large stands of pitch pine cloaking Pennsylvania's ridges and mountain benches, but today such stands are mostly gone. Either the trees died of old age, as pitch pines rarely live beyond a hundred years, or they were logged off. In Centre County, where I live, building companies sought out pitch pines during the housing boom right after World War II; the stiff, unbending wood went mainly for floor joists. Today most pitch pines grow as individuals scattered through the woods, and it's common to find pine knots littering the ground in forests where pitch pines have otherwise vanished. Sometimes the knots lie opposite one another in two lines, the trunk of the tree rotted to dust between them.

I spoke with district foresters regarding pitch pine in north-central Pennsylvania and in the Pocono region in the northeast, areas where *Pinus rigida* was abundant after destructive clear-cut logging and repeated wildfires of the early twentieth century. In the Poconos, most of the larger stands were cut between 1956 and 1964, in a harvest of mature and overmature trees. Today, the foresters told me, pitch pines have become so uncommon that field personnel marking out timber sales on state land are instructed to save any pitch pines they find. Generally the trees do not regenerate well after logging: deer eat the seedlings, and fires rarely arise to suppress competing growth. In some areas, foresters have begun replanting pitch pine. It's not a new practice: from 1911 to 1930, the state Department of Forests and Waters planted more than eight million pitch pine seedlings.

Pitch pine wood is hard compared with that of most other pines. The wood weighs 35 pounds per cubic foot, dry weight; a cubic foot of white pine, in comparison, weighs 25 pounds. Pitch pine lumber has been used widely for framing houses and barns. In Pike County, a barn floor made of pitch pine boards 2 feet wide and 1 1/2 inches thick served for more than a hundred years and was still in good enough condition that builders relaid the boards as flooring in a new house. Because of its high resin content, the wood withstands decay, and carpenters have used it for house sills, boats, mill wheels, and buckets. Between 1799 and 1801, the city of Philadelphia laid 45 miles of bored-out pitch pine logs as underground water pipes. Boxes, kegs, crates, railroad ties, mine props, and fence rails have also been made from pitch pine.

Early settlers called it candlewood; they split the heartwood into long slivers, useful for lighting the way to the barn at night or for carrying fire from one part of the house to another. They made torches by wedging pitch pine knots into the ends of hickory shafts. Sometimes they used the lanterns to "shine" deer: transfix the curious animals at night, allowing them to be shot. Another common name for pitch pine is jack pine, and it seems probable that the verb to "jacklight" a deer comes from this poacher's practice. Pitch pine wood made excellent charcoal. People distilled tar from the knots by heating them slowly in a pit and catching and then refining the resin that flowed out. At one time, according to Illick and Aughanbaugh, pitch pine tar was "the best axle grease to be had. Few wagons were seen without the ever-present tar bucket and tar paddle swinging from the rear axle."

I don't often burn pitch pine in my stove, because the wood lays down a particularly hard and flammable chimney soot. But I couldn't resist setting the pine knot I'd found onto a bed of coals one winter's night. Brilliant yellow flames flickered up as the dense wood immediately caught fire. The knot snapped and crackled and gave off plumes of black smoke. Flames raced up and down the knot, throwing warmth and light into the darkened room—warmth and light that sprang from years of sunshine locked up in the resin-drenched wood.

RED PINE

The red pines grew on a north-facing slope so steep in places that I had to haul myself about by gripping the springy boughs of mountain laurel. The pines' thick, straight trunks tapered slightly as they mounted to their crowns, dark green upright ovals composed of feathery needles tufting the branch ends. In the hazy August sunshine, the upper zones of the trunks and the thick, twisted branches were a light reddish orange. The color of its bark earns the red pine its name.

Lebo Red Pine Natural Area in Lycoming County surrounds a twelve-acre grove of old-growth red pines. At breast height, the trees' trunks are about 18 inches in diameter. The thick bark is covered with gray-brown, diamond-shaped plates separated by shallow interconnecting furrows. The outer surfaces of many of the plates had flaked off, revealing a ruddy orangish layer beneath. The bark of a nearby white pine looked almost black by comparison.

Red pine (Pinus resinosa) is not common in Pennsylvania. It is a tree of the north, with a range about 1,500 miles long by 500 miles wide. In Canada, it grows from Newfoundland to Manitoba. Red pine occurs in

New England, New York, Michigan, Wisconsin, and Minnesota. In the Northeast, red pine comes as far south as north-central Pennsylvania and the Appalachians of West Virginia, where it grows at elevations from 3,800 to 4,300 feet. Red pines are generally mixed in with trees of other species, but sometimes they grow in pure stands. Near where I live in Centre County, red pines decorate the campus of Penn State University, and they grow in cropfield rows on the rolling terrain at Black Moshannon State Park. According to some sources, planted stands now outnumber natural stands for this species.

The trees at Lebo Red Pine Natural Area were red pines planted by nature rather than man. Two centuries ago, a fire, probably started by lightning, swept up the slope above the First Big Fork of Trout Run. Onto this newly bared land, red pine seeds drifted.

Pinus resinosa produces large quantities of lightweight, broad-winged seeds that can travel up to 900 feet on the wind. Red pine's thick bark helps protect the tree against fire damage; mature trees are sometimes scorched as high as 40 feet without being killed, but if the fire or intense heat reaches the crown, the result is fatal. Red pine is not as perfectly adapted to fire as pitch pine and Table Mountain pine, lacking the serotinous, or heat-activated, cones of those other two species, but wherever red pines occur in a pure or a near-pure natural stand, you can be fairly sure that a fire paved the way.

On a powerline right-of-way that bisected the natural area, I found several small red pines, which gave me a close-up look at the needles: dark green (darker than white pine needles), slender, limber, bound in clusters of two. The needles are 4 to 6 inches long—the longest of any pine native to the Northeast. In comparison, needles of eastern white pine are 2 to 5 inches in length and packaged in bundles of five. A telling feature of the red pine's needles is that when bent double, they snap crisply. Each needle remains attached to its branch for three to four years.

Red pines thrive in poorer soils than do eastern white pines. They grow best in sandy or gravelly ground. They rarely grow in swamps but sometimes edge the wetlands. As they grow, some individuals develop taproots, long, central roots that probe deep for nutrients and moisture. Red pines have broad-spreading lateral roots that give good support and make the trees wind-firm.

Mature red pines stand 50 to 80 feet tall, with a trunk 1 to 3 feet in diameter. Huge specimens can become 150 feet tall and 5 feet in diameter. A red pine can live for around four hundred years. In a closed or densely grown stand, red pines become straight and free of lateral branches from

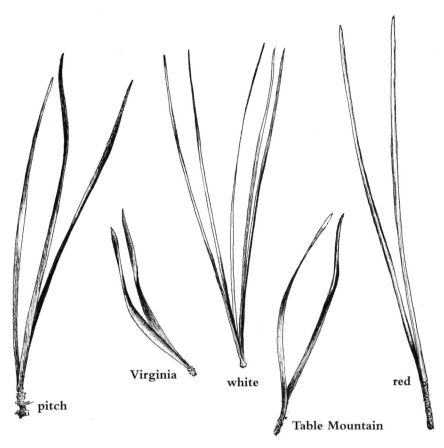

Needles of five pine species, drawn to scale.

ground level to three-quarters of the way up the trunk; in the full sun of an open stand, side branches may bend down nearly to the tree's base, and the trunk may be forked or strongly tapering. Most red pine branches extend out horizontally and tilt up slightly near the tip.

Red pine flowers from April to June. The pollinated cones grow and develop, but actual fertilization of the seed embryos does not take place until the following summer, after about thirteen months have passed. The cones are chestnut brown, about 2 inches long, and ovoid-conic in shape. Their scales lack spines or prickles. They ripen by mid-August to October of their second year. The cone scales expand, and the wind blows the fully developed seeds out from behind them. Although most seeds fall in autumn, trees may continue to drop seeds during the following winter, spring, and summer. During a good seed year in a mature red pine stand, each tree produces around two hundred cones. Good seed crops occur at three- to seven-year intervals, with light crops during intervening years and bumper crops every ten to twelve or more years. In a Michigan study, the soundness of seeds varied from 14 to 63 percent. After losing their seeds, the cones usually fall off the branches during spring or summer, although some may hang on for two or three years.

Red pines need direct sunlight to prosper. You may find hemlock and white pine seedlings growing beneath red pines, but rarely the reverse. In a mixed stand, hardwoods such as northern red oak and sugar maple may grow taller than red pines, ultimately shading them out.

Cedar waxwings, red-breasted nuthatches, golden-crowned kinglets, Blackburnian warblers, and pine warblers are some of the forest birds that nest in *Pinus resinosa*. In the Great Lakes states, bald eagles often build their bulky, heavy stick nests in the tops of large old-growth red pines. Because it produces seed crops fairly infrequently, red pine is less important as a wildlife food source than some other conifers. Red squirrels, white-footed mice, red-backed voles, and chipmunks eat large quantities of seeds in the years when they are available. Deer, mice, snowshoe hares, and porcupines feed on seedlings and bark.

Red pine wood is darker in color and harder than the wood of white pine; it is also heavier, at 33 pounds per cubic foot, dry weight, compared with white pine's 25. The green or undried wood of red pine, thoroughly impregnated with resin, is so dense that it sinks in water. Red pine gets used for general construction, structural framing members, flooring, outdoor furniture, and toys. Creosote readily penetrates the thick sapwood, and for this reason, red pine is often chosen for treated poles and pilings. Shipbuilders use it for masts, spars, and other fittings.

Pinus resinosa is frequently called Norway pine. Some sources claim that this title comes from the town of Norway, Maine, where red pine grew abundantly, but the nickname was in use before the town came into being. A more probable explanation is that early English explorers mistook the tree for Norway spruce, a valuable ship-building wood imported to Britain from Scandinavia. Red pine does not occur naturally in Norway or anywhere outside of North America.

SHORTLEAF PINE

Shortleaf pine *(Pinus echinata)* is one of the hard pines, so called because their wood is harder and heavier than that of eastern white pine. Most authorities recognize twelve species of hard pine native to eastern North America. These trees all carry their needles in bundles of two or three. Sometimes they are referred to collectively as yellow pines, owing to the color of their wood.

In the Northeast, the following species are considered to be hard pines: pitch pine, a Pennsylvania tree; jack pine *Pinus banksiana,* growing farther north and not in Pennsylvania; and red pine, in northern Pennsylvania, New England, southern Canada, and the Great Lakes states; as well as Table Mountain pine, Virginia pine, and shortleaf pine, three southern species that range north into Pennsylvania. Other hard pines of the South are pond, loblolly, longleaf, spruce, sand, and slash. Scots pine and Austrian pine are two European hard pines that have been widely planted and have become naturalized in the eastern United States. (For information on Scots and Austrian pines, see Common Introduced Trees.)

Shortleaf pine grows in twenty-two states, from south-central Pennsylvania and New Jersey south to Florida and west to Missouri, Oklahoma, and Texas. Fossilized pollen indicates that at one time it ranged as far north as Michigan. The tree grows its biggest in Arkansas, northern Louisiana, and the Piedmont Region of the southern states. It thrives in a variety of soils, although not usually limestone soils. In coastal New Jersey, shortleaf pine grows at elevations as low as 10 feet; in the mountains of North Carolina and Georgia, it ranges from the valley floors up to the ridgetops at more than 3,000 feet. On good sites in the heart of its range, a mature shortleaf pine may reach more than 100 feet in height and 3 feet in diameter. In Pennsylvania, shortleaf pine rarely ascends to the tops of the mountains; usually it grows at lower elevations. The largest specimen of *Pinus echinata* known in the Keystone State stands near the entrance to the Mont Alto campus of Penn State University in southern Franklin County. The tree is 75 feet tall and 102 inches in circumference.

Shortleaf pine is an important timber tree in the South, and loggers cut it for dimensional lumber, flooring, house trim, plywood, veneer, pulpwood, and barrel staves. Known as fat pine or lightwood, the resin-impregnated splinters of the heartwood have long been used to kindle hearth fires. The wood weighs 38 pounds per cubic foot.

Shortleaf pine is rare in Pennsylvania. When found, it is usually mixed in with eastern white pine, pitch pine, or Virginia pine, as well as various oaks. A state forester helped me locate one at Meeting of the Pines Natural Area, in Franklin County, about 10 miles north of the Mason-Dixon line. The pine was around 50 feet tall. We could not get a good look at the needles, clustered in the uppermost branches of the crown, straining toward the light in the forest canopy; thick-trunked oaks had surrounded and were now outstripping this and several other neighboring shortleaf pines. The conifers' role as successional or pioneering trees treats them to a swift early growth and often condemns them to a gradual decline as slower-maturing hardwoods overtake and then shade them out. According to the forester, an excellent grove of shortleaf pine stands on state land just west of Pennsylvania Route 997, opposite Irishtown Road south of Fayetteville in southern Franklin County.

If I'd had closer access to the needles, I would have found them slender and flexible, abruptly pointed, a dark bluish green, and 3 to 5 inches long. On shortleaf pine, most of the needles are in pairs, although some come in bundles of three. The needles last two to five years before falling off. The bark of shortleaf pine is a rich brown tinged with cinnamon red, broken into rectangular plates of varying sizes whose long axes generally run parallel with that of the trunk. Small holes, or resin pockets, pit the 1/2-inch-thick plates; some of the pockets are pitch-filled, while others may be empty. The outer surfaces of the rectangular plates peel off readily in thin, filmlike scales. Its thick bark protects the shortleaf pine from fire.

Cones of this species mature in two seasons. They are egg-shaped and 2 to 3 inches long, each scale tipped with a small, slender prickle. They release their winged seeds in late October and November. The average distance for seed dispersal is 250 feet from the parent tree, with a maximum of about a quarter mile. After shedding their seeds—twenty-five to thirty-five per cone—the empty cones may cling to the branches for several years. The numerous persistent cones are another trait useful for identifying shortleaf pine.

Birds and small mammals forage for the seeds. Squirrels sometimes cut down the cones and eat the seeds before the cones open naturally. Like other conifers, shortleaf pines offer resting and winter cover for many wild animals. In the South, shortleaf pines with red heart rot, a fungal disease, provide an important nesting habitat for the red-cockaded woodpecker, an endangered species.

VIRGINIA PINE

In Nittany Valley in my home county of Centre, where the soils are rich and limestone sweet, I do not find Virginia pine. But across the ridge in poorer Bald Eagle Valley, where I live, Virginia pine is abundant. It cloaks the shaley, infertile hills where people gave up on farming half a century back. It invades old fields from the edges. Its rough, scrimpy appearance contrasts greatly with that of the lofty, graceful white pine with which it often shares the land.

Virginia pine *(Pinus virginiana)* is also known as scrub pine and Jersey pine. It ranges from central Pennsylvania, central New Jersey, and the western end of New York's Long Island south to Mississippi, Alabama, and Georgia, achieving its best growth in the Piedmont Region of the Southeast. Virginia pine seeds itself onto depleted, eroded land; sandy areas; serpentine barrens, where soil chemicals defeat many other plants; and rocky hills and ridges. It is much less tolerant of wet soil than pitch pine. An excellent place to see Virginia pine in Pennsylvania is Pine Ridge Natural Area in Bedford County, on lands of the Buchanan State Forest. There, Virginia pines took over many marginal farms, including resettlement lands from which the federal government relocated farmers during the Depression years of the 1930s. Botanists consider Virginia pine to be a transitional or pioneering species, and today at Pine Ridge the coniferous pioneers are gradually giving way to taller, longer-lived trees such as oaks, hickories, and black cherry.

You can identify Virginia pine by its needles: bright green, 2 to 3 inches long, stiff and noticeably twisted, and bundled in pairs. The cones are 2 to 3 inches in length and covered with overlapping scales, each scale tipped with a slender but sharp prickle. Mature Virginia pines hold on to their cones for five to fifteen years after the fruits have released their seeds; the old cones turn a weathered gray-brown, sometimes falling apart on their stems. The bark of Virginia pine is thin (1/4 to 1/2 inch), dark reddish brown, and broken up into small, flat plates. People sometimes confuse the tree with Scots pine, a foreign species widely planted in eastern North America. But Scots pine does not hold on to its cones for long; its cones do not have prickles; and the bark on the upper branches is bright orange, whereas that on Virginia pine is dull brown. A destructive test can be made. Bend a 1/2-inch branchlet: if the tree is a Virginia pine, the tough, resilient branchlet will bend; if it's a Scots pine, the branchlet will snap.

A normal height for mature Virginia pines in Pennsylvania is 30 to 40 feet, with a trunk diameter of 18 inches. The largest Virginia pine reported to the American Forestry Association for its Big Tree Register is 101 feet tall and has a circumference of 111 inches, yielding a diameter of roughly 34 inches; it stands in Camp Crooked Creek, Kentucky. As I have seen them in south-central Pennsylvania, young Virginia pines are scruffy pyramids, while older specimens take on a flat-topped but still recognizably conical form. The overall impression is one of dishevelment, of thin foliage through which the background light filters evenly. Branching is horizontal and starts near the ground, although in a dense stand, the lower boughs die back as the trees get taller. To traverse a thicket of Virginia pines, the wise hiker seeks out a deer trail winding between the jabbing dead branches.

When growing in full sunlight, Virginia pines sometimes produce cones when only five years old. In April and May, female conelets become receptive to pollen released by male flowers. After a year has passed, fertilization takes place in June, in ovules pollinated thirteen months earlier; the cones mature by autumn and release their seeds for three months or longer, starting in late October. A healthy Virginia pine usually produces at least some cones each year, and heavy seed crops come along at intervals of three or more years. The seeds have small wings, and the wind blows them about. In a stand where the trees average 60 feet in height, most seed falls within 100 feet of the parent tree.

Even a thin layer of leaves or fallen needles will prevent seedlings from taking root. A light surface fire, erosion, or disturbance of the leaf litter by logging machines improves the chances of seedlings establishing themselves. They need direct sunlight for good growth and will die if heavily shaded. Virginia pine itself casts a dense shade and, as the years pass, produces a thick mass of needle litter, so it is not usual for the trees to reproduce themselves on the same site.

Under good conditions, a seedling may grow 4 to 8 inches in its first year, and by the end of ten years, it may be a 17-foot sapling. Virginia pines tolerate dry conditions, but their thin bark affords little protection against fire. The root system is generally shallow, and strong winds knock the trees over. Wet, heavy snow often breaks branches and flattens saplings.

Because of its many branches, Virginia pine makes knotty lumber. The wood weighs 33 pounds per cubic foot. It is soft and brittle. People burn it as fuel, and the stubby trunks are sometimes turned into mine props and railroad ties. Wild creatures find their own uses for Virginia pine. Rodents eat the seeds and gnaw the bark on young trees. In the snow that has sifted through a pine stand, I have found tracks made by ruffed grouse, mice and voles, red squirrels, rabbits, weasels, foxes, and deer—the creatures sheltering from inclement weather among the dense boughs or hunting for prey. Many birds nest in the screening foliage, from tiny warblers to crows, and also owls, which sometimes appropriate the crows' nests.

If Virginia pine is scrubby, it is also picturesque. In my mind's eye, I see its stark, immobile silhouette at dusk on a spring day, when the deciduous trees have not yet come to leaf, when the woodcock are circling in songful flight, spiraling down the dim sky to land in grassy openings of old fields inexorably returning to woods.

TABLE MOUNTAIN PINE

A hot summer's day on a wooded ridge: vultures tipping across the sky, monotonous chanting of a vireo high in an oak, a lizard basking on a heat-shimmering rock, a bobcat panting in a den beneath the boulders. From among the jumbled sandstone—the very spine of the ridge—protrudes a short, thick-limbed tree, a pine whose spare, bluish green crown is burdened with immense, prickly cones. The cones look out of proportion with the stunted tree. In the baking, desiccative heat, the cones' scales, drying, spread open a bit farther. From behind a scale on one cone, a seed slips out; the winged seed flutters down, slanting off eastward on the breeze.

Table Mountain pine *(Pinus pungens)*, also known as mountain pine, is a hardy tree that grows only in the Appalachians. Its range includes parts of eight states: Georgia, South Carolina, North Carolina, Tennessee, Virginia, West Virginia, Maryland, and Pennsylvania. In Pennsylvania, Table Mountain pine grows mainly in the south-central region, on dry uplands of the Ridge and Valley physiographic province; and on South Mountain, the northernmost extension of the Blue Ridge. The trees cling to exposed ridgetops, steep south- or west-facing slopes, shale hills, and rocky outcrops, rooted in the dry, infertile soil thinly skinning those difficult places. Table Mountain pines usually grow in discrete clusters in the predominantly oak woods, or as a single sentinel on some stark, lonely eminence. Its folk names tell of the tree's character and habitat: hickory pine, poverty pine, prickly pine, bur pine.

Table Mountain pine is distinguished by its cones, 2 to 4 inches long—as big as a good-size apple. They grow on the limbs in tight, whorled clusters of two to seven. The cones have bases that are slightly off-center, and short or

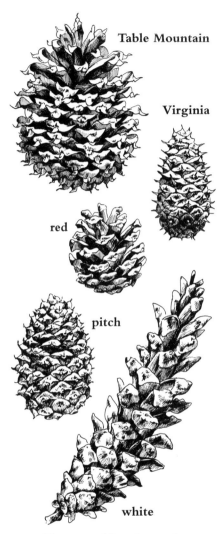

Table Mountain

Virginia

red

pitch

white

*The cones of five pine species,
drawn to scale.*

nonexistent stalks. A cone may stay on the branch for fifteen years or longer, with at least some of its seeds remaining viable all that time. Joseph Illick, in *Pennsylvania Trees,* describes a branch that was seven years old, $1^{1}/_{2}$ inches thick at its thickest end, and $3^{1}/_{2}$ feet long; it held no less than thirty-six cones. Each cone scale is armored with a stiff $1/4$-inch prickle, making the fruit look like a medieval mace. Writes the ecologist Charles Williams, who has studied Table Mountain pine for years, "I once had the painful misfortune to slip and fall on one of these botanical caltrops. Impalement led me to quickly respect the ability of the spines to protect the cone and its contents!"

The needles of Table Mountain pine come two per bundle. They are 2 to 4 inches long, stout, stiff, somewhat twisted, and sharp-pointed. The tree puts out sturdy horizontal limbs. If it grows on a slope, the longest, heaviest limbs will be on the exposed, downhill side of the tree's trunk. The trunk may be straight, bent, or leaning, beneath a rounded or irregular crown. Overall height is 30 to 40 feet, with a trunk diameter of 1 to 2 feet. Rarely does *Pinus pungens* achieve 60 feet. The largest Table Mountain pine known in Pennsylvania is at Meeting of the Pines Natural Area in Franklin County; it stands 78 feet tall and has a circumference of 80 inches.

André Michaux, the pioneering French botanist, named Table Mountain pine after Tablerock Mountain in North Carolina, where he first encountered it sometime before 1794. He wrote, "The Table Mountain pine has no valuable properties to recommend it to notice in Europe; it will serve only to complete botanical collections and to diversify pleasure-grounds." Table Mountain pine is grouped with the hard or yellow pines; its wood is brittle and knotty and similar in its qualities to that of pitch and Virginia pine. Settlers used it for fuel, rough lumber, and charcoal making, and they dressed wounds with turpentine collected from the tree. Today loggers cut Table Mountain pine for pulpwood, taking it indiscriminately along with oaks and other pines; some mills turn the pitch-impregnated trunks into landscaping timbers.

Pinus pungens is a fire-adapted species. The tree's thick bark protects its inner tissues from damage caused by flames and high temperatures. If a fire burns over a mountain, killing competing trees such as chestnut oaks and scarlet oaks and scorching away the built-up leaf duff that normally covers the forest floor, Table Mountain pine may seed itself onto the naked sites and promptly reforest them.

Like pitch pine, with which it often forms mixed stands, Table Mountain pine has serotinous cones: their scales, sealed shut by pitch, open after being exposed to high temperatures, such as those caused by forest fires. Cones of Table Mountain pine also open on summer and fall days when temperatures soar into the eighties and nineties, and hot winds blow. The seed kernels are about 1/4 inch long, with a thin wing about 3/4 inch in length.

The partially opened cones are food warehouses for white-breasted nuthatches, black-capped chickadees, tufted titmice, and various woodpeckers, which work the seeds free from behind the armored scales. Red squirrels seemingly ignore the cone's sturdy prickles, biting through the scales; writes ecologist Williams, "When the dinner is done, all that remains of the stout cone is a pile of scales and a core that resembles a corn cob." Williams also observed or found evidence of wild turkeys scratching for insects beneath Table Mountain pines, pileated woodpeckers excavating grubs or ants from old pine snags, and whip-poor-wills and ruffed grouse resting among the understory shrubs in Table Mountain pine stands. The red crossbill is a northern bird that sometimes migrates south and spends the winter in the Appalachians; during years when other conifers' seed crops fail, crossbills may subsist almost entirely on seeds of Table Mountain pine, some of whose cones invariably remain open.

Table Mountain pine hosts the mountain pine coneworm, a moth larva that feeds on the cones of this species and on nothing else. Southern pine beetles drill holes in the trees to eat the phloem, the food-conducting tissue. A pathogen called blue-stain fungus may invade the tree through the pine beetles' holes; the fungus shuts down water transport in the tree, killing it.

Ecologists believe the abundance of *Pinus pungens* in the Appalachians has long followed a pattern of expansion and decline. The pines cling to their rocky eminences; drought grips the land; fires caused by lightning or other factors denude it (Native American hunters periodically burned the forest to open the way for plants that would provide more food and cover for game); and the pines' wind-carried seeds quickly sprout, filling the openings. After the lumber industry ravaged the Appalachians in the late 1800s and early 1900s, fires fueled by logging debris burned off many square miles. Table Mountain pine and pitch pine quickly responded, perhaps becoming more abundant than they ever had been in the past.

In Pennsylvania, state agencies bought the logged-over land and encouraged new forests to grow while protecting the developing trees by suppressing fires. Gradually, because they were not held back by periodic wildfires, slower-growing hardwoods caught up to the pines, grew taller, and started shading out the conifers. Today ecologists recommend that forest managers reintroduce both high- and low-intensity fires to restore and maintain Table Mountain pine and pitch pine as key components of the eastern woods.

CEDARS

The names of many American trees have curious etymologies: European interpretations of Native American words; Old English or Germanic terms carried on through the centuries and applied to New World species, whether related or not to their Old World namesakes; names commemorating historical events or botanical features or antique uses; and names that recalled for early settlers the trees of their homelands, trees even of biblical and other far-off places.

The cedars belong to the last category. According to taxonomists, the true cedars are evergreen trees of the Old World genus *Cedrus,* which includes the famed cedars of Lebanon as well as certain trees in North Africa and the Himalayas. Our North American cedars are also evergreens, also fragrant and clean-smelling like Eurasian cedars. But they're not true cedars. The three species native to the Northeast all belong to Cupressaceae, the cypress family: red-cedar, *Juniperus virginiana,* fairly common in the Keystone State; and

Atlantic white-cedar, *Chamaecyparis thyoides,* and northern white-cedar, *Thuja occidentalis,* neither of which occur at present in natural populations in Pennsylvania.

Red-Cedar *(Juniperus virginiana).* This small to medium-size tree is actually a juniper, a member of the genus *Juniperus.* Its large range extends from roughly the hundredth meridian—known as the Dry Line, and running from South Dakota to Texas—east to the Atlantic coast, and includes all or part of thirty-six states from Maine to Florida, as well as southern Ontario. In Pennsylvania, red-cedar is found mainly in the southern counties, in fields taken out of farm production, early successional woods, serpentine barrens, and other dry to moist sites, although not generally in wetlands. The tree is also called red juniper, Virginia juniper, and savin, after a similar Old World species. Because of the color of its wood and bark, early French colonists named red-cedar *baton rouge,* "red stick."

Red-cedar can be a perplexing tree. It grows in two different forms and puts forth two different types of foliage.

Eastern red-cedars often spring up in old fields.
Many songbirds nest in their dense foliage.

A young red-cedar looks like nothing so much as a green finger pointed heavenward. (Is that why people transplant it so often in cemeteries: as an admonitory adornment?) The mature tree bears little resemblance to the upright, slender, youthful form, appearing conical but somewhat flattened at the top, wider and more hunkered-down around its stubby trunk. According to one observer, the young tree looks like an unopened umbrella, while the old tree is a half-opened bumbershoot.

The new, vigorously growing foliage of a red-cedar consists of thin, sharp-pointed needles that resemble the tip of an awl. These awl-shaped needles are three-sided and up to 1/4 inch long; often they bristle and flare out irregularly from the stems of seedlings that have been heavily browsed by white-tailed deer. The mature leaves are strikingly dissimilar: about 1/16 inch long, each overlapping the next like a reptile's scales and tightly pressed against the twigs, which branch out in dark green sprays. Often some of a red-cedar's boughs will show a rusty tint caused by old foliage that stays on the tree for several years after dying. To further complicate the situation, red-cedar becomes an ill-looking brown toward winter's end, and then greens up again in spring.

The reddish brown bark is whiskery, peeling off in long, vertical strips; *exfoliating* is the word botanists use to describe this quality. Extremely thin, red-cedar bark offers little protection against fire; the green foliage of the tree, however, does not burn readily. The trunk of an old red-cedar is often grooved, fluted, buttressed—anything but symmetrical and round.

Knee-high, waist-high, head-high, the young trees rise like columns from the tired soil of abandoned farms. Red-cedars can grow 40 to 60 feet tall, up to 100 feet on an excellent site. The oldest age reported for the species is three hundred years. The biggest red-cedar known in Pennsylvania stands in the Shawnee Presbyterian Church Cemetery at Shawnee-on-Delaware, Monroe County, in eastern Pennsylvania; it is 36 feet high and 67 inches around the trunk, with a 36-foot crown spread. Recently I found what may be an even larger specimen on a dry ridge in Huntingdon County. One other person and I clasped arms around the tree's trunk; we estimated a 10-foot circumference. The hoary giant had probably gotten its start in an open field that later became an oak woods; it didn't look as if the neighboring white and chestnut oaks would overtop the cedar anytime soon. The largest red-cedar known in the United States grows in Georgia, again in a cemetery. It is 57 feet tall and 242 inches—just over 20 feet—in circumference.

When Europeans arrived in North America, they found groves of tall, magnificent red-cedars, and it was not long before they learned from the native inhabitants, and discovered through trial and usage, how to employ the wood. Red-cedar is straight-grained, easy to split and plane, and long-lasting in contact with water and soil. Farmers used it for cabin logs and fences, craftsmen fashioned it into furniture, and shipwrights worked it into planks and parts for boats. Soft and uniform, red-cedar makes a good carving wood. My maternal great-grandfather, Addison Osgood Foote, was a Union soldier during the Civil War; his Wisconsin regiment mainly did guard duty on railroads in occupied Arkansas. I have a letter he wrote in which he describes whittling a set of chess pieces out of cedar wood.

For over a century, pencils were made from red-cedar: the wood is soft enough to be cut across the grain, which is how a mechanical pencil sharpener works, and light and fragrant in the bargain. In the early 1900s, as the supply of large red-cedars waned, pencil manufacturers bought old cabins, barn floors, and fence rails that had stood exposed to the weather for decades, their interiors still sound—before finally turning to the incense cedar of the American West. Today red-cedar is used mainly for fence posts, with the largest quantities cut in Tennessee, Kentucky, Alabama, Arkansas, and several other southern states. Because the aromatic wood seems to repel clothes moths, it often goes into chests, wardrobes, and drawer and closet linings. Red-cedar has whitish or yellowish sapwood and ruddy heartwood, and the two colors contrast dramatically.

In spring, small, inconspicuous flowers open at the ends of minute twigs. Male and female flowers generally appear on separate trees. By autumn the pollinated female flowers have developed into round, berrylike fruits 1/4 inch in diameter. Firm, sweet-tasting pulp encases a pair of seeds. The fruit is purplish blue, with a whitish powdery bloom; a tree full of fruit will have a noticeable bluish cast.

Anthonie Holthuijzen, a biologist working in southwest Virginia, explored the ecology of red-cedars for many years. In one study, he documented yellow-rumped warblers, cedar waxwings, robins, starlings, bluebirds, mockingbirds, downy woodpeckers, and wood thrushes eating the fruit. The cedar waxwing earned its name from its liking for red-cedar berries; a flock of these social birds can pick a large tree clean in a few days. It takes twelve minutes for a cedar seed to pass through a waxwing's system, Holthuijzen determined, and the digestion process renders the seed three times more likely to germinate than a seed in a berry that has simply fallen on the ground.

Birds spread cedar seeds across the land, tending to concentrate their leavings beneath perching sites. When Holthuijzen scraped 356 bird droppings off a 317-yard-long fence, he found they contained 1,006 red-cedar seeds. In some places, rows of bird-planted red-cedars stand between old fields, having outlasted the wire or wood fences that at one time divided the plots. Rabbits, foxes, raccoons, skunks, and coyotes eat red-cedar fruits, and the greenery helps sustain deer in winter.

Many birds nest in the dense foliage, including chipping sparrows, song sparrows, mockingbirds, cardinals, and robins. An even wider range of birds roost in red-cedars, shielded from inclement weather and predators' eyes. Leaf litter falling from cedars helps enrich depleted fields. Biologists have found that the soil beneath red-cedar trees hosts more earthworms than that beneath pine plantations.

Cedar-apple rust, a fungus disease, causes galls in *Juniperus virginiana.* During wet weather in spring, the fungus extrudes long, yellow, gelatinous growths whose spores may spread to apple trees, damaging their leaves. In some states, laws permit the eradication of red-cedars in apple-producing regions.

People have reportedly used red-cedar berries as flavorings for food. However, large quantities of the fruit are believed to irritate the urinary tract and kidneys. Native Americans of different tribes boiled the fruits and leaves to make elixirs for treating colds and coughs, and they drank an oil from the berries to relieve dysentery.

The related common or dwarf juniper, *Juniperus communis,* grows in Pennsylvania and the Northeast, and across Europe and northern Asia as well, usually as a shrub and rarely as a small tree. Its hard, pale blue berries are eaten by ruffed and sharptail grouse, bobwhite quail, ring-necked pheasants, and other birds and mammals. People use the berries to spice stews and to give gin its distinctive tang. The name *gin* comes from the French word for juniper, *genièvre.*

Atlantic White-Cedar *(Chamaecyparis thyoides).* This slim, upright cedar looks similar to red-cedar but occupies a different habitat. At one time, Atlantic white-cedar grew in bogs in Philadelphia and Bucks counties; a report made to the Philadelphia Academy of Sciences in 1886 noted that Atlantic white cedar "until very recently, was common along the Schuylkill and Delaware [rivers] and isolated specimens may still exist there." But no longer; the tree apparently has been extirpated by urban sprawl and development of the coastal plain habitat, little of which existed in Pennsylvania in the first place.

Atlantic white-cedar thrives in the muck of freshwater swamps from Maine to Florida. It reaches maturity in fifty to seventy years, growing 40 to 60 feet tall, with a trunk 1 to 2 feet in diameter. Prehistoric trunks of this tree 6 feet in diameter have emerged from wetlands, waterlogged but completely sound; in the past, loggers "mined" such wood in New Jersey swamps. The wood has been used for tubs, barrels, shingles, house siding, fencing, telegraph poles, and boat construction. When it weathers, Atlantic white-cedar becomes a soft pewter gray, rather than turning dark gray or black as the wood of red-cedar does. Charcoal from "swamp cedar" was used for making gunpowder during the American Revolution. Today the tree is a popular ornamental.

Northern White-Cedar *(Thuja occidentalis).* Some authorities say that northern white-cedar's other and perhaps better-known name—arborvitae, Latin for "tree of life"—stems from its longevity: this slow-growing plant can live three hundred to four hundred years. Or perhaps the name arises from an incident in Canada, in the winter of 1535–36, when tea prepared by Native Americans from the foliage and bark of an unidentified conifer (supposed to be northern white-cedar but possibly black spruce) cured the French adventurer Jacques Cartier and his fellow explorers of scurvy, thereby saving their lives.

No known native stands of northern white-cedar grow in Pennsylvania, although the tree has been "planted and/or naturalized at a few scattered locations," according to Ann Rhoads and Timothy Block in their definitive reference book, *The Plants of Pennsylvania,* published in 2000. Northern white-cedar grows naturally in Virginia, West Virginia, and Ohio, and in a broad band from Nova Scotia to southeastern Manitoba and south through parts of New England and New York. Horticulturists have bred more than fifty varieties for ornamental and landscape plantings.

In nature, northern white-cedar occupies two distinct habitats: rich fen peatlands, a type of swamp in which slow-moving water delivers a steady flow of nutrients; and dry, calcium-rich uplands, including soils near limestone ledges. Botanists believe that the correct soil pH—neutral or slightly alkaline—is more important to this tree than the amount of available moisture. Northern white-cedar grows slowly and can survive in dense shade. It fares poorly in, or is absent from, acidic swamps and bogs; there, black spruce usually becomes the dominant tree. In cedar swamps, northern white-cedar often grows in dense, pure stands.

The wood is similar to that of Atlantic white-cedar. It is light, at 20 pounds per cubic foot, dry weight, and works easily; it is long-lasting in contact with soil and water. Native Americans used it for the frames and ribs of bark-sheathed canoes. Several tribes prepared decoctions from the inner bark to ease menstrual cramps and alleviate rheumatism.

In the North, deer and moose often shelter in white-cedar swamps. In winter, deer "yard up" in the thickets, where they feed on the evergreen foliage. Snowshoe hares nibble on low branches. Red squirrels insulate their winter nests with strips of white-cedar bark, and various birds weave the fibrous strands into their nests. Red squirrels and pine siskins eat the seeds of northern white-cedar, which are borne in bell-shaped cones about 1/2 inch in length.

BROAD-LEAVED
TREES

COTTONWOOD

Eastern cottonwood *(Populus deltoides)* is an uncommon tree in Pennsylvania. State Forester Joseph Illick, in his 1928 *Pennsylvania Trees,* reported that cottonwoods grew in Lancaster County and on Presque Isle in Erie County, and that many had been planted elsewhere in the state as shade trees and ornamental specimens. *The Vascular Flora of Pennsylvania,* by Ann Rhoads and William Klein, published in 1993 and based on herbarium specimens, shows locations of cottonwoods as dots peppered around the fringe of the state; one suspects that at least some of those may be ornamentals. And Ann Rhoads and Timothy Block, in their monumental reference book, *The Plants of Pennsylvania* (2000), characterize the tree's distribution as "scattered." I do not know the eastern cottonwood from the wild, but rather from a line of old giants planted along the lane of a friend's farm.

Eastern cottonwood ranges from southern New England and Canada west to the Plains states, where it intergrades with the plains cottonwood, *Populus deltoides occidentalis,* a subspecies that continues west to the Rocky Mountain foothills. The eastern species grows in the Connecticut River valley, in parts of New York, and on the shores of several of the Great Lakes; it becomes more abundant starting in Ohio and moving west and south from there. The core of its range includes the humid lowlands of the Mississippi River drainage, where the tree makes its best growth. Eastern cottonwood ranges south to Florida and Texas and is absent from the higher Appalachians.

Cottonwoods rarely stray far from water. They prosper in moist, rich soils of floodplains and river bottomlands. They also thrive along stream banks and lake borders and in swamps. Planted as a shade tree, a cottonwood will grow if its roots—shallow but wide-spreading—find a reliable source of the moisture that this tree requires so abundantly.

Populus deltoides has a handsome form, which becomes particularly visible in winter: an expansive, open crown of very thick, often slightly drooping branches. Most cottonwoods stand 50 to 75 feet tall. Some achieve 100 or more feet, and observers have reported heights of 175 to 190 feet. Trunk diameters of 2 to 4 feet are typical, and really large specimens can be 4 to 6 feet across the trunk. Often a cottonwood forks into two or more stems a few feet above ground level. Young cottonwoods on excellent sites may add 5 feet to their stature in a single year and 40 feet in ten years.

Deep, vertical furrows mark the ashy gray bark of the mature tree. The leaf is strongly triangular, with a long, pointed tip. The best way to distinguish a cottonwood from one of the many hybrid poplars that have been planted is to look at the leaf. A hybrid will tend to have a more ovate leaf, or, if triangular, it will lack the truncate or straight-across base exhibited by the cottonwood. Cottonwood leaves are 3 to 5 inches long, rather thick, and have rounded teeth along their margins. They are a deep, shiny green above and pale green below. The leaves alternate along the twigs. When crushed, leaves and buds release a sweet aroma. The stalks of cottonwood leaves are long and laterally flattened, like those of aspens, causing the leaves to sway in the breeze. They make more of a rustle or a rattle, compared with the whisperings of the aspens' smaller leaves. In autumn, cottonwood leaves turn yellow; they fall early, often leaving the branches bare in September.

Unlike quaking aspen and bigtooth aspen, eastern cottonwood does not clone itself by sending up genetically identical shoots from its root system. However, a young tree will sprout vigorously from the stump if cut down, and cuttings planted in the ground grow readily. Cottonwoods can be less-than-ideal neighbors in cities, where their prolific, probing roots heave up sidewalks and clog sewers and drains. In rural areas, they make effective windbreaks and are planted for erosion control along ditches, riverbanks, and shorelines.

In March or April, just before its leaves unfurl, the cottonwood sets out flowers. Male and female flowers appear on separate trees. The fuzzy male blossoms are crowded together on drooping, yellow catkins; the deep red female blossoms are larger and displayed on drooping stems. Wind-blown pollen fertilizes the female flowers, which mature into elliptical capsules 3/8 inch long. The capsules split open around June, releasing many tiny seeds. Each seed has a tuft of downy fiber that acts as a parachute, carrying it several hundred feet or farther from its parent. I have visited midwestern towns in late spring, when the cottonwood fluff blew down the streets and piled up like snow in the gutters. The tree earns its name from its cottony seeds.

Trees start producing seeds when five to ten years old. Botanists have estimated that a single mature tree can release as many as forty-eight million seeds in one year. Plenty of the seeds fall in the water, and receding spring floods may deposit them on land. Writes David F. Van Haverbeke in the chapter on eastern cottonwood in *Silvics of North America,* "The cottonwood in the lower reaches of the Mississippi River may contain genes from many tributaries."

Seeds require abundant sunlight to germinate and grow. Cottonwoods often compete with willows to cover new sandbars and bare floodplains. When mature, they may stand among black ash, silver maple, American elm, hackberry, sycamore, and box-elder. Their life span is not long. Deterioration sets in as early as age seventy, with cracks and heart rot weakening and hollowing the trunk. Cavities in living cottonwoods are used for nesting and winter shelter by many animals, including wood ducks, woodpeckers, owls, opossums, and raccoons.

The heartwood of *Populus deltoides* is dark brown, the sapwood wide and white, and the soft but tough-to-split wood weighs a mere 28 pounds per cubic foot—about as light as aspen. Loggers cut it for plywood, paper pulp, excelsior, boxes and crates, matches, and interior parts of furniture. The wood warps and checks badly as it cures. When my great-grandfather Addison Foote claimed a homestead on the Kansas plains in 1871, he put up a house quickly, believed to be the first frame dwelling (as opposed to a sod house) built in Mitchell County, Kansas. Add was a good carpenter, but his material—the green or uncured wood of cottonwood, either the eastern or the plains variety—turned on him. Drafts were many in that humble abode. In later years, my great-grandmother, Sarah Gleason Foote, recalled that as a new bride fetched from Wisconsin, she spent much of her first winter in Kansas with her feet in the oven of the kitchen stove.

BIGTOOTH ASPEN

Twenty years ago, chain saws whined and log skidders growled in the hills around our thirty wooded acres. Where a forest of oaks and maples once stood, tangles of branches and leafy treetops littered the ground. Within a year, blackberries were pushing up between the stumps. And after another summer, new trees were evident on the sun-bathed slopes: bigtooth aspens *(Populus grandidentata),* straight greenish shoots lifting their apple green leaves skyward.

Botanists regard aspens as pioneer species, able to quickly establish themselves on abandoned fields or lands where logging, avalanche, disease, or fire suddenly wipe out a forest. In spring, aspen trees produce millions of tiny seeds, each tufted with white plant down. The wind scatters the seeds over miles. If they land on bare ground, the seeds germinate quickly and begin turning the land back into forest.

Two closely related species exist in Pennsylvania: quaking aspen, *Populus tremuloides,* has a scattered distribution mainly in the northern part of the state; and bigtooth aspen, *Populus grandidentata,* is abundant statewide. Quaking aspen prefers dry sites, especially sandy or gravelly soil. Bigtooth aspen colonizes dry, gravelly habitats, but it does best on rich, moist sites, including floodplains. Bigtooth aspen—also called large-toothed aspen, poplar, or popple—ranges from Nova Scotia west across southern Canada to Minnesota, and south to North Carolina and Kentucky. Both quaking and bigtooth aspen appeared on the logged lands around our Centre County home, with the bigtooth species the more abundant.

Bigtooth aspen is a small to medium-size tree. Most shoots top out at 30 to 40 feet, although specimens on excellent sites may grow as tall as 80 or even 100 feet. At maturity, the trunk is 1 to 2 feet in diameter, straight and with little taper, and often clear of branches for more than two-thirds of its height. The crown is narrow, rounded, and open, with horizontally spreading branches. One of the brawniest bigtooth aspens I've seen was holding its own in a patch of old-growth woods at Bark Cabin Natural Area, Lycoming County; it stood among tall red oaks and hemlocks, its crown claiming a share of the forest canopy high above. In general, bigtooth aspens are short-lived. Sixty years is reckoned a long life, although the root system, or clone, from which the stem may have sprung is often very much older. (See Quaking Aspen for an explanation of aspen clones and their potential antiquity.)

The bark of a young bigtooth aspen is pale olive green with a hint of gold. The bark is greenish because, like the leaves, it is living tissue, housing cells that contain the green pigment chlorophyll. During photosynthesis, chlorophyll captures the sun's energy and uses it to change water and carbon dioxide into energy-rich sugar for fueling the tree's life processes and growth. The life-giving gas oxygen is a fortunate by-product of photosynthesis. The dark, horizontal welts on the smooth bark of aspens and some other trees are lenticels, which are pores allowing the exchange of gases between the stem's internal tissues and the atmosphere. As an aspen ages, its bark thickens, becoming harder and

Both bigtooth aspen (shown here) and quaking aspen often grow as clones: interlinked stands of genetically identical trees sprouting from a common root system.

rougher and taking on a dark gray-brown color, sometimes resembling a chest-nut oak's bark, and sometimes turning almost black; this color change begins at the base of the trunk and proceeds upward. The upper trunk and the limbs keep their photosynthesis-capable bark with its distinctive green-gold color. A beautiful color it is, especially in winter when the low sun lights up the verti-cal gold stripes of a stand of aspens, often the only brightness in the woods.

As the tree's name suggests, bigtooth aspen has a leaf with large teeth along its outer margin. The quaking aspen leaf, by comparison, has many more, smaller teeth. The bigtooth's leaves are shaped like a heart, minus the deep notch. They are 3 to 4 inches long, deep green above and paler green below. The leafstalk, or petiole, is flattened and thin, like a ribbon, so that the least breeze sets the blade pivoting on its supple stalk. Bigtooth aspen is one of the first trees to leaf out in spring. According to J. H. White in *The Forest Trees of Ontario,* bigtooth aspen is "at once picked out in the forest when the leaves are unfolding in the spring by the downy appearance of the whole crown contrasted with the green of other species." In autumn, the leaves turn a soft yellow, with a few trees turning orange or red. A friend reports that aspen stands, when the leaves begin to fall, take on a distinctive fresh, clean, robust smell.

In winter, when leaves are not present, one can tell bigtooth aspen from quaking aspen by examining the leaf buds, located on the twigs and contain-ing the next year's foliage. On quaking aspen, the buds are shiny and less than 3/8 inch long; on bigtooth aspen, the buds are dull and longer than 3/8 inch.

Wild animals dote on both aspen species. In late March and early April, porcupines eat the drooping, fuzzy flower spikes, or catkins, some of the first new vegetation in the forest; in summer, they nip off branch tips, where the most nutritious leaves grow. Black bears climb into aspens to get at the new leaves in spring. Snowshoe hares and cottontail rabbits nibble the shoots and bark. Beavers prefer aspen to almost any other tree; the large, aquatic rodents gnaw down aspens, eat the tender growing tissues and the bark on the branches, and use the leftover wood to build their dams. White-tailed deer browse twigs and foliage. In north-central Pennsylvania, elk feed voraciously on aspen leaves in spring; in winter they zero in on the bark, stripping it loose with their teeth. Elk browse back the growing tips of aspen branches to the thickness of a human's little finger.

The conservationist Aldo Leopold, a Wisconsinite, wrote of the aspen in *A Sand County Almanac,* "He glorifies October and he feeds my grouse in winter." Several times I have watched ruffed grouse eating aspen buds. In the day's last light, three or four birds alight in a winter-bare tree. Their feathers fluffed against the cold, they clamber about on the swaying branches as they wrench off the energy-packed buds with their beaks—filling their crops quickly in anticipation of hawks and owls, then taking off in a thunder of wings and disappearing in the gathering dusk. Aspen buds and catkins are favorite foods of the ruffed grouse throughout the bird's range, which largely coincides with the range of bigtooth and quaking aspen in North America.

The wood of bigtooth aspen is soft, close-grained, brittle, weak, and fairly light: 29 pounds per cubic foot, dry weight. The heartwood is pale brown, the sapwood greenish white. The wood goes for crates, pallets, excelsior, matchsticks, tongue depressors, ice cream spoons, furniture parts, and interior house trim. Some aspens develop a rippling grain pattern, and such highly figured wood was once applied as a veneer on cabinetry and furniture. Aspen is often pulped, converted into paper for books and magazines. Since the 1980s, aspen has increasingly been manufactured into building products such as oriented strand board and I-beams, with chips or strands of the wood formed into sheets and structural members. (Another sign of the efficient and impoverished nature of our modern age: where before we built with solid planks of wood, now we use little chips glued together.)

Aspens belong to the willow family, Salicaceae, a group of species whose members contain the compound salicin in their bark. Salicin is the key ingredient in aspirin. In the past, Native Americans used aspen bark to treat fevers, coughs and colds, and menstrual pain.

On a recent February morning, I checked on the bigtooth aspens in the logged-off woods that have slowly grown back around our home. Two decades had passed, and already many of the aspens were dying. Dried-out fruiting bodies of wood-decay fungi studded the trunks; those of some trees had snapped off halfway up. I found where a woodpecker had chiseled out a nest cavity in a rotting snag. The places where the aspens looked healthiest were where the trees could still intercept sunlight: along the edges of old woods roads and log landings.

A process known as forest succession was taking place. The swift-growing aspens had stabilized the soil on the logged slopes. They had captured nutrients released by the rapid decay of leaf litter, spurred by the increased temperature of the forest floor. Enough sunlight had filtered down through their relatively open crowns to let slower-growing oaks and maples sprout from seeds or stumps. Over time, the oaks and maples had caught up with and were outstripping the pioneering aspens. As the aspens died, they would liberate their own nutrients to the benefit of other plants.

QUAKING ASPEN

If even a faint breeze stirs the air, the leaves of the quaking aspen *(Populus tremuloides)* will dance and flutter, twisting on their pliant stems. The silvery undersides of the leaves show themselves, and then the green upper surfaces display their slick sheen, in a ceaseless, energetic, back-and-forth flashing that makes the observer wonder if the tree itself is generating light rather than simply reflecting it.

The blade of the quaking aspen leaf—the main sun-catching part—is rounded, with a pointed tip. Small teeth rim the leaf's margin. The leafstalk is flattened, thin, and longer than the blade. The stalk acts as a pivot, presenting one side of the leaf to the wind, then the other. Some scientists suggest that this near-constant motion helps the leaf get rid of moisture in much the same way that a handkerchief waving in the wind dries faster than one hanging in still air. The aspen belongs to a group of trees known as the poplars, whose leaves all quake to some extent. Poplars grow rapidly, raising their crowns high and intercepting more sunlight than slower-growing trees. They need to process a large volume of water to shoot up so quickly, and perhaps the quaking habit is a moisture-shedding strategy that keeps their growth systems operating at full throttle.

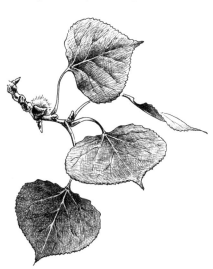

The stem, or petiole, of the quaking aspen leaf is ribbon-shaped and pliant, letting the leaf flutter in the slightest breeze.

Quaking aspen has a larger natural range than any other North American tree. *Populus tremuloides* grows from Newfoundland to Alaska, throughout New England and the Great Lakes states, and south in the Appalachian Mountains to Georgia and in the Rocky Mountains to northern Mexico. Aspens are extremely cold-hardy. They can survive temperatures as frigid as −80 degrees Fahrenheit. Forest ecologists suggest that aspens are genetically equipped to withstand winters of a severity unknown since the last ice age.

Quaking aspens quickly reforest unstable or damaged habitats such as fire-charred woodlands, avalanche slides, gravel banks, and cutover areas. They seed themselves on abandoned farmland. They prefer dry habitats but will sprout in most places and in almost all soil conditions except swamps. Aspens have a short lifespan— around sixty years—and are replaced by hardwoods and conifers that grow more gradually in the partial shade cast by the aspens' open crowns. Richly diverse shrub and herb communities often cover the ground beneath aspen stands.

Aspens are either male or female. Trees of both sexes put forth hanging fuzzy flowers, called catkins, in late March and early April before leafing out. The wind blows pollen from the male to the female flowers. Later the wind scatters the fertilized downy seeds that the female trees release. Seeds are tiny and light so that the wind can disperse them; they do not carry much energy with them, in contrast to a nut such as an acorn, which is chock-full of carbohydrates to be used by the new plant as it seeks to establish itself. The tiny roots of an aspen seed cannot penetrate through leaf litter. To survive, the seed must fall on bare ground.

In addition to reproducing sexually by means of seeds, aspens spread through vegetative reproduction, similar to the way a strawberry or a grass plant enlarges by sending forth runners, which themselves root and send up leaves. An aspen's roots radiate horizontally underground. From them, new shoots or stems—botanists call them ramets—grow vertically. These new shoots develop into trees, complete with branches, leaves, and bark. A root may snake along for 100 feet before sending up a stem, and each new stem then sends out its own roots that sprout more stems.

This unit of interlinked trees, all of them genetically identical, is called a clone. A typical clone may have a hundred stems and spread to a width of 80 or more feet. In Utah's Wasatch Mountains, researchers documented a quaking aspen clone that covered 106 acres and weighed an estimated 13 million pounds—nearly three times heavier than the world's largest giant sequoia tree. The scientists gave the clone a name—Pando, a Latin word meaning "I spread"—and proclaimed it "the most massive living organism in the world." East of the Rocky Mountains, clones are believed to be smaller, usually no more than a few acres in extent.

A clone's intricate root network can shuttle water and nutrients from one part of the organism to another, a strategy that lets aspens thrive in a patchy environment where other trees might die off. When fire or timber cutting kills a clone's standing shoots, the root system immediately sends up thousands of new stems. In the West, researchers have counted densities of four hundred thousand aspen stems per acre. Joseph S. Illick, author of

Pennsylvania Trees, found 24,792 stems per acre of quaking aspen on a lumbered tract in Lycoming County.

An individual aspen stem may live two hundred years and achieve a maximum height of 100 feet, although most stems do not live much beyond sixty or grow taller than 40 feet. But how old is the plant from which the tree may have arisen? A Minnesota clone has been aged at eight thousand years. Some researchers suggest that aspen clones may achieve an age of a million years or more. "In principal," writes botanist Michael C. Grant, one of the discoverers of Pando, "clones may even be essentially immortal, dying only from disease or the deterioration of the environment rather than from some internal clock."

In his 1993 article in *Discover* magazine, Grant noted that observant outdoor people can recognize clones and may be able to distinguish between the several clones that often merge to make up an aspen stand. The angle between individual branches and the main trunk tends to be a genetically determined trait: branches on the trunks of one clone may angle off at 45 degrees, while those of another clone may form 60-degree angles. Different clones may leaf out at slightly different times in the spring. (In general, quaking aspen leafs out earlier than its close relative bigtooth aspen, which is more abundant in Pennsylvania.) Autumn colors can vary from one clone to the next. Wrote Grant, "Some clones turn a brilliant, shining yellow. . . . Others manifest a deep, rich gold, vibrating with many overtones. The leaves of still other aspens turn red; some show a barely perceptible tinge, others a rich scarlet." (I myself have never seen a red or scarlet aspen leaf and wonder if this trait is limited to the West.)

The wood of quaking aspen is very light: 25 pounds per cubic foot, dry weight. Soft, weak, and brittle, it is used for all of the products made from the bigtooth aspen. Quaking aspen is the species most commonly logged for paper pulp, particularly in the Great Lakes states, with timber companies taking full advantage of its ability to sprout prolifically after clear-cutting.

Wildlife feeds heavily on the buds, bark, and leaves of quaking aspen. Birds such as black-capped chickadees, white-breasted nuthatches, tufted titmice, and woodpeckers dig out nest cavities in decayed, standing aspen trunks. Forest tent caterpillars and gypsy moth caterpillars eat the leaves of aspens, sometimes defoliating thousands of acres. Jack Schultz, a Pennsylvania State University entomologist who lives in Bald Eagle Valley not far from my home, discovered that aspens react chemically to insect attack. Soon after the caterpillars start chewing, the trees' remaining leaves produce bitter-tasting phenol compounds to discourage further feeding.

Quaking aspen is an attention-grabbing tree year-round. In winter, it shows off its attractive upright form and chalky white to pale yellow-green branches. In spring, the fuzzy catkins and pea green new leaves give *Populus tremuloides* a texture all its own in the forest tapestry. In summer, the perpetual shimmering of the coinlike leaves dazzles the eye of the beholder. The sound beneath an aspen stand is akin to rushing water, ceaseless and ceaselessly different, full of bright tones, pleasantly lulling. In fall, the trees light up the hills like the flickering flames of a thousand candles.

BLACK WILLOW

Rugged, ragged black willow *(Salix nigra)* slouches on the banks of streams in farming country, on the edges of swamps, in wet meadows, river floodplains, and bottomlands. Conspicuous and common once you start looking for it, black willow is also easy to overlook or dismiss, since it often appears straggling or in ill health, with a leaning trunk or several trunks splaying out from the same rootstock, branches quilled with shoots and sprouts issuing from knots and crooks, perhaps with a large limb or a split-away trunk moldering below, lying half in the water and half out. Yet black willow has its own intriguing beauty. Last autumn, soon after leaf-fall, I drove down a long valley where, along a meandering stream, stood one black willow after another. Each displayed a different form, each stood out against tan brush and golden cropfields as a complex, if disheveled, black silhouette.

Around twenty-five willow species grow in Pennsylvania, including seven introduced from Europe and Asia. (See Common Introduced Trees for information on the weeping willow.) They range in size from creeping shrubs to big trees, with black willow our largest native. Black willow gets its descriptive common name, and also the taxonomic name *nigra,* from its dark, almost black bark. The species ranges from Maine and southern Canada south to Florida, and west to South Dakota and Texas; in the South, black willow is sometimes called swamp willow. Pockets of black willows also occur in well-watered habitats in the desert Southwest, California, and northern Mexico. The species grows throughout Pennsylvania and is most common in the eastern and southern parts.

In Pennsylvania and the Northeast, mature black willows usually stand about 30 feet tall, with a trunk diameter of 10 to 20 or more inches. Some trees become 60 to 80 feet in height and have trunks 2 to 3 feet thick. The trunk or trunks are usually crooked or slanting; often they lean out over the

Black willow thrives in damp settings and develops
a wide, open, round-topped crown.

water from the bank of a stream or pond. The crown tends to be wide, open, and round-topped. In Pennsylvania, black willow sometimes takes a shrub form: many streambank bushes are classified as *Salix nigra*. In even-aged forest stands, particularly in the lower Mississippi Valley, *Salix nigra* can reach 100 to 140 feet tall and 4 feet in diameter, ascending in a single, straight trunk free of limbs for a considerable height.

The bark is thick, rough, and deeply furrowed, with wide ridges covered by thick scales. The leaves are 3 to 5 inches long and very narrow, only 3/8 to 3/4 inch in width. They stand off from the twigs on short stems; lance-olate in shape, they have round bases and taper to long points, with fine teeth on the margins. Sometimes they curve slightly to one side. Their surfaces are smooth, and a paler shade of green occurs on the undersides than on the upper sides. Twigs and branch ends—visible after the trees shed their foliage in autumn—are long, smooth, drooping, and, according to Joseph Illick in *Pennsylvania Trees,* bright reddish brown to orange in color; other sources say they are reddish olive, gray, gold, or yellow. These branchlets are brittle at the base, and high winds and ice storms often snap them off.

The branch ends are viable and are probably more important in the spreading and reproduction of *Salix nigra* than its seeds. If you take a fresh twig and put it in water, the underwater end will produce roots, and the exposed end will send out leaves. When twigs fall from a tree, they often land in the water and are carried downstream. Lodged against a bank, in silt or mud, they become new trees—no doubt the genesis of the great numbers of large riverbank specimens. Black willows also sprout freely from the stump and root system.

Willows are some of the earliest plants to flower in spring. Blossoms emerge in March or April, before the leaves expand. Male and female flowers arise on separate trees, in drooping catkins 1 to 3 inches long. Bumblebees, honeybees, and wild solitary bees gather willow pollen for their own sustenance; moving between male and female flowers, they cause pollination to take place. Willow pollen is quite fine, and wind shifts it between flowers; wind-aided dispersal often effects cross-pollination, and it can result in hybridization between species.

The conical fruit capsules split open in late spring or early summer, releasing thousands of seeds. The seeds are tiny and tufted with fine, long hairs; two to three million weigh 1 pound. Wind-blown seeds dry out quickly, and unless they land on damp, exposed ground, they become defunct within about twenty-four hours. Seeds dispersed by water last longer, but few of them end up in places where they can germinate. Young seedlings need full sunlight to grow.

The roots of *Salix nigra* require a constant supply of water during the growing season. The trees do best in wet areas that are not permanently flooded, at or slightly above the normal water level. Black willows shoot up quickly: a seedling may be 5 to 7 feet tall after its first growing season. Trees begin producing seeds at around age ten, with the optimum seed-bearing age spanning twenty-five to seventy-five years. Full-size and mature by fifty-five, black willows begin going downhill soon after that, usually dying before they reach eighty-five. Most large specimens have limbs broken off, causing breaches through which wood decay fungi enter.

Black willow root systems are shallow and branch extensively. They strengthen stream banks by binding the soil, helping prevent erosion and flood damage. They elevate the land by trapping silt: sometimes up to 20 feet of the lower part of a tree's trunk will end up buried in sediment. Black willows grow in pure stands or occupy their palustrine habitats in mixture with river birch, red and silver maples, box-elder, sycamore, eastern cottonwood, and other trees.

Several species of wildlife eat willow twigs, buds, and leaves, including grouse, deer, moose, muskrats, and porcupines. Black willow is a favorite fodder for beavers, which cut down young specimens and dine on the bark, twigs, and foliage. A host of insects feed on the leaves. Willow bark is rich in salicin, the pain-relieving ingredient in aspirin; Native Americans used this bitter substance to treat a variety of ills. They also fashioned the inner bark into ropes, bags, and fishnets. Twigs of willow, known as osiers, can be woven into baskets and wicker furniture.

The reddish brown wood weighs around 27 pounds per cubic foot, dry weight. It breaks down rapidly in contact with the soil. Although soft and too weak for structural framing, the wood resists splitting; at one time, it was a top choice for artificial limbs. Pioneers turned willow wood into charcoal, which they ground fine and used as a component in gunpowder. Black willow makes a poor fuelwood, burning quickly and yielding little heat. The wood from larger trees has gone into millwork, furniture, doors, cabinetry, boxes, barrels, toys, and paper pulp. Black willow is sometimes planted as a shade tree.

Wrote Joseph Illick in the 1928 edition of *Pennsylvania Trees,* "Very often one leaves a willow in despair because of the fact that it was impossible to identify it." More recently, George Petrides, in *A Field Guide to Eastern Trees* (1998), admitted that "identifying willows is often a difficult task even for the professional botanist." This confusion is caused by the way willows—both tree and shrub forms—cross-pollinate and produce hybrids, whose leaves, colors, catkins, bundle scars, and bud scales vary from those of their parents and fail to conform to published descriptions.

The Morris Arboretum of the University of Pennsylvania, the official arbiter of plant species in Pennsylvania, lists on its "Checklist of Pennsylvania Native Trees" black willow plus two additional willow species: peach-leaved willow and Carolina willow.

Peach-leaved willow, *Salix amygdaloides,* grows to 60 feet tall, often with a straight trunk and straight ascending branches. The leaves, broader than those of other willows, are shaped like those of the peach tree. Rare in the Keystone State, peach-leaved willow occurs in swamps and bogs and along wet shores in the northwestern part of the commonwealth. The species is abundant in the northern plains, replacing black willow along the Missouri River and its tributaries.

Carolina willow, *Salix caroliniana,* also called coastal plain willow and southern willow, is a common tree in the southeastern United States. It ranges as far north as southwestern and south-central Pennsylvania and is considered rare in our state. Carolina willow grows along riverbanks and shores and in low-lying woods.

Among the many shrub willows in Pennsylvania is pussy willow, *Salix discolor,* common in swamps and moist to wet woods statewide. All children should know of its catkins, whose coating of fine hairs feels like a kitten's soft fur. It is the immature male catkins that have this silken quality; as they mature, they send forth golden yellow, pollen-producing stamens.

BLACK WALNUT

Black walnut *(Juglans nigra)* raises its burly trunk and stalwart limbs above rich bottomland soil and on fertile hillsides. It ranges from southern New England—where outlying specimens crop up in Connecticut, Massachusetts, and Vermont—west across extreme southern Ontario to Minnesota, Nebraska, and Kansas, and south to Florida and Texas. The closely related butternut, *Juglans cinerea,* extends farther north and grows at higher elevations than black walnut. Black walnut occurs locally throughout Pennsylvania; it is more common in the southern half of the state than in the northern half, where it is absent over large areas. The finest black walnut I have seen stood on Thompsons Island in the Allegheny River in Warren County; its tall, straight trunk thrust a round-topped crown high into the canopy among the leafy tops of equally impressive white ash, butternut, hackberry, and black maple trees.

On a good site, a black walnut can become 70 to 100 feet tall and have a trunk 2 to 3 feet in diameter; black walnuts in North America's rich primeval forests are said to have stood 150 feet high, with trunks 6 and 8 feet in diameter. Woods-grown black walnuts develop straight trunks and gradually jettison their shaded-out lower branches through a process known as self-pruning. In the open—along a woods edge or in a fencerow or an abandoned field—black walnut forks low, its branches sprawling outward, sometimes drooping almost to the ground. Pure stands of black walnut are rare; usually the tree grows in mixture with other hardwoods.

Like the hickories, to which it is also related, *Juglans nigra* has compound leaves that alternate along the twigs. Each leaf is made up of thirteen to twenty-three leaflets attached to a central stalk called a rachis. In its entirety, the leaf of a black walnut measures 1 to 2 feet long. Each leaflet is 3 to 4 inches long by about 1 inch wide, stalkless, and shaped like a long spearhead with a pointed tip and finely saw-toothed edges. The leaflets all line up oppo-

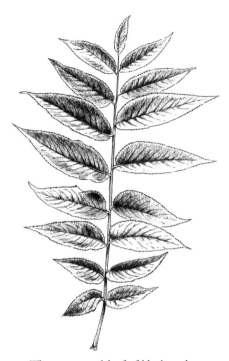

*The compound leaf of black walnut
has thirteen to twenty-three
tooth-edged leaflets attached to
a central stalk called a rachis.*

site each other, except for the terminal one at the rachis tip. Black walnut leaflets are hairless above and covered with many short, soft hairs on their undersurfaces. Crushed, they release a spicy scent. The leaflets are yellow-green to dark green above and paler beneath; they turn yellow in autumn, when black walnuts are among the very first trees to have their foliage turn color and fall.

As the tree's common name implies, the bark of the black walnut is dark: dark brown, charcoal gray, in some cases almost black. The bark is thick and rough, broken up by deep fissures running lengthwise with the trunk. You can get a real sense of the blackness of the bark by looking at the tree's leafless limbs silhouetted against the sky; note also the telltale zigzag twigs. Should you take a sharp knife and slice through a black walnut twig, you will see that its pith is chambered, interrupted by light brown partitions lined up like so many ladder rungs. In comparison, butternut also has chambered pith, but the partitions are closer together, darker, and heavier, whereas the hickories have solid, unchambered pith.

In deep, rich soil, black walnut sends down a large taproot and further buttresses itself with several substantial side roots; the best growth takes place on soils at least 30 inches deep. On most trees, the root system equals or even doubles the diameter of the leafy crown. When botanists excavated a nine-year-old black walnut in Indiana, it already had a taproot more than 7 feet long and lateral roots extending beyond 8 feet. Black walnut thrives on moist, sandy loam, and especially on soil having a limestone origin; it grows more slowly on acidic and shale soils. It does not survive for very long in poorly drained, swampy ground, although a mature tree can withstand up to three months of continuous flooding during the growing season. Black walnut does not flourish in places where its roots stub up against shallow bedrock, or on dry ridges and slopes. Seedlings need abundant sunlight and will not grow in the deep shade of the forest understory. On a good site, a young tree can add 3 to 4 feet of height per year; in twenty years, it may be 40 to 50 feet tall and may have a trunk 6 to 10 inches in diameter at breast height. Black walnut generally grows faster than the oaks and slower than tuliptree and white ash.

Black walnut flowers in May, before the tree's leaves have fully unfurled. A late frost may damage the flowers, ruining the year's nut crop. The greenish male and female flowers blossom on the same twig. The male flowers developed during the preceding year's growing season and overwintered as small cones; in May, the cones expand to become dangling 2- to 5-inch catkins. The female flowers, shaped like spikes, bloom in groups of two to five at the twig tips. The wind takes care of pollination. Female flowers usually blossom before male flowers on the same tree; this increases the likelihood of cross-pollination, in which another, separate tree provides the male pollen. Black walnuts can also pollinate themselves.

The rounded or slightly oblong fruit of *Juglans nigra* is 1 to 2 inches in diameter. It is technically a drupe, like the fruit of the plum—although in the case of the walnut, we discard the flesh and eat the seed's contents. A walnut consists of a fleshy outer husk; a woody, rough nut; and an oily, edible kernel. The fruit is a pale yellow-green becoming darker green in October and November; as the nuts ripen and fall, the outer husk becomes dry and brittle on the surface, black and mushy underneath. In the past, people used walnut husks to dye cloth brown. They also put the bruised husks in streams and ponds to stun fish for food, a practice now illegal.

Trees grown in full sunlight produce more fruit than those in forest stands; specimens younger than age twenty seldom yield nuts. Good nut crops occur about twice in every five years. Walnuts cling to the twigs singly, in pairs, and occasionally in threes. In autumn, the nuts drop off the twigs (you don't want to park your car beneath a loaded tree) or are cut down by squirrels. To separate the nuts from their viscous wrappers, grind the fruit underfoot, then pick out the nuts using fireplace tongs or while wearing rubber gloves. If you get the black muck on your fingers, the resulting dark stain can take weeks to wear off. After removing their husks, let the nuts dry for a week or two. Drying causes the nutmeat to shrink slightly, making it easier to extract from the hull. The woody nut is dark brown to almost black. Although thick and hard, the hull is not difficult to crack. Hold the nut edge-up, and tap the seam with a hammer. The twin-lobed kernel, or nutmeat, must then be teased out of its convoluted inner chamber. Black walnuts have a hearty flavor. They can be eaten raw or baked into cakes, cookies, and nut bread. The nutmeats, crushed and boiled, yield a rich oil.

Squirrels and other rodents avidly forage for the high-calorie black walnuts. Gray and fox squirrels use their large incisors to chip through a hull from both sides. Red squirrels generally gnaw from one end, and flying squirrels cut out four circular side openings. Chipmunks and mice also chew their way into the nuts to get at the energy-rich kernels. Gray squirrels hoard walnuts by burying them in the ground; after a winter or two, unrecovered nuts sprout in the spring and may become new trees. Walnut trees in fencerows are planted by squirrels using those corridors to move between wooded areas.

The sapwood of *Juglans nigra* is pale brown, sometimes almost white. The heartwood is what attracts human attention: a rich chocolate or purplish brown, sometimes with ample figuring, patterns of pale and dark wood that ripple through a board. Trees grown in the open tend to have more highly figured wood than forest-grown specimens. Black walnut wood is hard, strong, and durable. Dried, it weighs around 38 pounds per cubic foot. It splits easily and makes good firewood; the smoke from burning walnut is said to have a pleasant tea-leaf fragrance. Because of its beauty, strength, stability after drying, and the fact that it is easy to shape, craftsmen have long employed black walnut for fine products: furniture, house paneling, cabinetry, and gunstocks. Colonists in Virginia began exporting the wood to England as early as 1610. Settlers split black walnut for snake-rail fences, fashioned it into water wheels, and turned it into charcoal for making gunpowder. Cradles traditionally were made from valuable black walnut wood, as they held something wondrously valuable within.

Black walnut is one of the most highly sought-after timber trees in North America; it is now rarer than in times past, since so many trees have been cut for the market. Pennsylvania grows relatively little black walnut, and as a result a market has not developed here for moving the boards to customers. Today most commercial walnut comes from Missouri, Iowa, Illinois, Indiana, Michigan, Ohio, West Virginia, Kentucky, and Tennessee. The best wood goes for veneer: a machine rotates the log while a fixed blade slices off a thin scroll, which is later glued onto furniture, plywood, or other products. The United States exports black walnut to many countries, including England, Germany, Italy, and Japan. Top-grade walnut sawlogs fetch thousands of dollars, leading thieves to cut down trees and steal them. Even the hulls of the nuts have worth: the ground shells have been used to polish metal and clean jet engines, and as antislip agents in automobile tires.

The larvae of several moth species feed on black walnut foliage, including the caterpillars that later metamorphose into luna moths, night-flying insects with beautiful, pale green wings. Fall webworms often infest *Juglans nigra,* their messy silk nests cluttering the ends of the branches. The sap of black walnut is mildly sweet and can be boiled down to yield a syrup. Walnut attracts yellow-bellied sapsuckers, which cut feeding wells into the tree's bark in late winter and early spring; some trees are fairly ringed with the birds' peck holes.

Scientists have isolated a chemical called juglone from the buds, nut hulls, roots, leaves, and stems of black walnut. Under some conditions, juglone can build up in the soil beneath walnut trees, where it may inhibit the growth of competing plants, including black walnut seedlings. Horses are very susceptible to juglone; even the sawdust of black walnut, when used for bedding, can cause them to founder.

BUTTERNUT

Twenty years ago, after I had started building our house along a township road in rural Centre County, I took a hike along the dirt thoroughfare where it passed an old field. In the fencerow between road and field stood a walnut tree, its limbs heavy with fruit. There was something different about the tree. It looked scraggly, not sturdy and grand in the way of a black walnut. The bark was noticeably paler than a black walnut's. The leaves looked similar, but the fruits were oblong instead of round, and covered with sticky hairs. I took a few of the nuts home. Checking in my field guide, I concluded that I'd found a butternut tree *(Juglans cinerea),* also known as white walnut.

More resistant to cold than black walnut, butternut grows from southern New Brunswick and Quebec west to Minnesota, south through New England and the Mid-Atlantic states, in the Appalachians to northern Georgia, and west to Missouri and Arkansas. The nature writer Hal Borland called the butternut "New England's black walnut." The species is statewide in Pennsylvania; Joseph Illick reported in 1928 in *Pennsylvania Trees* that the butternut was more common in the northern part of the state than black walnut, and in the southern part it ascended in the mountains to higher elevations than black walnut. Illick judged butternut to be very common locally in parts of southeastern and southern Pennsylvania. Unfortunately, today the tree is dwindling rapidly across its range, the victim of a canker-causing fungus disease that some scientists predict will wipe out the species altogether.

Butternuts grow in lowland woods, in rich hillside pastures where the soil is underlain by limestone, and along streams and road edges. The trees occur singly or in small groups, never in pure stands, mixed in with basswood, sugar maple, American elm, red oak, and other hardwoods. *Juglans cinerea* grows best in sunny places and dies if it is shaded from above. A fast-growing tree, it usually does not live beyond seventy-five years.

A mature butternut is low and broad, its short, thick trunk branching into many stocky limbs; the overall form has been compared to that of an apple tree. Most butternuts stand 30 to 40 feet tall and have a trunk 1 to 2 feet in diameter. The occasional individual reaches 80 feet and has a 3- to 4-foot trunk. The crown on a healthy specimen is broad, deep, round-topped, and somewhat asymmetrical, and looks rather sparse and open. The outermost branches are dark, almost black.

Butternut sends down a long central taproot, plus a set of deep-extending lateral roots. Windstorms rarely knock the trees down, even though butternuts usually grow in open sites rather than in dense forest stands, where massed sylvan companions would blunt the force of gales. Wind-firm they may be, but butternuts often lose their stiff, brittle branches to storms and ice.

Pale gray bark covers the young trunks and branches. As a tree ages, dark fissures open between smooth, light gray bark ridges. Like black walnut and the hickories, butternut has opposite, compound leaves. Each leaf, 15 to 30 inches long, consists of a central stem, called a rachis, which is studded with leaflets standing opposite each other, usually with a single leaflet at the rachis tip. The leaflets are 3 to 5 inches long, have toothed margins and pointed tips, and number eleven to seventeen per leaf. In general, the leaves of butternut have longer stems and fewer leaflets than those of black walnut, leading to the butternut's feathery, sparse-appearing foliage. The overall color of the leaves is yellow-green. The leaflets are slightly hairy above and paler and cloaked with soft hairs on their undersurfaces. They emerge late in the spring, become tattered and dingy by midsummer, and after turning yellowish brown, fall off in early autumn.

The greenish flowers blossom in May, when the leaves are partly developed. Separate male and female flowers occur on the same tree, usually on the same branch. The male flowers crowd together in furry catkins 3 to 5 inches long. The female flowers, positioned near the twig ends, develop from shoots of the current season; the male flowers, farther back on the branchlets, derive from the previous year's growth.

Wind pollinates the female flowers. Over the summer, the fruits expand and lengthen, assuming the shape of a small lemon. Often three to five nuts hang in a drooping cluster. Green at first, the husk of a butternut turns brown as it ripens. It is furred with sticky, rust-colored hairs that will stain a person's hands brown. The husk conceals a rough, flinty shell 1½ to 2 inches long, studded with ridges and knobs and having a sharp point at one end. Inside the thick-walled shell lies the sweet, oily, edible kernel, which gives the butternut the folk name oilnut. Nuts missed by squirrels and human foragers, plus those buried by the rodents and then forgotten, germinate the following spring. Butternuts begin producing nuts at around age twenty; trees thirty to sixty years old yield the greatest numbers of nuts. Good crops occur about every two to three years.

The nuts of *Juglans cinerea* are delicious, like a mild black walnut with a hint of banana; I like them in cookies, muffins, and banana bread. In New England, they are used to make maple-butternut candy. You can free the kernels by hammering the nuts on their points. An old trick calls for half filling a burlap bag with butternuts, soaking the bag in hot water for half an hour, and hanging it up to cool; the treatment is supposed to make the nuts easier to crack and to keep the meats in larger pieces. The nutmeats tend to become rancid and need to be promptly harvested and used. Some foragers pickle butternuts, gathering the green immature fruits in June or July and preserving them in vinegar.

Native Americans ate butternuts raw, cooked, and ground into a meal for baking cakes or thickening porridge. The Iroquois extracted the

black walnut

butternut

The nuts of black walnut are rounded; those of the butternut are oblong and covered with a sticky husk.

seed oil, cooked with it, and used it to dress their hair. Butternut sap can be boiled down and concentrated to make a sweet syrup; compared with sugar maple sap, it takes four times as much butternut sap to make a given volume of syrup. At the outset of the Civil War, secessionist soldiers boiled butternut twigs, leaves, buds, and fruits to make a dye that imparted a tan color to their uniforms. Those troops, as well as Southern civilians and Confederate sympathizers in the North, henceforth were known as "butternuts."

The outer sapwood of butternut is narrow, rarely more than an inch in depth. The heartwood is a rich chestnut brown, often with a beautifully intricate grain pattern, especially in boards sawn from branch crooks. The wood is lighter in color than black walnut, which is why butternut is sometimes called white walnut. The wood is soft, rather weak, and weighs 25 pounds per cubic foot. Carvers and woodworkers find it easy to shape and finish to a high luster. The wood is stable and rarely warps or cracks, and it darkens with exposure to the atmosphere. Butternut has been made into furniture, cabinets, paneling, the interiors of carriages and sumptuous private railroad cars, and carved church altars.

In 1928, Illick wrote in *Pennsylvania Trees* concerning butternut that "the old trees are very susceptible to the attack of wood-destroying fungi." Heart-rot fungi invade butternuts through wounds where storms and ice have damaged the branches. Since Illick's era, a new and deadlier menace has arrived. It's not known whether this canker-causing fungus of genus *Sirococcus* is a recent accidental import or a native species that has mutated into its present lethal form. In the last thirty years, it has swept through the butternuts of North America, leaving few trees uninfected.

Scientists postulate that storms blow spore-laden moisture droplets far and wide. The tiny, microscopic spores of the fungus enter young twigs through leaf scars and lenticels and get into older stems through wounds and natural bark cracks. As the infection progresses, rain splashes the spores from lesions high in the tree to branches lower down. Diseased wood becomes dark and mushy, with most of the damage hidden beneath the bark. As cankers girdle branches or trunk, they destroy the outer cambium layer and disrupt the flow of nutrients and water. The branches gradually die back, and after several years, most trees perish. Butternut canker fungus renders the nuts infertile and kills trees of all ages. At present, there is no known treatment for the disease.

The fungus was first reported from Wisconsin in 1967. An estimated 58 percent of Wisconsin's butternuts and 91 percent of Michigan's butternuts died over the next fifteen years. By 1986, approximately 77 percent of butternuts in North Carolina and Virginia had perished. So many butternuts have died across the species' range that the U.S. Fish and Wildlife Service has added *Juglans cinerea* to the list of candidates for protection under the Endangered Species Act. Scientists are trying to locate trees that have natural resistance to the fungus; they hope to take grafts and preserve the trees' gene plasm. Mike Ostry, a forest pathologist with the U.S. Department of Agriculture and a leading researcher into butternut canker disease, has suggested that butternut is more likely to become extinct than the beleaguered American chestnut.

The butternuts near my home on Mountain Road have not borne nuts for several years. Although they still send out leaves, dead limbs stand starkly in their crowns, and dark cracks interrupt their bark. I wonder if I'll ever taste their fruit again.

HICKORIES

Five different hickories grow in the Northeast. A pair of similar species thrive in fertile lowlands: shagbark and shellbark hickory. Two others—pignut and mockernut hickory—grow more often in upland areas. Bitternut hickory occurs frequently in bottomlands along streams and also in mountainous terrain. Taxonomists place the hickories in Juglandaceae, the walnut family, all of whose members reproduce themselves through nuts: large, energy-packed seeds protected inside husks and hard shells. Other trees in the group include black walnut, butternut, and pecan.

The hickories have pinnately compound leaves, with an odd number of leaflets (five, seven, nine, or eleven) arranged in twin rows, each row opposing the other on either side of a central stalk called a rachis, with the "odd" leaflet extending from the rachis tip. The leaflets have many small teeth on their margins; they are shaped like lance heads and are broader than the leaflets of butternut and black walnut. The compound leaves of hickories alternate along the trees' branches. Next year's foliage and female flowers lie folded up inside large twig-end buds, which are helpful to the amateur naturalist seeking to confirm a hickory's identity. The leaves turn various shades of yellow in autumn. Both the foliage and the four-part nut husks give off a spicy, nose-tickling smell when scratched or crushed.

Hickories produce male and female flowers on the same tree. The male flowers are furry and 3 to 5 inches long. They dangle in groups of three from a common stalk; often several stalks cluster together. The shorter female flowers look like hairy spikes. Wind brings about pollination. Over the summer, the female flowers develop into highly nutritious nuts that, by autumn, are eagerly sought by woodland creatures ranging in size from mice to black bears; human foragers hunt for them as well.

The nuts of the hickories are rounded to pear-shaped and vary in size and pleasantness of flavor. Hickories usually produce at least some nuts each year and send forth bumper crops every two or three years. Squirrels help disperse the different species across the landscape: the rodents bury excess nuts to eat in the future, and nuts that go unrecovered sprout and become seedlings during the next growing season.

As they mature, hickories send down long central roots deep into the soil; these taproots anchor the trees against storm winds and let them take in water during drought. Hickories grow slowly and may live for two hundred to three hundred years. If young trees are cut down, they usually sprout from the stump.

Hickories range across eastern North America and eastern Asia. Fossils show that they once grew in Greenland, Iceland, and Europe, but they died out in those places during the ice ages. In North America, the hickories and other trees gradually withdrew southward and then extended their ranges northward again when the ice sheets melted. Scientists speculate that the north-south orientation of the Appalachian mountain chain made such movements possible, as seed-carrying birds and mammals moved easily along valley corridors. In Europe, the major mountain ranges lie on an east-west heading, preventing plants with heavy, hard-to-transport nuts from shifting north again after the ice withdrew.

Shagbark Hickory *(Carya ovata)*. This large tree generally reaches a height of 50 to 75 feet, with a trunk 2 to 3 feet in diameter; old specimens on excellent sites can be 120 feet tall with a 4-foot breadth. Shagbark hickories make their best growth on rich, moist soil in full sunlight. The species ranges from southern Maine and Quebec west to Minnesota and eastern Nebraska, and south to Georgia and Texas; outlying populations exist as far west as northeastern Mexico. In Pennsylvania, shagbark hickory is statewide, most common in the southeastern and southwestern quadrants. In mountainous regions of the commonwealth, *Carya ovata* can be locally common in fertile valleys. Shagbark hickories also grow on rich hillsides and along streams and the borders of swamps.

The most dramatic aspect of this hickory is its pale gray bark, aptly described by the shagbark title: as the tree expands its girth over the years, the bark shatters into long, strap-shaped plates running up and down on the trunk. The plates can be as wide as 3 to 6 inches. Often they warp away from the trunk at both ends, while remaining attached in the middle. The strips cover the lower trunk, giving it a decidedly whiskery appearance; this roughness often extends to the main branches. Fallen bark strips usually litter the ground beneath the tree. Ecologists suggest that the rough, rugged surface works as a defense against creatures that lust after shagbark nuts. Maybe it thwarts a few raccoons and opossums, but judging from the number of squirrels I see clipping nuts in the crowns of shagbarks, it's not a wholly effective deterrent.

As a shagbark hickory's girth expands, its bark shatters into long, strap-shaped plates running up and down the trunk.

The compound leaves of shagbark hickory are 8 to 14 inches long and divided into five, rarely seven, leaflets. The two leaflets at the base of the rachis are not as large or long as the upper pair and the terminal leaflet. The leaves turn a bright candle-flame yellow in early fall.

Shagbark hickory flowers in May, after its leaves are almost fully developed. The nuts ripen in the fall. The thick husk gradually splits into four pieces, exposing a whitish nut with a faint point. The nut is egg-shaped and about an inch long; a relatively thin shell surrounds the delectable kernel. A good way to shell a hickory nut is to hold the huskless nut on its side on a hard, unyielding surface (a vise works well); position the nut so that the seam around its perimeter faces up; and tap the seam with a hammer. Use a nutpick to tease the meat out of the two convoluted inner chambers.

Shagbarks begin bearing nuts when they are twenty years old and produce good numbers of nuts from age forty onward. Bumper crops occur about every third year. Human foragers should plan to harvest in early October, after winds have shaken the nuts to the ground. Hickory nuts are excellent in a white or yellow cake, or in a plain cookie, from which their subtle sweetness emerges; baking helps bring out the flavor. Many wild animals eat the nuts, including all species of squirrels, chipmunks, opossums, wild turkeys, and wood ducks.

Yellow-bellied sapsuckers chisel feeding wells into thinner areas of the tree's bark and lap up the sap that oozes out. You can find older trees that have deep scars almost ringing their trunks, horizontal grooves left by the drillings of sapsuckers. The brown creeper—a small, inconspicuous forest bird that spends most of its life hunting for insects and other invertebrates in tree bark—often chooses shagbark hickory for a nest site, hiding its elongated, hammocklike nest behind a curl of bark.

The word *hickory* comes from *pohickery,* an Algonquian Indian word. Native Americans pounded the nuts, boiled them, and then strained the liquid, preserving the oily essence, which they added to other foods, including cornmeal cakes and hominy. The early settlers put hickory to many uses. They fashioned tool handles and wagon hubs and carved hinges from the tough, elastic wood. Some made mauls from hickory roots, further hardening the heads of those crude implements by holding them in the heat of a fire; the mauls were then used to pound in iron wedges and gluts for splitting chestnut logs into fence rails.

Some woods are stronger than hickory and a few are harder, but no other American species equals it in combined strength, hardness, and stiffness. Hickory is a third stronger than white oak and twice as shock-resistant: the wood of the shagbark is reputed to be the strongest of all the hickories. People use it for tool handles, flooring, furniture, cross-country skis, charcoal making, and parts for musical instruments. Shagbark hickory wood weighs almost 52 pounds per cubic foot, dry weight. Its fuel value exceeds that of any other American tree except black locust. One cord of hickory—a stack 4 feet wide by 4 feet deep by 8 feet long—releases as much heat as a ton of anthracite coal or 175 gallons of fuel oil.

Shellbark Hickory *(Carya laciniosa).* Shellbark hickory is similar to shagbark. In the past, the two were called shellbark hickory and big shellbark hickory, the latter name denoting *Carya laciniosa,* on account of its very large nuts. One way to tell the two species apart is by their compound leaves: those of the shellbark are generally larger, at 10 to 22 inches in length. Another clue is the number of leaflets, usually seven and sometimes nine for the shellbark, as opposed to five (rarely seven) for the shagbark.

Shellbark hickory has a smaller range than its shagbark cousin, centered on the Ohio and Mississippi river valleys and extending east into Pennsyl-

vania and New York. Shellbark hickory grows as far west as Iowa and eastern Kansas, and south to Arkansas and Tennessee. In Pennsylvania, the tree
is found in the southern half of the state, mainly east of the Allegheny
Mountains. In *Pennsylvania Trees,* Joseph Illick judged shellbark hickory
"probably most common in Northampton, Bucks, and Montgomery counties." Even more than the shagbark, the shellbark thrives on damp, rich soil
in low-lying sites that may temporarily flood in the spring. Occasionally
shellbark grows on fertile hillsides.

The bark is similar to a shagbark hickory's, except the shellbark's is usually a bit less shaggy; "flaky" is an adjective often used to describe it. The
two trees have a similar overall form. In a dense forest setting, shellbark hickory grows a tall, slightly tapering trunk that is free from branches for much
of its length. Another name for *Carya laciniosa* is kingnut, and its nuts are
indeed the largest of all the hickories, up to 2$1/2$ inches long. Twenty-five to
thirty-five nuts make a pound; in contrast, it takes a hundred shagbark nuts
to make a pound, and approximately two hundred pignut hickory nuts.

Neither loggers nor timber users differentiate between the wood of
shellbark and shagbark hickory.

Pignut Hickory *(Carya glabra).* A medium-size tree, pignut hickory stands
50 to 60 feet tall and is 2 to 3 feet across the trunk at breast height. The
maximum size is about 90 feet tall and 4 feet in diameter. Most pignut hickories grow in mixed oak-hickory woods, and the crown of a forest-grown
specimen tends to be oblong, tall,
and narrow, with short, spreading
branches; limbs lower down on the
trunk may droop. Pignut hickories
have five and occasionally seven
leaflets per compound leaf; the
overall length is 8 to 12 inches. The
leaves are hairless, dark glossy green
above and paler below. Pignut hickories are some of the tardiest trees
to set forth foliage in spring.

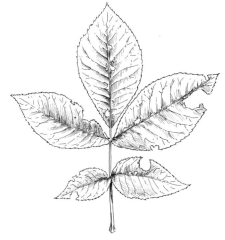

The bark is dark gray, with shallow fissures and tight, narrow ridges,
hard and tough and about $2/3$ inch
thick. The bark rarely peels off from
the trunk, or exfoliates, as the botanists

*Leaves of pignut hickory have
five to seven leaflets.*

say, and never as dramatically as in the shagbark and shellbark species, but on older pignut hickories, it sometimes fragments—just enough that a white-breasted nuthatch can wedge one of the tree's own nuts between the plates, using them as a natural vise while hammering and picking away the shell to get at the nutmeat.

Pignut hickory ranges from southern New England to central Florida and from northern Illinois to Louisiana. It is more common in southern than in northern Pennsylvania. It thrives on dry ridges and hillsides and rarely grows in damp settings. It is the only hickory in the woods around our home, on a dry bench a few hundred feet downslope from the Allegheny Front. Here, as on most upland sites, pignut hickory is less common than the red, black, white, chestnut, and scarlet oaks with which it mingles.

The somewhat pear-shaped nuts are 1 to 2 inches in length. Their skin is usually quite thin, a bit less than 1/8 inch. Some of the nuts are sweet-tasting, but others are insipid or bitter—from the same tree, no less, which doesn't inspire one to gather bucketfuls and devote the time needed to extract the small nutmeats, especially when one can drive down into the valley and pick from beneath shagbarks. Squirrels and chipmunks avidly eat the nuts of this tree, and at one time farmers turned their pigs loose to feed on them, giving rise to the common name. Another moniker is broom hickory, bestowed by early settlers who fashioned brooms and scrubbers out of narrow splits of the wood.

I'm always on the lookout for dead and dying hickories in our woods. I like to cook venison on an outdoor grill over a slow-burning hickory fire; placing the lid tightly on the cooker ensures that the steaks become infused with that wonderful smoky flavor. Typical for hickory, the heavy wood of this species burns with a fierce, steadfast heat. On frigid winter nights, I fill our heating stove with oak, then top the load off with a thick billet of hickory. Come dawn, the house will be toasty, the hickory a bed of glowing coals from which I can start the morning fire.

Mockernut Hickory *(Carya tomentosa).* Mockernut hickory ranges from southern New England west to Arkansas and south to Texas and Florida. *Carya tomentosa* grows mainly in moist, open woods, valley forests, and rich soils collected at the bottoms of slopes; it is uncommon in floodplain bottoms. In Pennsylvania, mockernut hickory is most abundant in the southeast and is absent from parts of the northern tier. Mockernut hickory probably gets its name because its fruit appears to be promisingly large, but wrapped inside a thick, green husk and a thick, hard shell, the nutmeat is disappointingly small.

The tree grows 50 to 75 feet tall, with a diameter of about 2 feet. The dark or light gray bark remains tight and deeply furrowed. The large, rounded buds on the twig ends seem to be covered with grayish brown felt. The leaves, 8 to 12 inches long, are compounded of seven to nine leaflets. Foliage and twigs are resinous and fragrant. The Latin species name describes the hairy, matted-wool quality of the leaf stalks and the undersurfaces of the leaflets—characteristics that make this tree easy to identify when in foliage. Flowers appear in May, when the leaves are half developed. The resulting nuts are sweet-tasting.

The white-breasted nuthatch will sometimes wedge a hickory nut into the tree's ridged bark, then use its beak to hammer the shell apart.

The wood of mockernut hickory has a large proportion of white sapwood; for this reason, the tree is sometimes called white hickory. As useful as any of the other hickories, it goes for tool handles (including scythes), furniture, flooring, baseball bats, and skis.

Bitternut Hickory *(Carya cordiformis).* Bitternut hickory stands 50 to 75 feet tall, with a trunk diameter of 1 to 2 feet; some specimens grow as large as 100 feet and have a trunk 2½ to 3 feet broad. Stout side branches grow upward; they sprout slightly drooping branchlets, forming a broad, rounded crown. The bark is light gray, tight, and a bit scaly or roughened by shallow fissures and narrow ridges. The leaves are 6 to 10 inches long and have seven to nine (rarely eleven) leaflets. Each leaflet is 2 to 6 inches in length: the smallest of all the hickories. In winter, the twigs end in sulfur yellow buds.

Carya cordiformis ranges farther north than any other hickory (marginally farther than shagbark hickory) and is the most abundant hickory in Canada. It occurs from Quebec to Minnesota and south to Florida and Texas. Across its range, bitternut hickory is probably the most abundant and uniformly distributed of all the *Carya* species. It is present throughout Pennsylvania; in the southwestern corner of the state, where it is particularly common, bitternut hickory often grows to a large size. It thrives in low, moist, fertile soils along streams, in woodlots, and on mountain slopes.

Many autumns ago, as a neophyte forager, I filled a bucket with smooth, pale hickory nuts that had already shed their husks. Back home, I started shelling my gleanings. Fortunately, I tried a taste before I got too far. I popped the kernel into my mouth—and spat it out immediately. The nut was incredibly bitter, and a few cautious taste tests persuaded me that the rest of the batch was just as bad. Thus was I introduced to bitternut hickory. It's believed that most wild animals find the nuts unpalatable, although rabbits have been seen eating the kernels. Apparently the tree depends on gravity and on water transport for the dissemination of its seeds.

The wood of bitternut hickory is judged slightly less strong than that of our other hickories. It is reputed to be the best of its clan for smoking meat.

ALDERS

If one follows the definition of a tree used by the U.S. Forest Service— a woody plant attaining a height of 13 feet or more, and having a single trunk at least 3 inches in diameter at breast height, or 4$^{1}/_{2}$ feet above the ground—then the alders do not qualify. They are mere shrubs. But a book of trees that does not include these swamp dwellers is, to my way of thinking, incomplete.

I have spent many hours in the damp, tangled depths of alder thickets, watching birds, hunting grouse and ducks, and simply being off on my lonesome in a fascinating natural setting. Two alder species are native to Pennsylvania; both grow along streams, lake margins, and bogs. **Smooth alder** *(Alnus serrulata)* occurs mainly in the southern two-thirds of the state. It is sometimes called hazel alder, common alder, or tag alder. On a continental scale, it ranges from southern Maine south to Florida and west to Missouri and Texas. **Speckled alder** *(Alnus incana)* is more common in northern Pennsylvania. It too is known as tag alder and also gray alder. It spans the continent from Labrador to the Yukon and extends south as far as West Virginia and Iowa. Altogether, seven alder species occur in North America. The alders are closely related to hornbeam, hop-hornbeam, and the birches.

Alders grow best in wet but well-drained soil that is sandy or gravelly. They require full sunlight. The egg-shaped leaves are 2 to 4 inches long. The leaves have prominent veins and toothed edges; they feel thick and leathery to the touch. Some have a rippled or wrinkled aspect. In summer, they are a deep glossy green, darker on top than on the bottom. In autumn, they turn bronze-yellow or simply take on a brownish cast before they wither and fall.

I had never noticed which type of alder, speckled or smooth, grew in the bog at Black Moshannon State Park near my central Pennsylvania home; I made a late-winter foray to find out. Rain dimpled the tannin-dark stream as it wound through a meadow where last year's grasses and sedges lay pressed down by snow, most of which had melted. Highbush blueberry shrubs and hummocks of knee-high leatherleaf dotted the bog. I came to a shrubby tree composed of eight crooked branching trunks, all sprouted from a central clump. It was a speckled alder: the bark on twigs, stems, and trunks was a deep reddish brown heavily stippled with pale yellowish speckles. The speckles are lenticels, pores that permit the exchange of gases between the plant's interior tissues and the surrounding air.

Dangling from the alder's twigs were cylindrical structures about 1/8 inch thick and an inch long, tight-wrapped and dormant. Nearby—in some instances even on the same twig—were smaller, cone-shaped structures also protected by winter scales. The larger structures were male flowers, and the smaller ones were female. In early April, before an alder leafs out, its flowers open and expand into furry catkins. The wind carries pollen from the male to the female flowers. Over the summer, the fertilized female flowers develop into cones, which open in autumn and release small, winged seeds. I noticed that many of last year's cones still clung to the tree; rounded, woody, and about 1/2 inch long, their opened scales devoid of seeds. They looked like miniature cones of red pine or pitch pine.

Most alders stand no taller than 10 feet, although the occasional specimen will reach 20 or 25 feet. The trunks, or stems, are rarely larger than 4 inches in diameter. Eight, ten, twenty stems per clump: often they curve outward before bending up, on account of heavy snow having flattened them when they were young. Some of the alders at Black Moshan-

Alders carry their seeds in small cones. The developing fruits appear farther out on the twigs than last year's cones.

non had large, thick trunks, up to 8 inches across about a foot above the ground. The stems were not tall, however; generally they were topped with dead, rotting limbs much excavated by woodpeckers, and from their remaining sound woody tissue, near the ground, many new stems rose. I wondered how old those thick trunks might be, how many densely packed growth rings lay beneath the weathered bark.

Alders have shallow root systems. Like aspens, alders can reproduce vegetatively. Their roots radiate out through the mucky soil, then send up other stems several feet away from the parent plant. This underground root network with its attached, aboveground stems is called a clone. The roots of neighboring alder clones mesh with each other and sometimes even graft together. Along a stream, interwoven alder roots help anchor the soil and prevent bank erosion.

The roots serve another function, important to the ecology of the bog. They possess nodules, small bumps located just beneath the surface of the soil, in which nitrogen-fixing microorganisms live. The alders supply the microbes with organic food. In turn, the microbes give the alders nitrogen in a form that the trees can use. Such a mutually beneficial relationship is called symbiosis. The microbes release nitrogen into the bog soil, a highly anaerobic and acidic environment where nitrogen, essential for plant growth, is scarce. Alder leaves are also rich in the element, and when the stems shed their leaves in the fall and the leaves break down, more usable nitrogen enters the soil.

Along the creek at Black Moshannon, I found a clump of alders that beavers had been feeding on. The small stems were nipped off 6 inches to a foot above the ground. Beavers eat buds and bark of alders and use the remaining woody parts for building or repairing their dams and lodges. White-tailed deer browse on alder, although it is not a preferred item in their diet; some sources call it starvation food. Cottontail rabbits and snowshoe hares feed on alders, and ruffed grouse take buds and catkins. In autumn, goldfinches, chickadees, redpolls, and pine siskins eat alder seeds.

Alders may be more important to wildlife as cover than as a food source. Woodcock rest on the ground in alder stands, probing their bills into the soil in search of earthworms, a favorite food, while overhead the crowded, interwoven branches shield them from hawks and owls. Deer hide amid the dense growth; in October and November, I find alder stems much scuffed and frayed by buck deer, who, seized by the rut, slash their antlers at the pliant trunks. In spring and summer, birds nest in alder thickets. The alder flycatcher gets its name from this favored habitat. Yellow-bellied flycatchers, yellow warblers, common yellowthroats, red-winged blackbirds, and swamp sparrows also nest in alders. Ducks rest on small streams and potholes in alder thickets.

"No commercial value," according to the tree texts: the trunk of the alder, be it smooth or speckled, is insufficiently straight and thick to yield marketable timber. Yet the plant offers much more.

BLACK BIRCH

Two decades ago, scarcely a black birch could I find on our land. But after successive gypsy moth defoliations killed about one in every five oaks, I began seeing more birches, rising in the scattered small clearings where the foliage of the now-skeletal oaks no longer shaded the forest floor. Today, having cut many of the dead oaks for firewood, I've begun turning to the birch, thinning out a few trees here and there, particularly in one area where all the oaks were killed and where black birch *(Betula lenta)* and black-gum now compete for light and space. The birch has proven to be as good a firewood as oak: easy to split, quick curing, clean burning. The heat, baking out of our cast-iron stove in visible shimmering waves, isn't a bit less comforting.

Betula lenta, also known as sweet birch or cherry birch, is a common tree throughout Pennsylvania—and becoming more common every year. It grows in a variety of habitats, from rich, moist lowland forests to bone-dry, rock-strewn ridgetops. The species ranges from southern Maine to Ohio and south in the Appalachian Mountains to northern Georgia and Alabama. The tree achieves its best growth in the southern Appalachians.

Two characteristics make black birch easy to identify. Its bark is dark brown to purple to black, smooth and shiny when young, and becoming rough and plated with age, but not peeling off in papery layers like the bark of other birches, although sometimes thick flanges of it stand off from the trunk. The bark has prominent lenticels. It looks much like that of black cherry, *Prunus serotina,* with which black birch often shares the same habitat, but the two are distinguishable by the simple expedient of snapping off a twig: if the broken wood smells acrid, or doesn't have much of an odor at all, it's cherry; but if it fills your nose with the clean fragrance of wintergreen, black birch it must be.

Black birch generally grows 50 to 80 feet tall, with a trunk 1 1/2 to 2 feet in diameter. The leaves, extending from short spur branches, are alternate, sometimes in pairs; their length varies from 2 to 6 inches. The shape is elliptical, pointed at the tip and often with a slight notch at the base; the edges are

As black birch ages, its bark thickens and breaks up into scaly blocks and plates.

finely toothed with sharp-tipped projections. Nine to a dozen or more veins branch out prominently from each side of a central midrib; turn the leaf over to see this veining in detail. The leaves are a dark dull green above and a lighter yellow-green below. Dappled light comes streaming through the partial canopy of wind-flickering birch leaves; I can stand beneath a black birch for minutes on end, watching this ever-changing spectacle. In autumn, the leaves turn yellow before dropping.

Black birch seedlings can be hard to tell from those of yellow birch, but the black birch has a more pronounced wintergreen taste. Like most birches, black birch sprouts prolifically from the stump. Ground fires damage the tree, owing to its thin bark, and even a light scorching at the base of the trunk may open the way for attacks from disease organisms and insects. One place where I have seen black birch growing in tremendous abundance is Sweet Root Natural Area in southern Bedford County, near the Mason-Dixon line. At Sweet Root, an old-growth hemlock stand succumbed to old age, drought, and an infestation of the hemlock woolly adelgid, an insect pest. During the summer of 2000, on that unrelievedly rocky site—a steep, rubble-strewn cove opening into the side of Tussey Mountain—I found black birch and basswood seedlings nearly as thick as bamboo.

Black birch flowers in spring, before its leaves come out. The male flowers are arrayed on drooping catkins 3 to 4 inches long, carried on the twig tips; the shorter female catkins are about an inch long and sit higher on the same twig. Writes Bernd Heinrich in *The Trees in My Forest,* "Trees improve their odds of fertilization by dispersing astronomical numbers of pollen grains. More than five million are released from a single birch flower or catkin, and each tree has hundreds of thousands of flowers." The pistils of the female flowers possess enlarged sticky areas to snag pollen grains out of the air. There is only a brief period of time when the sexual union can occur. "If flowers waited until after the leaves unfurled," writes Heinrich, "then they would be partially shielded from the wind and there would be less chance for successful transfer of pollen between flowers."

The female catkins develop into brown, barrel-shaped seed packets that stand erect on the twig. The seeds mature in autumn. The catkins shed the tiny, lightweight, two-winged seeds, which blow about on top of the snow in winter. Trees begin producing seeds when about forty years old; they yield bountiful crops every year or two. I often see bands of dark-eyed juncos foraging on the forest floor in our woods and suspect they are picking up black birch seeds. Ruffed grouse also eat the nutlets, and moose and cottontail rabbits browse the twigs. Deer feed on black birch, but not avidly.

In spring, birch seeds germinate in moist mineral soil, in humus, and on rotting logs. Seedlings need light shade for two or three months during their first summer. They grow best in succeeding years when protected by side shade or partial overhead shade. In general, black birch is a shade-intolerant species, and as a tree, it must become a part of the forest canopy to survive.

Oil of wintergreen is a potent aromatic extract originally gotten by distilling the vegetation of a creeping forest plant called wintergreen. The oil has been used in small quantities to flavor medicines and candies, and provide the fragrance for disinfectants. People discovered that black birch yields the same substance, in much greater volumes than the smaller plant. It takes around a hundred saplings to distill a quart of wintergreen oil; at one time black birch was considered endangered, because so many were being cut and chipped for distillation. As late as the 1950s in Pennsylvania, wood-fired birch stills dotted the forest, mainly in the northern counties. According to one source, the average production of oil was about 2 quarts per cord (a cord of wood measures 4 feet by 4 feet by 8 feet), with the best yield coming early in spring after the sap had started to run. The concentrated liquid is said to cause death if taken internally. Today manufacturers produce oil of wintergreen through a different process, using wood alcohol and salicylic acid. Black birch sap can be turned into a syrup that is not as sweet or thick as maple syrup; it can also be fermented into birch beer.

The wood of black birch is heavy, at 47 pounds per cubic foot, hard, and dark brown with thin, yellowish sapwood. (The 4-inch-diameter saplings I've been cutting for the stove are essentially all sapwood, with the faint beginnings of dark heartwood at the core.) The properties and appearance of black birch are similar to those of yellow birch, and often the two woods are not separated by loggers. Black birch polishes to an attractive sheen. It is used for furniture, cabinets, and millwork.

Because so many oaks have died from gypsy moth defoliation, because black birch is such an aggressive seeder, and because it is not heavily browsed by deer, *Betula lenta* promises to become a much more prominent tree in Penn's Woods.

YELLOW BIRCH

Yellow birch by moonlight is a strange, otherworldly tree. The bark is pale and silvery, with thin, ragged strips curling away from the trunk, catching and reflecting the moon's glow. The effect is heightened when snow covers the ground: the tree is lit from below, as well as above, so that it stands like a great, glimmering ice sculpture displayed on a field of pure white.

Yellow birch *(Betula alleghaniensis)*—also known as silver birch and curly birch—is a large tree of cool, moist uplands. Forest-grown, it develops a tall, straight trunk with little taper, which supports a short, rather narrow crown. In a more open setting, the crown broadens and, with its drooping lower branches, takes on a rounded shape.

Betula alleghaniensis, formerly *Betula lutea,* occurs from Newfoundland across southern Canada to Manitoba, in Minnesota, and south to Iowa in the west and extreme northern Georgia in the Appalachians. At the southern end of its range, it grows mainly on steep slopes at high elevations where temperatures remain cool. In Pennsylvania, yellow birch is common on the Allegheny Plateau and rare or absent in the southeastern and southwestern counties. Small clusters occur along streams and in other moist habitats, including the borders of swamps. *Betula alleghaniensis* often grows in company with black birch, eastern hemlock, red maple, sugar maple, American beech, and American basswood.

It's easy to confuse yellow birch and black birch seedlings, because they have similar leaves, and both give off a distinctive wintergreen odor when their foliage and twigs are crushed, although the odor is not quite as strong in yellow as in black birch. But as the trees grow larger, they become easily distinguishable. Know yellow birch by its silvery-gray to yellow-bronze bark, marked with narrow, horizontal dark lines, and by the small, shreddy curls standing off all over the trunk. On old specimens, the bark may darken to brown or almost black, becoming thick and breaking up into flat plates.

Yellow birch is the largest of the native birch species. Mature trees regularly grow 60 to 80 feet tall, with a trunk 2 to 3 feet thick; occasionally a specimen will achieve 100 feet, with a trunk 4 or 5 feet in diameter. The root system goes moderately deep and consists of several strong, wide-spreading laterals.

The leaves of this species are typical for the birches: 3 to 4 inches long by $2^1/2$ inches wide, elliptical in shape, distinctly and doubly saw-toothed on the margins, and ending in a sharp point. They alternate along the stems, sprouting singly or in pairs. Dull green on their upper surfaces and light yellow-green below, they turn a vivid yellow in autumn.

Yellow birch puts forth flowers in April, before its leaves emerge. Male and female catkins appear on the same branch. The male catkins, which formed during the previous growing season, expand to a length of about 3 inches. The female catkins are greenish and $2/3$ inch long. They stand erect, farther back on the twig. Wind accomplishes the pollination.

The female catkins develop over the summer into egg-shaped cones $3/4$ to $1^1/4$ inches long, covered with hairy scales guarding small, winged seeds. In autumn, the scales expand, releasing the seeds, which skate away on the wind. In *The Trees in My Forest*, Bernd Heinrich writes that yellow birches gradually shed their seeds throughout winter: "I've seen them strewn like pepper across the snow for a hundred yards, creating a long thin shadow." The seeds can tumble along for miles on top of the snow.

The survival of any tree's offspring, Heinrich says, "depends on energy supply, either that which they carry along, or that which they

Yellow birch seeds sprout readily on stumps. After the stump rots away, the tree remains standing on stiltlike roots.

acquire from sunshine. Birch seeds carry minimal supplies. That is why they must find sun." Yellow birch seeds germinate readily on bare soil, especially earth exposed by a forest fire; abandoned fields and logged-over tracts are also hospitable sites. Yellow birch can tolerate more shade and thrive on a wider variety of soil types than can its close relative the paper birch.

Seeds and seedlings of yellow birch do not usually survive on thick leaf litter, since they lack the energy reserves sufficient to root downward through the detritus. Sometimes they grow in strange places: a scrap of moss on a rock, mats of soil and sod held up by the roots of a blown-down tree, or the rotting summit of a stump left after logging. If a seedling finds enough nourishment and sunlight on such a perch, it gradually sends its roots to the ground. I have seen yellow birches whose roots looked like great, gnarled hands fingering down over a moldering stump; if the stump has rotted away, the tree is left standing on stilts above a stump-size void.

Yellow birches produce large seed crops about every third year. Usually at least some of the seed cones remain on the trees over winter, and they attract local resident birds, including ruffed grouse. Red squirrels and other rodents also eat the seeds. In spring, yellow birches provide sweet sap for yellow-bellied sapsuckers. Seedlings and saplings of *Betula alleghaniensis* are a favorite food for white-tailed deer.

In Canada, yellow birch is sometimes called hard birch; the name bespeaks its tough wood. It is the most important hardwood lumber tree in eastern Canada and the most valuable of all the birches. The heartwood is brown to reddish brown and the sapwood white; the wood weighs about 41 pounds per cubic foot, dry weight. Most birch furniture is made from this species; often the wood is stained to resemble mahogany or cherry. Other uses include flooring, interior finish, boxes, veneer, and fuel. In times past, people fashioned ox yokes and sledge frames from the relatively light but strong wood. Because it remains stable after it has cured, yellow birch was the top choice for wagon-wheel hubs; it kept a tight grip on the spokes so that they did not work loose. People also made a root-beer-like beverage from the sap.

As with other birches, the bark of yellow birch traps moisture, and the wood, once a tree has perished, quickly rots. Often a standing dead tree becomes little more than a cylinder of bark wrapped around a core of rotten punkwood. Indians dried this decayed cellulose and carried it with them for use as tinder in which to start a fire by friction.

Modern travelers in wilderness settings can start their own fires through the agency of yellow birch. Like that of paper birch, the bark contains combustible oils. Take several silvery curls from a dead-and-down tree, construct a tepee of twigs over them, and hold a match to the bark. Even if your kindling is damp, the intense heat from the flaming bark will dry it and set it alight.

RIVER BIRCH

This small to medium-size tree has collected many names. The one most widely used, river birch, describes the species' usual habitat: sandbars and banks of rivers and streams; *Betula nigra* also grows in floodplains, wet woods, swamps, and along lake and pond margins. Another name, water birch, points out this riparian, or water's-edge, preference. The name red birch comes from the dark red color of the branchlets, and cinnamon birch from the pinkish brown bark of young trees. Older trees display evidence for another common name, black birch: over the years, the bark on those mature specimens darkens to a deep gray that approaches black.

Betula nigra is the most southerly of North American birches. It grows from southern New England, along rivers in Massachusetts and Connecticut, west across New York to Minnesota, and south to northern Florida and eastern Texas. It is most abundant in the hot, humid Southeast. In Pennsylvania, river birch stands are scattered along the main courses and tributaries of the Delaware, Lehigh, Schuylkill, and Susquehanna rivers in the eastern, southeastern, and central regions of the state. I first met this tree while canoeing on the West Branch of the Susquehanna in northern Centre County, where ragtag bunches of river birch huddle on low islands and silty banks.

In the South, particularly the Gulf states, river birch may grow to 90 feet or taller and have a 5-foot-diameter trunk. The tree rarely gets taller than 30 to 50 feet in Pennsylvania, with a trunk diameter of 1 to 2 feet. The 1928 edition of *Pennsylvania Trees,* by Joseph Illick, includes a photograph captioned "The Largest River or Red Birch in Pennsylvania," taken near Avis, Clinton County. The specimen shows the classic mature form of *Betula nigra:* a short bole dividing, around 15 to 20 feet up, into three or four spreading, divergent limbs, which arch upward to a narrow, oblong, and irregular crown.

The leaves of river birch are alternate, never across from each other; they occur singly or in pairs. A typical leaf is 3 to 4 four inches long and 1 to 2 inches wide, with six to ten pairs of lateral veins. The leaf margins are coarsely double-toothed, broken up into sawtooth projections, each of which is further divided into smaller points. The leaves shine dark green above and show a pale yellowish green to almost white below. The undersides are usually hairy or velvety, as are the leafstalks, twigs, and buds. The twigs, when snapped off, do not give off a wintergreen scent, as do those of the closely related sweet birch and yellow birch. Not a brilliant fall tree, river birch displays dull yellow foliage in autumn.

When I canoed along the West Branch, what caught my eye on those adolescent river birches was their bark: papery, scaly flakes peeling back to show the inner layers, whose color was a rich pink-brown, like a pale mahogany. The inner bark possessed a lustrous sheen that reflected the sunlight almost as brilliantly as did the river's surface.

River birches flower in April or May in Pennsylvania. The male flowers are arranged on yellowish catkins about 3 inches long that droop near the twig tips. Farther back on the twig, and standing upright on a short stalk, is the greenish female flower, which appears at about the same time as the tree's leaves. The wind carries pollen from the male to the female blossoms. The female catkins develop during spring and summer, becoming brownish, roughly cylindrical, 1- to 1 1/2-inch cones that remain erect on their stems. Botanists call these cones strobiles, a name that describes their overlapping scales.

River birch is the only North American birch that does not produce its seeds in autumn. The strobiles release small, hairy, winged nutlets in late spring or early summer. Good seed crops occur almost every year. Seeds that are not eaten by wild turkeys, ruffed grouse, songbirds, or rodents are transported by wind and water. They germinate rapidly in moist, alluvial soil. A pioneer species, river birch needs full sunlight and grows vigorously when it gets it.

A dense streamside thicket of river birch helps prevent bank erosion. Floods and floating ice can damage or scour away the young stands. River birch often grows alongside sycamore, red maple, silver maple, and black willow. Mature specimens develop cavities that provide nesting space and shelter for wood ducks, woodpeckers, black-capped chickadees, white-breasted nuthatches, and squirrels. River birch has no serious insect pests. *Betula nigra* can tolerate acidic conditions; in southern Ohio, researchers found it growing thickly on stream bottom areas that coal-mine drainage had rendered too acidic for other species. This perhaps helps explain the presence of the river birches I spotted on the upper reaches of the Susquehanna's West Branch, into which many acidified tributaries drain. Foresters sometimes plant river birch to help reclaim soils turned topsy-turvy by mining.

The wood is 36 to 40 pounds per cubic foot, dry weight. It is soft but strong. The heartwood is light brown and the sapwood pale. People use river birch wood for furniture, barrels, basket hoops, woodenware, and paper pulp; in bygone days, it was fashioned into ox yokes and wooden shoes.

At maturity, river birch can be a handsome tree; in the Northeast and Midwest, it is sometimes planted as an ornamental. In the 1860s, Prince Maximilian of Austria judged river birch the most beautiful of the trees he viewed while touring in North America before he was installed as the emperor of Mexico by Napoleon III.

PAPER BIRCH AND GRAY BIRCH

A cold, rainy morning on the shore of a Minnesota lake. The canoeists rise and emerge from their tent, and cast about for tinder to make the morning fire. No better way to ignite it than with a curl of bark from a fallen paper birch. Despite the dampness, orange flames leap from the bark as soon as the match touches it; black smoke ascends in little clouds; the bark fizzles and sputters as the fire consumes it. The concentrated heat dries kindling twigs and sticks, which also come ablaze—and the first steps have been taken toward a cup of coffee and a hot breakfast.

Paper birch *(Betula papyrifera)* is a decidedly northern tree. It spans the continent from Labrador to Alaska. From near the northern limit of tree growth, it extends southward in the East to New York, Pennsylvania, and various high-altitude outposts in the Appalachians as far as North Carolina. It grows in a variety of soils and topographies and seems to do best in areas where average summer temperatures do not top 70 degrees Fahrenheit. In Pennsylvania, *Betula papyrifera* occurs mainly in the northeastern and north-central regions, on rich forested slopes, in rocky woods with cool soils, in cutover areas, and on the borders of lakes, streams, and swamps. Most paper birches become medium-size trees 50 to 75 feet tall and 1 or 2 feet in diameter. Some paper birches in the virgin forests towered to 120 feet, and a pair of 107-foot-tall giants have been documented recently in northern Michigan.

Its white bark makes paper birch one of our handsomest trees, known through paintings and photographs to many people who have never seen it in the wild. In young paper birches, the bark is brownish, but it begins to turn white after about ten years. The white bark builds up in paperlike layers marked with narrow horizontal lenticels, portals between the interior wood tissue and the outside air. The papery bark scales off in lines going around the

The white bark of paper birch is marked with black chevrons showing where branches have died and fallen off.

trunk, not up and down it. Beneath the loose paper, the tree's inner bark shows creamy to pinkish or orangish white. A note to prospective fire-starters: never peel bark from a living tree, because the white layer will not be replaced, and the trunk will bear ugly dark scars for the rest of its life. Take instead the wrapper from a fallen log; although the wood may be damp and rotten, the bark that encases it retains the volatile oils.

On white trunks of paper birches, dark triangular markings, or chevrons, show where branches have died and fallen off. The closely related gray birch, *Betula populifolia,* also found in Pennsylvania, has whitish bark as well, but its bark is tight and nonpeeling and usually displays a greater number of large, black chevrons at the bases of the self-pruned branches. Plant physiologists believe that these two cold-climate trees evolved their white coverings to reflect radiation throughout the entire light spectrum, keeping the trunks from warming up prematurely on sunny winter days.

The leaves of paper birch are 2 to 5 inches long, 1 to 3 inches wide, and roughly oval in shape; their edges are double-toothed, and the tips taper to a point. Five to nine veins branch off on each side of a central rib. The leaves are dark green and smooth above and paler below, with tiny patches of hair, visible through a magnifying lens, where the veins join the rib. The leaves turn yellow in autumn. After falling, they break down quickly, releasing calcium, nitrogen, phosphorus, magnesium, and potassium.

In paper birch, the root system is shallow. However, high winds and ice buildup are more apt to shatter the trunk or branches of a tree than uproot it. Since the bark is thin and highly flammable, even a large tree may be torched by a moderate groundfire. Although *Betula papyrifera* does not clone itself from its roots, as some other birches do, a young and vigorous tree will send up stems from its stump if the trunk is injured, cut down, or burned. Compared with trees that grew from seeds, sprouts tend to mature earlier, after about 50 or 60 years, and deteriorate sooner, after 70 to 90 years. Paper birches rarely live beyond 140 years.

Flowers, borne on catkins, appear around April or May, before the leaves emerge. The male flowers stand on long, drooping catkins near the twig tip, and the greenish female flowers blossom on short, upright catkins farther back on the same twig. The wind shifts grains of pollen from the male to the female reproductive structures. Plant geneticists have discovered that hybridization between the birches is common. Paper birch hybridizes with almost every other native species in its genus. This causes a blending of outward traits and physical characteristics and is the reason why paper birches can be hard to tell apart from similar gray birches.

In paper birch, the female flowers become cones 1½ to 2 inches long, narrowly cylindrical, and dangling from stalks. The small, winged seeds ripen in late summer and early autumn. Most seeds disperse on the wind, from September through November. Some may lie dormant on the forest floor for a year or longer, but those that end up on bare soil, humus, or rotting wood will germinate in the spring. Because the seeds are so tiny, the newly sprouted seedlings lack a nutritious reserve, such as an acorn supplies, and are very delicate. They grow better in partial shade than in the glare of full sun. After a year, seedlings rooted in humus may be 4 to 16 inches tall.

Ruffed grouse eat the seeds and buds of paper birch. The seed-filled catkins also feed black-capped chickadees, redpolls, pine siskins, and fox sparrows. White-tailed deer, snowshoe hares, moose, cottontail rabbits, beavers, and porcupines all eat the twigs or bark. Yellow-bellied sapsuckers chip holes into the bark, returning to feed on the sap that pools in the excavations; red squirrels gnaw similar wells to gain access to the sweet sap. Hal H. Harrison, in *A Field Guide to Birds' Nests,* notes that black-throated green warblers often incorporate strips of birch bark into their nests, making the nests "easier to find in dark coniferous forests."

Native Americans boiled the sap of paper birch to make a sweet syrup, and they passed on this bit of woodlore to explorers, traders, and settlers. Perhaps no other eastern tree gave the continent's original inhabitants so many products. Different tribes used birch wood for snowshoe frames and fuel; the sturdy, resinous, waterproof bark they fashioned into shelter coverings, boxes, cups, emergency snow goggles, and horns for calling in bull moose during the rut, or mating season. Their sophisticated technology included the making of birchbark canoes, among the most beautiful vessels ever crafted by human hands. Bark canoes are light and strong: the Indians used them in heavy rapids and also on the ocean. Large sheets of bark peeled away from mature trees were wrapped around a wooden frame fashioned out of cedar, birch, or maple. Canoe makers employed the split roots of black spruce or white pine in sewing the sheets together; the holes they caulked with spruce gum. Notes John McPhee in *The Survival of the Bark Canoe,* "The bark of a birch-bark canoe is always inside out. The side that touched the wood of the tree is the side that touches the river." Another name for *Betula papyrifera* is canoe birch.

The wood, weighing 37 pounds per cubic foot, is softer and not as strong as that of yellow birch and black birch. People have used it for tongue depressors, toothpicks, clothespins, spools, broom handles, toys, and paper pulp.

Several paper birches grow on our land, all of them in a 5-acre strip that, after it was logged, we bought and added to our property. Now twenty years old, the birch trees are 5 inches in diameter at breast height and 25 to 30 feet tall. When I checked on them recently, I failed to find any catkins, even though paper birch may begin to flower and produce seeds when as young as fifteen years. Optimum seed-bearing ages are forty to seventy.

Foresters rank *Betula papyrifera* as a shade-intolerant species. Among its usual associates in the Northeast, only the aspens, pin cherry, and gray birch are considered less shade tolerant. Over time, the black cherry, red maple, and mockernut hickories growing with the paper birches on our land will probably overtop them, shade them out, and cause their decline. In the interest of having a diversity of species in our woods, I may cut those competing trees for firewood, sparing the paper birches, whose trunks, shining like beacons on dull days, so please my eye.

Gray Birch *(Betula populifolia).* People often loosely refer to both paper birch and gray birch as white birch. Gray birch is a smaller, bushier tree, usually 15 to 30 feet tall, with a diameter of 9 to 18 inches. The bark, dull silvery gray to chalky white, does not peel or separate into layers as readily as the bark of paper birch. A greater number of black chevrons—inverted V-shaped markings at the bases of living and sloughed-off branches—adorn the trunk of gray birch. The leaves of the two trees differ somewhat: those of gray birch are more triangular and have longer, sharper-pointed tips. Gray birch leaves possess slender stems, and, like aspen leaves, they tremble in the breeze.

Gray birch ranges from Nova Scotia and southern Ontario south in the Appalachians to North Carolina. In Pennsylvania, it is found chiefly in the east, on abandoned fields, strip-mined land, hillsides, rocky slopes, and burned areas, often on dry and infertile soils. Other names for the species include wire birch, poverty birch, old-field birch, and poplar-leaved birch.

The tree grows rapidly. During its brief life, it functions as a nurse tree, shading and protecting seedlings of other species, such as white ash, yellow birch, and white pine, which ultimately succeed it.

Seeds of *Betula populifolia* are small, oval, and winged. Gray birch often grows as a clump of leaning trunks emerging from an old stump. Trunks and limbs are fairly flexible; when wet snow builds up on them, they bend all the way to the ground, only to spring up again unharmed when relieved of the snow load. My friend Jim Finley admits: "Sometimes children and old foresters will climb into the top of a gray birch and 'ride' it to the ground."

Donald Culross Peattie, in *A Natural History of Trees,* calls gray birch "a stunted sister" of the more graceful paper birch, and otherwise gives it short shrift. Hal Borland, in *A Countryman's Woods,* recognizes the role gray birch plays in forest succession; he notes that the gray birches so common on the reverting fields of his New England region "are of slight importance in man's economy, but nature's economy needs them."

HORNBEAM

I encounter hornbeam in the seepy lowland places visited by migrating woodcock, where fog collects on October mornings; where, in what was cow pasture decades ago, probe marks of the cocks' bills stipple the damp, worm-inhabited earth. Hornbeam *(Carpinus caroliniana)* is a small tree. Its bark, thin and smooth, looks like it was shrink-wrapped onto the trunk. The tree crooks and leans, its wood fluted and ridged like a tensed muscle—hence the name I first learned for the tree: musclewood. The autumn foliage is scarlet and jack-o'-lantern orange, among the fieriest hues in the eastern woods.

The name hornbeam connects two old words: *horn,* meaning "hard" or "tough," and *beam,* cognate with the German *baum,* as in *tannenbaum,* meaning "tree." *Carpinus caroliniana* has many other aliases: blue-beech, for the way its slick bark resembles that of American beech, although the beech's bark is pale gray, whereas that of hornbeam is a darker bluish gray tinged with brown; ironwood, because its wood is extremely hard; and water beech, since it grows in swamps and along lakes and streams.

Hornbeam ranges from southern Maine and Quebec west to Minnesota and Iowa, and south to Florida and Texas. It also grows in Mexico and Central America. Statewide in Pennsylvania, hornbeam is a fairly common component of the understory in oak-hickory and beech-birch-maple forests. It grows best

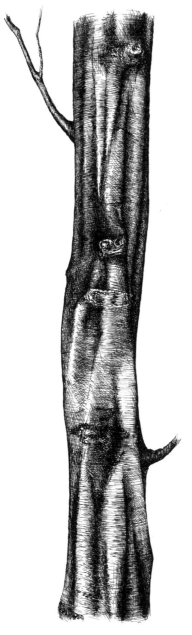

American hornbeam bark forms a smooth skin over the fluted, ridged trunk. Another name for the tree is musclewood.

on rich, moist sites but can tolerate a range of habitats, including drier hills, slopes, and ridges. In parts of its range, hornbeam forms pure stands in abandoned fields.

Smaller than the closely related hop-hornbeam, hornbeam generally grows 10 to 30 feet tall and up to 8 to 12 inches in diameter. A large specimen was reported in 1988 from Valley Forge National Park in Chester County: 56 feet tall, with a 58-foot crown spread and, at 2 inches above the ground, a circumference of 84 inches, for a diameter of more than 2 feet. The current national champion cited by the American Forestry Association stands 69 feet tall in Ulster County, New York. Botanists consider hornbeam to be a slow-growing but rather short-lived species.

When it grows as a single-trunk tree, the crown becomes wide and round-topped, with ascending branches. Near their ends, the side limbs may dip downward. Many hornbeams fork near the ground and take on a shrubby form. The leaves are egg-shaped, with rounded or wedge-shaped bases, 2 to 5 inches long, and have pointed tips and doubly saw-toothed margins. Dull, dark blue-green above, the leaves show a paler green below. On their undersurfaces, small hairs cloak the veins and vein angles.

Male and female flowers appear on the same branch, in April or May, just as the leaves are unfolding. The male catkins are 1/2 inch long, the female catkins 2/3 inch. Wind spreads male pollen to the female flowers. During summer, the female catkins develop into small nutlets enclosed by leaflike bracts, which are loosely stacked in pairs along slender stalks. The fruits ripen from August to October. The nutlet is about 1/3 inch long, and its attached bract, or wing, looks like a thin-lobed maple leaf. The graceful, three-pointed bract functions like the blade on a maple samara, giving the seed the buoyancy it needs to travel on the wind. The clustered bracts may remain hanging on the trees into winter.

Large seed crops arrive at three- to five-year intervals. The nutlets can germinate on leaf litter and establish themselves in the shade beneath mature trees. Seedlings on wet muck will survive if the soil dries out for at least part of the growing season. Although shade-tolerant when young, hornbeams need an opening in the canopy—a dominant tree felled by disease or wind—to achieve full size. Because of their small stature and protected position in the understory, hornbeams rarely get uprooted by wind. Particularly in the South, when overstory trees are removed by logging, hornbeam may grow in densely, preventing the larger trees from reproducing themselves.

Songbirds, ruffed grouse, ring-necked pheasants, bobwhite quail, wild turkeys, and squirrels eat seeds, buds, or catkins. Cottontail rabbits, beavers, and deer nip off leaves, twigs, and stems. Chickadees and other small birds nest in cavities in dead hornbeams.

Early settlers in New England made leak-proof bowls and dishes out of the tough wood, which, wrote William Wood in *New England's Prospects,* "requires much paines in riving as is almost incredible." The wood is close-grained, hard, and heavy, at 45 pounds per cubic foot. Since the trunk is so small, the tree is rarely sawed into boards; instead, people fashion it into tool handles, levers, wedges, and mallets. It can be burned as fuel, and charcoal made from hornbeam was once used in making gunpowder. The wood rots quickly in contact with the ground, precluding its use as a fence post.

Had I a wet patch of woods, I'd transplant some hornbeams there, so I could look at their fluted bark and quirky branch pattern year-round and, in autumn, treat myself to the emphatic brilliance of the leaves.

HOP-HORNBEAM

It's easy to overlook hop-hornbeam *(Ostrya virginiana),* a small tree that hides in the shade of loftier hardwoods. I don't encounter it often, but when I do, I stop and spend a few pleasant minutes examining the shreddy, brown-gray bark, which reminds me of some wild animal's pelt. If it's winter, I bend down a branch and look at the male catkins, which dangle in triplets, tight in their dormancy, waiting to expand in spring. In autumn, I ruffle the papery, rattling seedcases—they look like massed, tiny brown-paper bags—whose nutlets feed some of my favorite birds.

The *hop* part of the common name is from the resemblance of the tree's pendent fruit clusters to the fruit of the cultivated hop plant, used in brewing beer. Hornbeam means "hard tree." The word came across the Atlantic with early immigrants who knew—and used—a related tree in England. Other names for this species are eastern hop-hornbeam, leverwood, and ironwood. It is related to American hornbeam, *Carpinus caroliniana,* and both of the hornbeams belong to the large birch family, Betulaceae, which includes the birches and alders.

Hop-hornbeam ranges from Nova Scotia west to southern Manitoba and the Black Hills of South Dakota, and south to Florida and Texas. Although its range is extensive, nowhere is it a particularly abundant tree; generally hop-hornbeam is scattered through hardwood forests, and it also grows along woods edges. In Pennsylvania, *Ostrya virginiana* is statewide. Look for it on dry, gravelly slopes and ridges, and on moist sites in stream valleys. It prefers cool, shady places and thrives on limestone soil. It is more common in oak-hickory forests than in beech-birch-maple woods. The last time I encountered hop-hornbeam, I found a handful of specimens growing in company with American hornbeams in a grassy clearing along a remote stretch of the Hammersley Fork in southern Potter County.

Mature hop-hornbeams rarely grow taller than 30 feet or broader than 18 inches across the trunk. A specimen 73 feet tall and 3 feet in diameter was reported from Michigan in 1976. The crown tends to be high, open, and rounded, formed by wide-spreading branches that support ascending branchlets. Tough and resilient, the branches resist damage from ice, snow, and wind. The thin bark is made up of many small, flat scales that are usually loose at both ends while remaining attached to the trunk in the middle.

The foliage and twigs much resemble those of American hornbeam. The birchlike leaves are 3 to 5 inches long, dull yellowish green above and paler green below. Long-oval in shape, they sport sharp tips and double serrations, large teeth further divided into smaller teeth; the leaves stand at the ends of short, hairy leafstalks. Rutherford Platt, in *Discover American Trees,* calls hop-hornbeam leaves "flannel soft." They are thin, but firm and tough, and turn a dull yellow in autumn.

Hop-hornbeams begin to flower and fruit at around age twenty-five. As the leaves unfold in April, the 2-inch-long male catkins extend their pollen-laden stamens. Female catkins flower on the same branch, blooming fully about one month after leaf development began. The female catkins are usually paired on a single stem and are shorter and smaller than the male structures. Wind takes care of pollination.

In summer, the growing fruits are green; as they ripen in September and October, they turn brown. They look like loose, papery pinecones about 2 inches long and an inch wide. They are composed of a dozen or more bladderlike bracts, each holding a single flat nutlet. The bract expands to become a buoyant, inflated sac about 3/4 inch long. The sacs detach from the stem, and the wind disperses them during fall and early winter. The hairy stems remain attached to the branches. Thirty thousand hop-hornbeam seeds weigh 1 pound.

Ruffed and sharp-tailed grouse eat the nutlets, as do wild turkeys, ring-necked pheasants, bobwhite quail, finches, grosbeaks, woodpeckers, and squirrels. Ruffed grouse also eat the buds and male catkins in winter. White-tailed deer browse foliage and twig tips, but not very avidly. Beavers readily cut and eat hop-hornbeam: a study in Ohio found that hop-hornbeam was the third most utilized food, after alder and aspen.

Hop-hornbeam seeds usually germinate the spring after they are shed. Seedlings grow fast, even in the shade, and may be 7 feet tall after five years. As a more mature tree,

The fruit of hop-hornbeam (top) looks like a loose, papery pine cone. Hornbeam (bottom) sets out a series of three-pointed bracts, each bearing a single nutlet.

hop-hornbeam has a slow to medium growth rate. In some areas, foresters try to poison or grub it out in favor of more commercially valuable species. This approach ignores hop-hornbeam's value to wildlife and its contribution to the diversity of the eastern woods. Donald Culross Peattie, who often assigned human characteristics to trees, called hop-hornbeam "serviceable and self-effacing." He points out, in *A Natural History of Trees,* that as an understory species, the tree "gives shade or, rather, redoubled shade to the wild flowers and the mosses."

Hop-hornbeam sends down a long taproot. The tree dies if flooded: *Ostrya virginiana* was the third most flood-sensitive of thirty-nine tree species compared in a Tennessee study. Cut, burned, or injured trees send up sprouts from dormant buds on the trunk; they do not root-sprout. Studies have shown that hop-hornbeam is very sensitive to air pollutants such as sulfur and nitrogen oxides, chlorine, and fluorine. Reports John Eastman in *The Book of Forest and Thicket,* "Because it cannot tolerate salt, winter salting of roads and subsequent soil leaching make this a tree that is seldom seen from a car window."

Hop-hornbeam wood is extremely hard—harder even than hickory, black locust, and persimmon, although not quite as unyielding as dogwood. It is considered 30 percent stronger than white oak and weighs 50 pounds per cubic foot. Some Native American tribes made bows from hop-hornbeam. Settlers used it for ox yokes, fence posts, tool handles, mallets, rake teeth, sled runners, and levers for moving heavy loads.

BEECH

I have found exactly one beech in our woods. It grows on a dry, rock-studded, south-facing slope—hardly a favored site for its tribe—surrounded by chestnut oaks and black oaks. Although overtopped by the taller oaks and standing in their shade, the beech tree appears to be in good health. Tier upon tier of bright bluish green leaves extend from its apex to within a few feet of the ground: this in contrast to the oaks, whose leaves cluster in their topmost branches. Even though there are no other beech trees in the forest for hundreds of yards around, I have a pretty good idea how our solitary specimen got here.

American beech *(Fagus grandifolia)* ranges across southern Canada to Wisconsin and south to Florida and Texas—including essentially all of the eastern United States. Beeches prefer rich, moist soils of both uplands and lowlands and occur as scattered individuals or in small, pure stands. In the middle latitudes of its range, American beech shows up more abundantly on cool, moist, north-facing slopes than on drier, south-facing aspects. In the southern Appalachians, the tree grows at elevations as high as 6,000 feet. Before the ice ages, *Fagus grandifolia* grew as far west as California and probably flourished over most of North America. Today a subspecies survives in the mountains of Mexico. Our American species is similar to *Fagus sylvatica*, the European beech. The oaks and American chestnut are close relatives of beech trees.

American beech is statewide in Pennsylvania, most abundant in the northern tier of counties and generally absent from the intensively farmed limestone valleys farther south. Beech has no aversion to limestone soil; in fact, the species makes its best growth on "sweet" limestone loam in the Midwest. Early in our country's history, pioneers learned that beech trees signaled good soil, and settlers homed in on, and cleared for agriculture, the great beech forests that blanketed parts of Ohio, Kentucky, Indiana, and central Michigan.

Beech trees typically stand 60 to 80 feet tall (old-growth specimens can reach 120 feet), with a diameter of 2 to 3 feet. Forest-grown beeches often show a different form than individuals growing in the open. In the woods, a beech tends to be tall and slender, free of branches for a long way up from the base, yet with a deeper crown than many of its sylvan neighbors. Where it gets more sun, as in an old field, a beech will have a short, thick trunk with many long side limbs; the lowest branches droop toward the ground, those in the middle spread out horizontally, and the branches in the crown extend upward, forming a dense, symmetrical crown. The roots are shallow and wide-spreading; often they protrude above the ground for a few feet before angling down into the soil.

The most distinctive aspect of American beech is its bark. The thin, smooth, pale gray covering gleams in the shadowy woods. The bark must be unusually elastic, because it never breaks up into plates and furrows like the bark of most other trees as their girth expands with age. Beech bark gains character as it becomes blotched with lichens and scarred with graffiti produced by animals' claws. I recently encountered a Tioga County beech amply written over by climbing black bears and raccoons. The most famous inscription ever made on a beech is *D Boone cilled a bar on tree in year 1760*, carved into a tree along an old stage road in Tennessee. When the tree toppled in 1916, scars from the inscription were still visible on its trunk. The tree was estimated to be 365 years old.

Leaves of American beech remain on the tree during winter,
slowly fading to a pale tan.

Slender, sharp-pointed, many-scaled, bronze-colored beech buds are almost an inch long—about five times as long as they are thick. Rutherford Platt, in *Discover American Trees,* likened them to "tightly rolled spindles."

From the buds unfurl leaves that are 3 to 6 inches long by 1 to 3 inches wide. They have a rather stiff, leathery texture. Beech leaves are short-stemmed and ovate, with a central vein from which prominent parallel side veins extend outward, each side vein ending in a large, sharp tooth on the leaf margin. Leaves or leaf clusters, with two or three leaves together, alternate along the twigs. I can detect a definite blue tint in the dull green upper surfaces of beech leaves, whose paler undersides are glossy and reflective; summer sunshine beams through the translucent blades. In autumn, beech leaves turn a clean, soft yellow. In winter, they hang in the tree for months, slowly fading to a pale tan like ancient parchment.

Beeches flower in April or May, just before and during leaf emergence. Male and female flowers appear on the same tree. The yellow-green male flowers form a globe-shaped mass that hangs on a long stem. The paired female flowers are 1/4 inch long, short-stemmed and urn-shaped, and bordered by reddish scales; wind brings about their pollination. Spring frosts can ruin the tender beech flowers.

Beechnuts are protected by somewhat prickly husks. The nuts drop following frosts in September and October. They are triangular, shiny brown, and no bigger than a fingertip. The sweet meats make an excellent trail snack. If you find the nuts in quantity, you can make them into a flour. Mash the kernels, let the resulting paste dry, and grind it; substitute it for half the flour in any muffin, biscuit, or bread recipe. Unless carefully dried, the fresh nuts keep but a few weeks; after that, they turn rancid. The nuts contain about 22 percent protein and were a key item in the diets of several woodland Indian tribes, including the Iroquois.

Beechnuts are the main mast crop produced in the northern hardwood forest, a biome composed largely of beech, birch, and maple trees, though in some areas northern red oak, also a mast producer, joins the species mix. American beech starts bearing substantial amounts of nuts when about forty years old and large quantities by age sixty. Notes Donald Culross Peattie in *A Natural History of Trees,* "Fruit is abundant, in general, only every third year on any one tree, and commonly a heavy or a light harvest of the nuts prevails over a whole region." Other sources report good crops once every three to seven years.

Many wild animals eat beechnuts. Squirrels climb into the trees' crowns and cut down the nuts in early autumn. Gray squirrels bury nuts singly to store them; red squirrels fill middens—storage sites in hollow stumps, rock crevices, and voids inside brush piles—with caches of nuts; and chipmunks stockpile the mast in their burrows. Bears shinny into beech trees, sit in

branch crotches, and draw outer limbs in toward themselves while they feed, sometimes snapping the branch ends and leaving a messy tangle. Opossums, raccoons, red and gray foxes, white-tailed deer, and mice consume beechnuts, as do wood ducks, ruffed grouse, spruce grouse, bobwhite quail, wild turkeys, grosbeaks, and other birds. Before humans drove them to extinction, passenger pigeons in their colossal flocks subsisted largely on beechnuts; the cutting of beech forests to create farmland, along with unrestricted hunting, snuffed out the species by the early 1900s.

Blue jays are particularly fond of beechnuts and flock to areas with nut-laden trees. The birds chip apart some of the nuts and eat them on the spot. A jay will collect surplus nuts, stuff them into its expandable throat

When black bears climb beech trees to feed on nuts, they leave claw marks on the smooth bark.

and esophagus, and carry the food back to its home territory, up to several miles away. A single bird may make hundreds of trips, carrying up to fourteen beechnuts per journey. Back home, the bird caches the nuts by pushing them into soft soil or covering them with plant debris; in winter or early spring, the bird returns, remembers the storage spots, digs up the nuts, and eats them. The jays do not remember all the nuts they hide, and some of the birds perish before they can retrieve their hoards. Since jays are very adept at selecting only sound, germinable nuts, they end up planting a lot of beech trees.

Biologists theorize that jays' nut-caching habits helped the American beech and some oak species move rapidly northward following the last ice age, reforesting areas denuded by the glaciers. Nut dispersal by jays remains ecologically important today, especially in places where human activities have fragmented forests, isolating patches of woods with grassland, farmland, and highways in between, barriers against the movements of small seed-dispersing mammals such as squirrels and mice. Jays help maintain the trees' genetic diversity by transferring their seeds between forested areas.

Which returns me to the solitary beech on our land. The whole mountain here was logged in the late 1920s. It's likely our beech was planted by a blue jay some time after the clear-cut logging, when the oaks had begun to resprout from their stumps. American beech is shade-tolerant, and even if the oaks had enjoyed a head start of a decade or two, a jay-planted beech could have survived in the understory. That it received a reasonable amount of sun during its early years is shown by the tree's open-grown form, with the branches reaching all the way to the ground. Today its uppermost limbs extend into the canopy, where several surrounding chestnut oaks died following gypsy moth infestations in the 1980s.

After falling from the tree or being buried by a squirrel or jay, a beechnut remains dormant over winter. It germinates the following spring or early summer. Seedlings prosper in partial shade and protected small openings; in direct sun, the soil may dry out too much for them to survive. Seedlings can germinate beneath ferns and raspberries and gradually extend up through such cover. Beech is considered to be as shade-tolerant as sugar maple. Beech seedlings grow slowly in deep, shady woods. In an old-growth hemlock and hardwood stand along East Tionesta Creek in northwestern Pennsylvania, foresters monitored the height of beech seedlings. The seedlings were 1 foot tall at age six, 2 feet at age ten, 5 feet at age twenty, and 7 feet at age twenty-five.

A beech requires twice as much water for transpiration and growth processes as some of the more drought-resistant trees, such as the oaks. Like an oak, a beech—especially a young one—will sprout from the stump if cut down. And like an aspen, a beech will also reproduce by sending up sprouts, or suckers, from its root system, particularly on a marginal or dry site. Altogether, forest scientists believe more beech reproduction comes from sprouting than from seeds. Wherever beech limbs touch the ground, they send down roots, a process that botanists term layering. A tree's roots form a dense mat; most are shallow, but some roots may penetrate 5 feet deep in good soil. The root system of American beech is shallower than those of yellow birch and sugar maple, two species often found growing with *Fagus grandifolia*. Deer seldom feed on beech twigs or vegetation if other trees are available. In overbrowsed forests in northern Pennsylvania, beech may become dominant when deer suppress other tree species.

Beeches are very susceptible to death from flooding. Late spring frosts severely damage the trees, and their thin bark makes them vulnerable to injury caused by fire, logging operations, insects (including notably a pest called the beech scale), and humans with pocketknives. Once its trunk is breached, a beech may be invaded by fungi causing bark disease and heart rot. As beeches age and their trunks thicken, wood-decay fungi often render them hollow. These spaces provide a habitat for cavity-nesting birds such as black-capped chickadees, tufted titmice, woodpeckers, and owls, and also porcupines, squirrels, opossums, raccoons, and, in really big, old trees, black bears.

The wood of American beech is a light reddish color. It is hard, strong, and tough, but not durable in contact with the soil. Difficult to season, it tends to warp and twist while seasoning. It weighs 43 pounds per cubic foot when dry. People have used it for pallets, railroad ties, flooring, shoe lasts, butchers' blocks, veneer, containers, clothespins, hangers, tool handles, and charcoal. When heated with steam, beech bends readily and later holds its shape, making it a favorite choice for bentwood furniture. Although tough to split, beech makes an excellent fuelwood, burning slowly and releasing ample heat.

In Europe, beech bark gave early humans a ready-made drawing and writing surface, a prehistoric book. Our word *book* derives from the Anglo-Saxon *boc,* meaning a letter or a character, which in turn comes from an older word, *beece,* for beech.

CHESTNUT

When several hundred acres surrounding our land were logged in the 1980s, the sudden burst of sunlight energized certain trees along our boundaries. The trees included about a dozen American chestnuts *(Castanea dentata)*. The trees—saplings, really—sprang up from the root systems of chestnuts that had been blighted back in the 1920s, as a fungus, accidentally brought to North America from Asia, swept through the eastern woods. The pathogen killed essentially all of the upper growth but left alive the root systems of some of the trees.

As they grew, our new chestnut saplings donned a thick raiment of lovely, spearhead-shaped leaves. They reached 20 feet tall. One year they even managed to bear a few nuts; I had to act quickly to get a taste before the squirrels cleaned them up. Then orange-red fungal cankers appeared, killing the inner wood tissues and girdling the saplings' 4-inch trunks. It wasn't long before the trees became lifeless snags. Now, fifteen years after the chestnuts enjoyed their brief resurgence, I can't find a single one on our land.

Today American chestnut exists mainly as a shrub or a small tree. At one time, it was the most abundant large tree in the East, making up almost 25 percent of all hardwoods. In some areas, four of every ten trees were chestnuts. The species ranged from Maine to Georgia, Alabama, and Mississippi, and from the Atlantic coast west to the Appalachian Mountains, where, foresters judged, it achieved its best development in the uplands of western North Carolina and eastern Tennessee. In Pennsylvania, American chestnut grew statewide; it was most common in the eastern, southern, and central regions, where it mingled with oaks and hickories. Chestnut thrived on many different types of soil, although not on limestone soil or extremely wet muck, from lowlands bordering rivers to ridges and mountaintops.

A mature chestnut stands 60 to 80 feet tall, with a trunk 3 to 4 feet in diameter. On an excellent site, this fast-growing tree could soar to 100 feet or higher, supported by a trunk up to 10 feet broad. The leaves are 5 to 9 inches long and 2 to 3 inches wide. Prominent side veins parallel one another, each ending in a small, forward-curving spike. Shiny yellow-green above, the leaves are paler below; they change to a rich yellow in autumn. The bark on young trees, such as the ones that sprouted on our land, is smooth and greenish; on old trunks, it becomes fibrous, with deep fissures divided by flat-topped ridges covered with dark brown scales. Occasionally I will find a sizable chestnut in the woods; the most recent one was in summer 2000. It grew at Bruce Lake Natural Area in Pike County, in the

Pocono Mountains of northeastern
Pennsylvania. The tree had a trunk
nearly a foot in diameter at breast
height. It was as tall as its neighbors,
mainly white oaks and chestnut oaks.
Spiny husks lay on the ground;
apparently the tree had produced
nuts, although in this instance the
squirrels and deer had beaten me to
them. Unfortunately, the tree's trunk
showed the telltale orange stippling of
the blight fungus near a branch stub.

*In autumn, the spiny husk of
the American chestnut opens
to reveal the ripe nuts.*

Chestnuts flower in June or July,
which is late enough that frosts rarely
damage the blossoms. Flowers of
both sexes occur on the same tree. Whitish or yellow-green male flowers stand
on upright, 6-inch catkins at the base of the leaf; the insect-pollinated female
flowers occupy shorter catkins. The fertilized female flowers develop into
fruits consisting of a bur 2 to 2 1/2 inches in diameter, covered with 1/2-inch-
long spines, and usually containing two or three seeds. The seeds, known as
chestnuts, are a shiny dark brown, flattened on one side and pointed at one
end. The nuts are 1/2 to 3/4 inch long. They have a rich, sweet taste.

Wayne Harpster, an elderly friend and neighbor of mine, wrote and
published a small book, *Come Walk with Me,* about growing up in rural central Pennsylvania during the first half of the twentieth century. This is from
a chapter entitled "Nutting": "Looking at my father's diary for Monday,
October 9, 1911, I saw this entry: 'Cool this morning. A grand day. The
children and I picked 41 quarts of chestnuts.'" To get the chestnuts, Wayne
wrote, his father cut "a long, thin pole that had a limb at the large end. The
limb would then be cut back to make a seven- or eight-inch hook that
could be hooked over a higher limb on the tree. As our dad would climb,
he would reach up and hook the pole above him. This would leave both
hands free for climbing. As he got up to where the opened burs were hanging, he would take the pole and switch or trim the limbs, causing the burs
and chestnuts to fall to the ground." ("Those things sure hurt if they hit
you!" Wayne once told me.)

"When the tree was completely switched, father would climb down
and we would all go under the tree to hunt the nuts." During that era, people gathered nuts for their own use and sold any surplus. In cities, vendors

roasted chestnuts on the street; passersby would purchase bags of the warm, delicious nuts.

Deer, bears, squirrels, chipmunks, wild turkeys, bobwhite quail, and many other wild creatures, including the now-extinct passenger pigeon, ate chestnuts, as did hogs and other farm animals. Squirrels and chipmunks probably helped replant the trees by burying the nuts, as they do with oaks' acorns.

The yellowish brown wood of American chestnut was even more valuable to humans than the tree's nuts. Softer, lighter (at 28 pounds per cubic foot), and easier to work with than oak, it was employed for general construction and for a range of products, including wagon tongues, house trim, furniture, and shingles. People used the rot-resistant wood for fence posts and rails (chestnut splits easily), utility poles, and mine timbers. Bark and wood of chestnut supplied tannin used for tanning leather. Chestnut makes a good fuelwood; it gives off sharp pops as it burns. Loggers were still harvesting lumber from long-lasting chestnut snags decades after the blight killed the trees. So tenacious is the wood of American chestnut that I still run across stumps of trees sawed down in the 1920s and 1930s, including several on our land, which remind me of gravestones on the forest floor.

The chestnut blight fungus, *Cryphonectria parasitica* (formerly called *Endothia parasitica)*, came to North America from Japan or China at the beginning of the twentieth century on imported Asiatic chestnut seedlings. The blight was first noticed in 1904 on trees at the Bronx Zoo in New York. In Pennsylvania in 1913, the legislature established a Chestnut Tree Blight Commission and appropriated $275,000—a huge sum at that time—for research and control, including chemical spraying and felling trees ahead of the plague. But the fungus spread inexorably, and *Castanea dentata* exhibited no natural immunity to the foreign pathogen. By the 1950s, the chestnut had been virtually wiped out across the species' range in what some ecologists have termed "the greatest botanical disaster in history."

Scientists have since learned that the blight fungus produces two types of spores, which can be thought of as microscopic seeds: a dry disk carried by the wind, and a smaller form that is washed down the trunk by rain and enters breaks in the bark—scrapes, branch stubs, woodpecker and insect holes—spreading the infection within the tree. The smaller spores are sticky; they cling to the feet of birds and may be transported for many miles. In attacking the inner bark, the fungal cankers split the wood and girdle the stem, killing the tree above the lesion. After a stand of chestnuts is infected, 95 percent of the trees die within ten years.

Periodically, the root systems of "dead" chestnuts send up sprouts, especially when they receive direct sunlight, after logging or storms remove tall
neighboring trees that have cast their shade on the chestnuts. Studies indicate that most chestnut sprouts today come not from the stumps of dominant forest trees, which were mainly killed outright by the blight, but from
old seedlings and former low-growing stems that had never become part of
the forest canopy. The root systems of those survivors have a limited life
span, and many are now finally dying themselves.

For decades, scientists have worked to create a blight-resistant American chestnut through cross-breeding, introducing genes from resistant
Asian *Castanea* species. State forestry departments and private conservation
groups, including the American Chestnut Foundation, are poised to begin
planting hybrid variants in eastern forests. It is unlikely that chestnuts will
ever again dominate the eastern woods, but they may be able to survive
with human help.

The poet Robert Frost wrote these hopeful and perhaps prophetic lines
about the American chestnut:

> It keeps smoldering at the roots
> And keeps sending up new shoots
> Till another parasite
> Shall come to end the blight.

Recently, a weakened, or hypovirulent, form of chestnut blight has
emerged. It seems to infect the normal robust form of *Cryphonectria parasitica* with a virus, weakening it so that a tree can withstand its effects and wall
off the invading fungus behind new bark tissue. Today researchers are study-
ing methods of spreading the hypovirulent form in nature.

RED OAK AND BLACK OAK

In early October 2001, while cutting firewood on my land, I had to watch
out for acorns. The oaks in our woods were dropping nuts—and none
more prolifically than the red oaks, which, from their lofty, wide-spreading
branches, showered their big acorns down on the ground and on anyone and
anything that happened beneath them. There were times when I was very
glad to be wearing my hardhat. I needed to watch my step in places: it felt
like I was walking on marbles. That fall was the most productive autumn for
acorns in my memory.

Northern red oaks *(Quercus rubra)* are some of the largest trees in the Northeast. A mature specimen will tower 70 to 90 feet, with a 2- to 4-foot trunk diameter. There are red oaks on record 150 feet tall, with trunks 5 feet across. The classic woods-grown red oak has a long, straight trunk topped with ascending branches that support a small, narrow crown. When a red oak grows in the open—in a field, shading a city street, in a park—it forks nearer to the ground, its short, thick trunk dividing into a network of stout branches holding up a deep, spreading crown. Many species of hardwoods display these contrasting growth patterns, but in red oaks, the difference between a tree that must compete for light and one that is bathed in it is particularly striking.

Northern red oak is one of the northernmost of our oak species; bur oak, *Quercus macrocarpa,* grows marginally farther to the north in Canada's Manitoba province. Red oak ranges from Nova Scotia west across southern Canada to Minnesota, south through the Carolinas to Georgia and Mississippi in the east and through eastern Kansas and Oklahoma in the west. It is the common oak of New England. In the Southeast, red oak is present in the Appalachians but absent from the coastal plain and the piedmont. Red oak has been widely planted in England and in western Europe, where it has become naturalized and is now expanding its range. Red oaks thrive under a variety of moisture conditions and soil types. They grow throughout Pennsylvania. The common name describes the color of the tree's wood.

Genus *Quercus,* the oaks, numbers around eighty-five species in North America. Botanists separate the oaks into two broad categories: red oaks and white oaks. Prominent among the red oaks are northern red oak, *Quercus rubra;* black oak, *Quercus velutina;* scarlet oak, *Quercus coccinea;* and pin oak, *Quercus palustris.* Members of the white oak group include eastern white oak, *Quercus alba;* chestnut oak, *Quercus montana;* post oak, *Quercus stellata;* yellow or chinkapin oak, *Quercus muhlenbergii;* and bur oak, *Quercus macrocarpa.* The leaves of species in the red oak group have angular lobes that end in bristle tips, in which the veins jut out beyond the leaf margin in the form of needlelike points. These points, some scientists suggest, may help drain away moisture, thwarting fungal growth that might cloud the leaf's surface and disrupt photosynthesis. Leaves of trees in the white oak group have rounded, flowing margins on their lobes, which are not equipped with bristles. It takes two years for the acorns of the red oaks to mature; the acorns are laced with tannins, bitter chemicals that deter some foraging animals. White oak acorns ripen in a single growing season, and have a lower tannin content, making them more attractive to wildlife.

The leaves of northern red oak are 5 to 9 inches long by 4 to 6 inches wide. They are divided into seven to nine lobes, each of which may end in several points equipped with bristle tips. The gaps or sinuses between the lobes extend about halfway in from the leaf's margin to its midrib. When unfurling from their buds, the young leaves are a pink color. By summer, they are dull green on their top surfaces; often the midrib has a yellowish or reddish tint. The foliage of red oaks turns different colors in fall, including dark red, orange, and bronze; the leaves on some trees simply become dull brown before dropping off. In some cases, the leaves remain hanging on their twigs into winter.

Members of the red oak group hybridize frequently, resulting in individuals whose leaves and other vegetative and reproductive structures are intermediate in form between those of their parents—halfway between the leaves of red oak and black oak, for example. This situation can cause confusion for amateur botanists, and it prompted Donald Culross Peattie into making the following pronouncement in his book, *A Natural History of Trees:* "The leaves and acorn cups of Red Oak are so variable that it is hard to identify the tree, hard to describe it, and hard to illustrate it with certainty." Leaves may even vary in shape on the same tree. In addition, the leaves of a seedling or a sucker shoot may be different—usually larger, and with shallower sinuses, giving a greater overall surface area—than the leaves of a mature tree.

On young trees and stems, the bark is greenish brown and smooth. Mature red oaks have thick, dark brown bark, whose surface is broken up by shallow fissures into long, vertical ridges that run into and connect with each other. Often the ridges are broadly flat-topped. They look like they've been pressed down by a clothes iron; their smooth surfaces shine with reflected light. The inner bark, just below the hard outer layer, is a light reddish color.

Red oaks prefer moist soil, which can be sandy, loamy, rocky, or with a strong clay component. They do not grow in swamps. Wide-spreading lateral roots—and in some cases, deep-plunging taproots—anchor the tree and procure water. *Quercus rubra* is the fastest growing of all the oaks. In one year, a seedling can rise 19 inches. The same seedling at age ten can be 18 feet tall. And by age fifty, the resulting tree may tower up 50 to 60 feet. Red oaks are intolerant of shade when young. Both youthful trees and adults sprout prolifically from the stump or root system if logging or fire kills the aboveground portion of the plant. Although red oaks withstand cold better than most other oaks, they are more susceptible to drought than their *Quer-*

cus relatives, and extended dry periods can kill them. On a good site, a red oak may live three hundred years or longer.

Red oaks grow in pure stands and mixed in with maples, American beech, basswood, white ash, black birch, tuliptree, black cherry, hickories, pines, and many other species. In my woods, fairly typical for the central Pennsylvania uplands, the mix of oak species includes scarlet, black, white, and chestnut, as well as red.

Flowers emerge in May, when the leaves are about half developed. The yellow-green male flowers are borne on a slender, hairy string 4 to 5 inches long; the structure is technically known as an ament and is also called a catkin. The female flowers are an unobtrusive pale green, rounded and smaller than the dangling male catkins. The male flowers usually are concentrated in a tree's upper branches, while the female blossoms emerge lower in the tree. The male flowers put out tremendous quantities of yellow pollen, which drifts and blows freely through the air. In a predominantly oak forest, the pollen will cover all flat surfaces and lie in a skin on backwaters of streams and lakes. In our woods, we always wait until the oaks are done flowering before we clean the house windows in spring.

Red oak acorns are a lustrous medium brown color and are furred with minuscule pale hairs. The nut has a flat base and a narrow tip. The broad, shallow cup looks like a saucer; it covers less than one-third of the base of the nut and is made up of many tightly overlapping reddish brown scales. Red oak acorns range from about 3/4 to 1 1/4 inches in length. The ones in our woods are about as big as the last joint of my thumb. As Peattie notes, wonderful variation exists in red oak acorns: in their color, shape, size, and weight. The ecologist Bernd Heinrich checked a series of acorns in his three-hundred-acre Maine woodland and found weights ranging from 0.85 to 7.47 grams. Variation is the raw material of natural selection; notes Heinrich in *The Trees in My Forest,* "If, for

Acorns of northern red oak drop during autumn, then lie dormant on the forest floor until spring, when they germinate.

example, gray squirrels disperse and bury the smaller acorns more than the larger nuts, then trees growing where the squirrels are abundant will reproduce more if they have small nuts."

Red oak acorns mature at the end of their second growing season; an individual tree can potentially bear a nut crop every other year. The nuts fall just before the leaves let go of their stems and come drifting down. The fallen leaves bury the acorns, hiding some from foraging wildlife while leaving others exposed for seed-dispersing animals. The acorns don't germinate until the following spring, in contrast with the white oak's strategy of immediate autumn germination.

Oaks often seem to be in some sort of mysterious synchrony, with many trees—even of different species—producing bumper crops in the same year. A superabundance of acorns defeats seedeaters such as deer, bears, mice, chipmunks, and squirrels, so that some nuts remain to sprout. Large acorn crops spur population increases in deer mice and other rodents; those populations plummet in years when acorns are scarce. Ruffed grouse, ring-necked pheasants, bobwhite quail, wild turkeys, woodpeckers, crows, blue jays, tufted titmice, white-breasted nuthatches, brown thrashers, towhees, and grackles all eat acorns. The nuthatch uses its beak to hammer the shell open. The wild turkey swallows acorns whole and lets its muscular gizzard break up the nuts. The grackle has a hard ridge or keel in the roof of its mouth; the bird rotates an acorn against this projection to slice through the nutshell.

Blue jays flock to forests where red oak acorns are plentiful. A jay will load its expandable throat and esophagus with several nuts, then fly back to its home territory and there bury the acorns beneath leaf duff, soft soil, or grass, for eating in late winter or early spring. Acorns that jays fail to recover, and that squirrels do not dig up and pilfer, germinate and may become new trees. Scientists believe that blue jays' transporting and burying of acorns helped oak trees march northward after the last ice age ended, around ten thousand years ago, when the *Quercus* species remained only in the south. Squirrels are major seed dispersers for all the oaks, including northern red oak. Acorns from trees in the red oak group, of which *Quercus rubra* is a member, have high levels of bitter-tasting tannins. Where red oak and white oak acorns lie side by side, squirrels tend to eat the white oak acorns immediately and cache the red oak acorns for future use.

Native Americans of many tribes had different ways of dissolving the water-soluble tannins from the nutmeats of red oak acorns. They buried the acorns in the mud of a swamp for a year, stored them beneath sand in fresh water, and pounded them into a meal and then let a stream run through the fragments for a day.

More than a thousand species of insects are known to eat red oak foliage, including moth caterpillars, leaf miners, June beetles, and walking-sticks. Other insects lay eggs in the developing flower. The larva then lives in the nuts and chews its way out through the shell, leaving a telltale hole. By far the most destructive insect pest is the gypsy moth, whose caterpillar larvae defoliate millions of acres of oak forests yearly. A Eurasian insect, the gypsy moth was brought to Massachusetts in the mid-1800s by a French entomologist who wanted to breed hybrid silk moths and establish a silk industry. Some of the moths escaped, and the insects have been expanding their range ever since. The leading edge of the infestation passed through central Pennsylvania in the 1980s; in my mind I can still hear the sound of the caterpillars' droppings, like a light rain pattering on the forest floor. Gypsy moths prefer the foliage of oaks over all other trees. The caterpillars may denude whole forests by early summer; the trees leaf out again, squandering valuable energy. If moth populations remain high and larvae strip trees several years in a row, the stress may ultimately kill the trees, which perish within one to three years of defoliation. In my woods, more red oaks died than any other species, perhaps because they could not withstand the dual burdens of defoliation and drought.

Red oak wood is heavy, strong, and hard; the heartwood is a light reddish brown, the sapwood paler. The wood weighs around 40 pounds per cubic foot, dry weight. In the past, people considered red oak wood inferior to that of white oak. The red was lighter, more difficult to season without twisting and cracking, more porous, not as rot-resistant. It went for rough construction, clapboards, and slack cooperage (barrels not meant to hold liquids). Today red oak is used for railroad ties, since its porosity helps it absorb preservatives, and for paper pulp. The better grades now bring a much higher price than white oak. Its attractive color and handsome grain pattern make red oak a top choice for furniture, cabinets, flooring, and house trim.

A closely related species is southern red oak, *Quercus falcata,* also called Spanish oak, whose range centers on the southeastern states. Botanists have found it in about five Pennsylvania counties, in dry to moist woodlands on or near the coastal plain in the extreme southeastern part of the state. The tree is 50 to 80 feet tall at maturity. The leaves differ noticeably from those of northern red oak. In the southern species, they are 4 to 8 inches long, generally with three main lobes set off by a rounded base. Shiny green on their upper surfaces, they are coated with down on their lower side. In 1683, in a letter to the Free Society of Traders in London, William Penn listed "Spanish oak" as one of the many natural resources found in his new colony.

Black Oak *(Quercus velutina)*. Black oak can be difficult to distinguish from northern red oak, with which it frequently hybridizes. Black oak is a common dry-woods species found throughout Pennsylvania, except in the extreme north-central counties. On a continental scale, it ranges from southern New England to the midwestern states and south to Florida and Texas—a slightly more southerly distribution than that of northern red oak.

Black oaks grow 50 to 80 or more feet tall. They often occupy sandy and rocky ridges and slopes, and seldom occur in rich bottomlands. The leaves bear a strong resemblance to those of northern red oak, but are judged to be somewhat thicker, wider at the top sinuses, and more of a yellow-green color on their undersides. They are also quite variable. According to Joseph Illick in *Pennsylvania Trees,* "No other oak produces so many differently shaped leaves on the same tree." The bark is darker and lacks the broad, glossy-topped ridges of northern red oak. Big black oaks that I have seen in the forest—and had identified for me by trained foresters—possessed thick bark broken by deep fissures, most of which ran vertically but some of which crossed the trunk, making for an extremely rough, almost checkered surface.

The inner bark is yellow to orange and charged with tannin; in the past, people used it to tan, or cure, leather and to dye cloth yellow. Many birds and mammals eat the acorns of black oak, which form part of the mast crop that sustains so many woodland creatures in Pennsylvania and other parts of the Northeast.

PIN OAK

Pin oak's species name, *palustris,* is a Latin word describing a bog or marsh and signals the tree's preferred habitat: palustral, or swampy, land. Look for this medium-size tree in wet woods, river bottomlands, and the fringes of swamps. Pin oaks *(Quercus palustris)* do best in soil saturated for part of the year, such as lowlands that flood in late winter and early spring. They also grow on clay soils underlying poorly drained upland sites.

Pin oak belongs to the red oak group, along with northern red oak, black oak, scarlet oak, and several other species. *Quercus palustris* ranges from southern New England west to Iowa, Missouri, and eastern Kansas, and south to North Carolina, Tennessee, Arkansas, and eastern Oklahoma. It is fairly common in eastern and southern Pennsylvania, sparsely distributed in the western part of the state, and rare or absent in the northern counties.

A mature pin oak stands 50 to 90 feet tall and has a trunk 1 to 3 feet in diameter; the largest specimens on record exceed 100 feet in height and possess trunks more than 5 feet in diameter.

I have a special fondness for deciduous trees in winter, a time when one can see and truly comprehend the form of an individual specimen. Winter-bare pin oak is one of my favorites. Unlike other oaks, *Quercus palustris* sends up a central stem that does not fork. This mastlike shaft rises straight to the top of the tree, narrowing as it ascends. The trunk appears thick, relative to the size of the branches projecting from it. Branches near the crown fan upward; those near the middle of the tree extend horizontally; and ones lowest on the trunk dip downward, reaching back toward the ground. The overall shape is conical. Filling in this complex, distinctive symmetry is a host of smaller branchlets, particularly in the lower half of the tree: short, thin, strong, flexible twigs that resemble pins closely enough to have earned this oak its most widely accepted name. Other monikers are water oak and swamp oak.

The lower branches of pin oak droop toward the ground, giving the tree a distinctive winter silhouette.

The angular leaves of pin oak strongly resemble those of scarlet oak. They are 4 to 6 inches long and 2 to 4 inches broad. Five to seven tapering lobes, each with a few sharply pointed teeth, stand separated by deep clefts; these gaps between the lobes extend almost the whole way to the midrib and are rounded at the base. As a member of the red oak tribe, pin oak sports tiny bristle tips at the ends of the lobe teeth. The leaves are shiny dark green above and light green below; on their undersurfaces, at the angles where the conspicuous side veins join the midrib, grow tufts of pale hairs. The leaves turn a rich deep red in autumn; some usually hang on the tree, dead and brown, into winter.

The bark is gray to gray-brown, hard, thin, and fairly smooth, broken by shallow cracks. Between the cracks, low ridges stand covered with small scales. The bark on young trees is smooth and shiny, light brown to reddish in color.

Pin oaks flower at the same time that they are putting out leaves in spring. Individual trees have both male and female flowers. The male flowers are grouped in dangling, hairy catkins; the bright red female flowers stand at the ends of short stalks. Wind carries the male pollen to the female flowers. The resulting acorn takes two years to mature. It is about 1/2 inch long and equally broad, notably rounded in shape. A scaly, saucer-shaped cup covers between one-quarter and one-third of the nut. Inside the acorn lies a pale yellow kernel that is suffused with bitter-tasting tannin compounds. Despite their bitterness, the acorns are sought out and eaten by deer, squirrels and other rodents, wild turkeys, woodpeckers, and ducks, especially mallards and wood ducks, which walk about on dry land picking up the nuts. In *The Book of Swamp and Bog,* the Michigan naturalist John Eastman reports finding pin oak acorns cached by blue jays in the ragged seedheads of cattails in autumn.

Pin oak has a shallow, fibrous root system; although it does not send down a taproot, the tree is fairly resistant to summer drought. A shade-intolerant species, it pushes up quickly in wet areas where logging has removed other trees. Pin oaks as young as twenty years can produce acorns; the trees rarely live longer than a century. In poorly drained soil, pin oaks may grow in nearly pure stands. They also mix with hardwoods such as American elm, silver and red maples, hackberry, basswood, and shagbark and shellbark hickories.

The wood is fairly heavy, at 43 pounds per cubic foot, dry weight. It has a reputation for warping and checking, or cracking, badly while curing; thanks to the tree's prolific branching habit, many small knots interrupt the grain. Pin oak gets used for cheap construction, railroad ties, barrels, crates, and pallets. The tough, stubby, pinlike twigs were used as pegs to hold together the big, squared-timber frames of old barns.

Pin oak, with its intriguing, graceful form, makes an excellent street or lawn tree. Since its root system is shallow, pin oak is easier to transplant than other oaks, and its fast growth habit allows the tree to fill a site quickly. It is disease-resistant and wind-firm, and it tolerates polluted air fairly well. I particularly admire specimens in their middle years: old enough to have developed those elegant, drooping lower branches, yet not so large that they have broadened and lost that upward-striving, conical silhouette.

SCARLET OAK

A scarlet oak on the edge of our pasture seems to both celebrate and pro-long autumn each year. As the maples are dropping their vermilion foliage, fires have begun to smolder among the scarlet oak's greenery. By early November, the tree is a rich maroon—a red with depth and staying power. As November wanes, and the leaves are stripped from the other species of oaks, and winds chase them across the tan grass, color remains in the tight-clinging leaves of the scarlet oak, a diminished red like the dregs of last night's wine. Finally the leaves go brown; but even then, as the first snows fall, they remain attached to their twigs, ragged, sere, talkative, refusing to let go.

Scarlet oak *(Quercus coccinea)* belongs to the red oak group. It is com-mon throughout Pennsylvania, except in the northernmost counties. The species ranges from Maine to Michigan, and south to South Carolina, Georgia, Alabama, and Mississippi. It is found in all or part of every state east of the Mississippi River, with the exception of Wisconsin and Florida; west of the Mississippi, it is limited to southern Missouri. A hardy, fast-growing tree, it takes root on dry slopes and ridges, often on sandy or stony soil. The best specimens thrive on deeper soils that have accumulated at the bases of slopes. On poor sites, *Quercus coccinea* seems to grow more rapidly than any other of its oak associates, which include northern red, black, white, and chestnut oaks.

A medium-size to large tree, scarlet oak usually tops out at 70 to 80 feet. At maturity, its trunk is about 2 feet in diameter. The trunk is often straight and has a noticeable taper to it. The crown tends to be rounded, open, and shallow. As the tree grows taller, its lower branches become shaded out and die; often they remain attached for years, barkless stubs jut-ting out from the trunk. Branches high in the tree stretch upward, while those in the middle and lower parts stand out horizontally or droop toward the ground. The branches lack the pinlike twigs of the closely related pin oak. The bark of scarlet oak is dark, thin, and broken into grooved fissures, which stand between ridges neither as rough as the bark ridges of black oak nor as flat-topped as those of red oak.

The leaves are 3 to 6 inches long by 2 to 5 inches wide and strongly resemble pin oak leaves. They are deeply divided almost to the midrib into seven (rarely nine) lobes. The lobes broaden toward their tips and end in sev-eral bristle-tipped teeth. The notches, or sinuses, between the lobes have broad, rounded bottoms deeper than those of any other oak, except perhaps pin oak; they give the scarlet oak's foliage an angular, ragged appearance. The

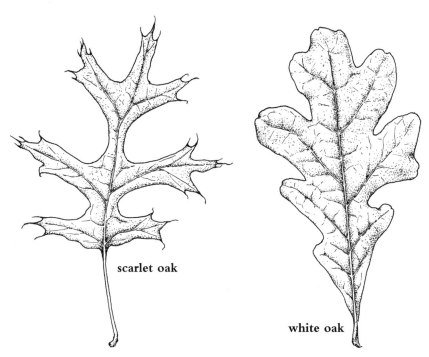

scarlet oak

white oak

*Scarlet oak is a member of the red oak group, whose leaf lobes
end in sharp bristle tips. White oak belongs to the
white oak group, whose leaves lack the bristle tips.*

leaves are a bright shining green above and a paler yellow-green below, and
usually have tufts of hair in the angles where the veins diverge from the midrib.

The leaves, when they emerge around May, are bright red. When the
leaves are about one-third developed, the flowers open, both sexes on the
same tree: male flowers attached to dangling catkins 3 to 4 inches long, and
reddish female flowers on short stalks. The wind blows pollen, released by the
male flowers, to fertilize the female flowers. Scarlet oak hybridizes with northern red oak, *Quercus rubra,* and with the shrublike bear oak, *Quercus ilicifolia.*

A scarlet oak acorn takes two growing seasons to mature: a flower fertilized in May of one year becomes a ripe acorn by autumn of the year
following. The acorn of *Quercus coccinea* is short-stalked or seated directly
against the twig; it stands solitary or as one of a pair. The acorn is egg-
shaped, 1/2 to 1 inch long, 5/8 to 7/8 inch in diameter, and reddish brown.
A deep, bowl-shaped cup encloses a third to half of the nut; the cup is
formed of smooth, close-fitting scales that often end in a fringe around
the cup margin.

Seed production in scarlet oaks varies greatly from year to year; occasionally the trees produce bumper crops. Scarlet oak is a member of the red oak group, all of whose acorns are invested with bitter-tasting tannin compounds, likely evolved to deter mammals from eating too many of them. However, the digestive systems of some acorn eaters, including squirrels, have adapted to resist the ill effects of tannins, which interfere with protein absorption. Squirrels, deer, bears, chipmunks, mice, wild turkeys, blue jays, and other birds all relish scarlet oak acorns. Squirrels and jays scatter-hoard the nuts, burying them beneath leaves and in loose soil. Unrecovered acorns sprout, perpetuating the scarlet oak and other oak species.

Of four common northeastern oaks—scarlet, red, chestnut, and white— scarlet is the least tolerant of shady environments. Scarlet oak seedlings grow well in open woods or areas recently cleared of forest vegetation by windthrow, fire, or logging. Once the canopy closes, with trees linking their crowns overhead, scarlet oak seedlings can arise only in gaps where sunlight touches the forest floor. For this reason, scarlet oak tends to fade from the scene and become uncommon in mature woods. Because it has thin bark, scarlet oak is easily damaged by fires, even fires of low intensity. If not killed outright, the tree's bark may be breached, allowing pathogens to enter. After it has reached adult size, scarlet oak is often attacked by fungi, leading to heart rot, which weakens the trunk so that a windstorm snaps it.

A friend of mine cruises timber for a small sawmill, and he often gripes when, at a timber sale, foresters mark scarlet oak simply as red oak, the way it has traditionally been sold and marketed. The wood of scarlet oak is strong; heavy, at 46 pounds per cubic foot; and coarse. It is considered inferior to that of northern red oak, because it often has large knots that make it difficult to use for furniture, flooring, and interior trim. Scarlet oak has gone into farming implements, boats, wagons, barrel staves, and firewood, with a few trees sound enough to provide stock for finer products. These days, my friend tells me, a market exists for railroad ties up to 24 feet in length, used in switching yards where a single track diverges into two; scarlet oak, which often has a long, straight bole, finds an application there.

WHITE OAK AND SWAMP WHITE OAK

L ast fall I cut down a small white oak *(Quercus alba)* on our land. Dead at least five years, it would, I knew, make excellent firewood: hot-burning, long-lasting fuel to keep the stove pumping out heat through a cold winter's night. After bucking the tree into stove lengths, I noticed how dense the annual growth rings were on the log closest to the stump. I left that billet unsplit; when I got back to the woodshed, I fetched a ruler and a hand lens.

The billet measured 8 1/2 inches in diameter. Starting from the center, I began counting my way out. The rings were so narrow in places that I needed the magnifying glass to distinguish them. At every tenth ring, I made a pencil mark. By the time I reached the outermost rings on the log, my count was one hundred. I lost a few rings at the perimeter, laid down during the last years of the tree's life, now flaking away and obscured by wood rot. I figured the tree was 105, maybe 110 years old.

The white oak had been a seedling around 1890, a quarter century after the Civil War ended. It had sprouted from an acorn dropped by a now dead and vanished white oak—perhaps a huge, venerable tree, although I doubt many old-growth specimens survived in our valley at the end of the nineteenth century. The oak grew slowly during its first several decades; one ten-year span measured only 1/4 inch, the rings so narrow they almost blended into each other. Today I doubt whether such a seedling would survive for long—not with the scores of deer that haunt our woods, ready to nip off any tender new growth. Back in the 1890s, though, deer were rare in Pennsylvania, almost wiped out following a century of unrestricted market hunting.

According to an elderly neighbor, much of the land in this area, including what is now our tract, was logged between 1928 and 1930. Obviously the white oak was too small to be worth cutting then. I could see how the growth rings widened considerably after the logging. Some measured 1/8 inch, which meant that the tree, flourishing in the now-abundant sunlight, expanded its girth by 1/4 inch a year, ten times as fast as it had grown before the logging. Things slowed down again for the white oak in the 1940s, when other trees apparently outstripped it in the race upward to the forest canopy to claim the bounty of sunshine. Indeed, another white oak, now 13 inches across, and a tall black oak, its trunk a strapping 22 inches in diameter, both towered over the dead white oak's stump.

The small white oak survived a gypsy moth infestation in the 1980s, when every oak in our woods was stripped of its leaves two years running.

However, I could not tell which growth rings might have reflected the gypsy moth scourge; everything was so crowded together, there at the end, as the tree's life dwindled and finally wound down. Perhaps the stress caused by defoliation represented the final straw.

Eastern white oak ranges from Maine across New England and southern Canada to Minnesota, and south to Florida and Texas. Although it grows in sandy and gravelly soil (ours is rocky and thin), white oak does best in rich, deep, moist soil. The species thrives in lowlands, hill country, and mountains, sometimes occurring in pure or nearly pure stands. White oaks do not colonize bone-dry ridges, chestnut oaks replacing them there, or poorly drained flats and wet bottomlands, to which swamp white oak is better adapted. Joseph Illick, in *Pennsylvania Trees,* judged the species abundant in eastern, central, and southern sections; common locally in parts of northern and western Pennsylvania; and absent from the Allegheny River watershed in Potter and McKean counties.

Quercus alba is the exemplar of the white oak group, a complex of species whose leaves have rounded instead of angular lobes and lack the pointed, needlelike extensions at the lobe ends, called bristle tips, that distinguish the red oaks, the other major oak group. White oak acorns contain fewer tannin compounds and are not as bitter-tasting as the acorns of the red oaks. White oak acorns mature in a single growing season, whereas those of red oaks take two growing seasons to ripen.

Under normal conditions, a mature white oak will reach 70 to 80 feet tall, with a trunk 3 to 5 feet across. The potential exists for greater growth: there are records of specimens 150 feet tall, with trunks 8 feet in diameter. In a closed forest stand, the trunk of a white oak typically becomes tall and straight, with little taper; the limbs cluster at the top of the tree, forming a compact crown. Open-grown white oaks look like another species altogether. The trunk divides near the ground into many stout branches, which twist and crook as they extend outward up to 50 or more feet, and upward to form a deep, broad crown, often with an irregular shape but sometimes quite symmetrical and covering an impressive area. Look for such behemoths in farm fields, where they were left to provide a patch of shade for the plowmen and horses or oxen of yesteryear.

White oak leaves are 4 to 9 inches long by 2 to 4 inches wide. They have three to nine—usually seven—ascending lobes that are blunt-tipped and separated by deep, round-based gaps. The shape suggests the part of a topographic map you would get if you snipped along a single contour line surrounding a hilly upland drained by numerous streams. Leaves in the tree's crown often are slender, with deep lobes; those on lower branches tend to be broader and less deeply lobed. The leaves are bright green above, and gray-green or whitish green on their undersurfaces. They turn a deep dark red in autumn, a hue similar to that of scarlet oak, although not usually so brilliant. Often they remain attached to their twigs into winter.

The pale bark gives the tree its name. It is made up of small, irregular scales or patches that often are only loosely attached. On small branches, the bark may be light green, reddish green, or almost silvery and not patchy. Extremely pale, almost white,

Farmers of yesteryear left white oaks standing in fields to provide shade for plowmen and their teams.

roughly circular areas on the trunk are harmless surface fungi, saprophytes that get nourishment from dead and decaying organic matter. Black, stringlike strands beneath the sloughed-off bark of a dead white oak are the mycelia of *Armillaria mellea,* a root-rotting fungus whose gilled fruiting bodies are the choice edibles known as honey mushrooms.

In May, the boughs of winter-bare white oaks turn red and then fade to a silvery pink as the leaves emerge and expand. When the leaves are about a third developed, the trees set out flowers. Male flowers are creamy-green, clustered on hairy, stringy, drooping catkins 2 to 3 inches long; the short-stalked female catkins are shaped like spikes. Flowers of both sexes blossom on the same tree. The wind blows the male pollen to the female flowers. The resulting acorns are a shiny pale brown, oval, rounded at the tip, and range in size from 1/2 to 1 inch long, averaging about 3/4 inch; a bowl-shaped cup encloses the nut's base for a quarter of its overall length. The nuts take about four months to ripen. They fall off in September and October of the year in which they were formed.

Lacking a strong tannin defense, white oak acorns germinate quickly after they fall; before freezing weather, their first small roots have penetrated the soil, with the shoot remaining dormant until the following spring. Animals avidly search out these sweet-tasting nuts, which, at about 6 percent protein and 65 percent carbohydrates, constitute a high-energy foodstuff. More than 180 species of birds and mammals consume white oak acorns, including squirrels, chipmunks, mice, deer, bears, raccoons, blue jays, wild turkeys, quail, grouse, woodpeckers, nuthatches, and ducks.

Native Americans of many tribes sought out white oak acorns, whose low tannin content made the nuts more palatable and easier to use than red oak acorns. The Indians boiled the nuts to remove the water-soluble tannins, then ground them into a meal used in baking bread. Acorns from some white oaks are sweet enough to eat out of hand.

Growing in open light, a white oak as young as twenty years may produce nuts. Trees between the ages of fifty and two hundred are the most prolific acorn producers. In Virginia, botanists monitored a single sixty-nine-year-old white oak and found that it bore more than sixty thousand acorns in one year; the tree was 69 feet tall and had a 25-inch trunk diameter. Typical good production for a mature forest-grown tree is probably closer to ten thousand acorns. A stand of white oaks can yield more than two hundred thousand acorns per acre. Several years may pass when trees bear few or no acorns; then every four to ten years, they produce a bumper crop. Investing their resources in vast quantities of acorns on an irregular schedule is a strategy that overwhelms seed predators: by dropping more acorns than local wildlife can consume, the odds are improved that at least some acorns will germinate and sprout. How trees synchronize their acorn production is a mystery scientists have yet to solve.

Of all the oaks, *Quercus alba* is the most shade-tolerant. It sprouts relatively well even beneath the canopy of a mature forest, allowing the species to maintain its numbers or increase in a wooded stand. Seedlings and saplings wait, growing slowly, until a taller tree dies and comes crashing down; then they press toward the light. White oak seedlings, saplings, and even pole-size trees are able to persist under a shady forest canopy for more than ninety years—which is about the age of that smallish, stunted white oak I cut up for firewood recently.

After one growing season, seedlings may be 3 to 4 inches high, with a taproot $1/4$ to $1/2$ inch in diameter, reaching down more than 12 inches. As the tree enlarges, the central taproot disappears and is replaced by several deep, spreading lateral roots, usually within 21 inches of the ground surface, plus a system of fibrous rootlets. White oak grows faster than hickory and beech, and slower than tuliptree, black walnut, white ash, and sugar maple. Among oaks, white oak grows faster than chestnut but not as rapidly as scarlet, northern red, and black. Young white oaks sprout prolifically when cut down or damaged by fire. But once the trees get to be over a foot in diameter, the likelihood of such stump sprouting falls to only 15 percent.

White oaks are extremely long-lived; individual trees six hundred years old have been recorded.

White oak wood is pale brown, with lighter sapwood. Extremely strong, hard, and heavy, it weighs around 46 pounds per cubic foot when dry. In his 1928 *Pennsylvania Trees,* Joseph Illick characterized white oak as "the most valuable of all oak wood"; today red oak and black oak exceed it in value, because their ruddier color makes them more popular for furniture and flooring. In the past, white oak went into boats and ships: the nascent American navy built its famed heavy frigates, including the USS *Constitution,* largely out of white oak. American sailors dubbed the *Constitution* "Old Ironsides" after her stout white oak hull turned aside British cannonballs during the War of 1812.

Because it resists decay, white oak has been used for log houses, barn frames (our horse barn has white oak posts made from trees cut on our land), covered bridges, railroad ties, and fences. Another name for white oak is stave oak: the traditional choice for barrel staves, especially for tight cooperage, vessels that hold whiskey and other liquids. Because the pores of white oak are plugged with woody cells, liquids cannot seep through them. Red oak, on the other hand, makes loose cooperage, because its pores are not watertight.

Botanists have documented hybridization between *Quercus alba* and seven other species in the white oak group, including these Pennsylvania natives: swamp white oak, bur oak, basket oak, chestnut oak, post oak, and yellow oak.

Swamp White Oak *(Quercus bicolor).* Recently I found several swamp white oaks growing at Ruth Zimmerman Natural Area, Berks County, in southeastern Pennsylvania. The trees were scattered throughout a wooded tract near a slow stream, rooted in ground that squelched underfoot. They were typical for the species: 60 to 70 feet tall, their trunks approaching 2 feet in diameter, with grayish brown bark fissured into long, flat ridges that were broken up into small scales. Their leaves swayed in the breeze, showing dark green upper surfaces, then flashing back the October sunlight from their bright, pale undersides—demonstrating why taxonomists assign the species name *bicolor* to this lowland dweller.

Swamp white oak is neither as common nor as widespread as eastern white oak. It ranges from southern Maine west to Minnesota, Iowa, and Missouri, and south to North Carolina and Tennessee. In Pennsylvania, it occurs mainly in the southern half of the state and in the northwestern counties. It grows in wet woods along streams and the borders of swamps, although not in the standing water of open swampland. Think of it as the counterpart to pin oak, the major wetland-dwelling species in the red oak group.

Quercus bicolor sometimes grows alongside pin oak. It also mixes in forest stands with American elm, hackberry, shagbark and shellbark hickories, silver and red maples, basswood, and other species. Long-lived trees, swamp white oaks can survive more than three hundred years. The wood of this species is similar to, and not differentiated from, that of eastern white oak.

Swamp white oak leaves are 4 to 9 inches long. They look like the leaves of chestnut oak, but with slightly deeper lobes. The lobes separate four to ten prominent, rounded teeth on each side of the leaf. The leaves have soft, whitish hairs on their undersurfaces. Branches of this tree often show a distinctive pattern: upper ones abundant and erect, middle ones sticking out horizontally from the trunk, and lower ones curved down, intermingled with dead branches that remain attached to the trunk for some time. Notes John Eastman in *The Book of Swamp and Bog,* "Small branches shed their bark somewhat like sycamore trees."

The acorns of swamp white oak stand in pairs at the ends of stems an inch or so long. The nuts are 3/4 to 1 1/4 inches long, egg-shaped, and have a bowl-like cup. Swamp white oaks produce bumper acorn crops every three to five years. The sweet-tasting nuts are relished by wild turkeys, squirrels, deer, ducks, and other animals that live in wetlands or dabble along the edges of those productive habitats.

CHESTNUT OAK

In central Pennsylvania, where I live, a series of long, parallel mountain ridges runs on a northeast-southwest heading. The ridges are wooded, and between them lie cleared agricultural valleys. I would estimate that oaks make up one-half to three-quarters of the trees on the ridges, especially on the drier, sun-catching slopes facing the southeast. Of the oaks, at least half are chestnut oak, which perhaps makes *Quercus montana* the most numerous tree hereabouts. It is probably the most common species in my own thirty-acre woods.

Chestnut oak ranges from southwestern Maine across parts of New England and extreme southern Ontario west to southeastern Michigan, and south to Georgia and Mississippi—a more limited distribution than that of many other eastern oaks. *Quercus montana* reaches its maximum size on rich, moist soil of mountain slopes in the Carolinas and Tennessee. Chestnut oaks grow in lowlands but are more notable for colonizing dry uplands, including sandy, gravelly, and rocky habitats. On ridges, they sometimes form pure stands. In Pennsylvania, the species is statewide, more common in the south than in the north. Two folk names describe the tree's habitat preferences: mountain oak and rock oak. The Latin species name, *montana,* remarks the tree's affinity for mountains. An alternate binomial is *Quercus prinus.*

When mature, a chestnut oak stands 60 to 80 feet tall, with a trunk 2 to 3 feet in diameter. Under excellent growing conditions, an old specimen can become 100 feet tall and 6 feet in diameter. In forest stands, where many individual trees shoot up in competition for light, a chestnut oak will become tall, with a straight trunk; in a more open area, the tree will fork low to the ground and form a broad, open crown. In the thin soil of a wind-scoured ridge, *Quercus montana* can become stunted, almost like a bonsai specimen, with a bent, twisted trunk and gnarled, crooked limbs. Add in the rough, blocky bark that is normal for the species, and you have a truly rugged-looking plant. The bark is thick, gray-brown to black, and broken into long, broad, vertical ridges, sharp-angled uplifts that are themselves interrupted and offset by horizontal-running faults. At the bottoms of the fissures between the ridges, a layer of inner bark may show pale tan or cinnamon red in color.

The crenate leaves of chestnut oak resemble the toothed foliage of the American chestnut, *Castanea dentata,* a similarity that earned the oak its common name. The leaves are thick and leathery, 5 to 9 inches long by 2 to 4 inches wide, generally oval in shape, and bordered on each side with ten to sixteen coarse, rounded teeth, which lack the points that adorn the lobes rimming the leaf of American chestnut. In chestnut oak, the leaves are a glossy green above, paler and slightly hairy on their undersurfaces. They turn yellow or bronze in autumn.

In May, when the new leaves are expanding, chestnut oak puts out flowers, both male and female on the same tree. The greenish yellow male flowers look like bulky knots studding the hairy, stringlike, 2- to 3-inch-long catkins. The female flowers cluster in small groups on short stalks. As with all oaks, wind takes care of pollination. Chestnut oak is a member of the white oak group, whose acorns mature over a single growing season. The pollinated female flowers develop into acorns, which mature and fall to the ground in September and October. In the spring, late frosts sometimes kill the flowers, reducing or eliminating acorn production for that year. Heavy seed crops occur every few years, with most trees in a given area simultaneously producing a bumper crop.

The dangling flowers of chestnut oak appear in May in Pennsylvania,
when the trees' leaves are about one-third developed.

The acorns hang by themselves or in pairs on the twigs. The oblong
nuts are among the largest of all oak acorns, 1 to 1^1/$_2$ inches long and nearly
1 inch across. They are smooth, shiny, chestnut brown or light brown, with
a thin cup made of knobby, hairy scales; the cup covers about one-third of
the nut. Chestnut oak acorns are relatively low in tannin content (tannins
are bitter-tasting compounds that deter foliage- and nut-consuming animals), another trait of acorns from the white oak group. Some sources say
Quercus montana has the sweetest-tasting acorns of all the northern oaks.

On November 15, I picked twenty chestnut oak acorns at random from
beneath a tree I can see out my office window. The nuts had fallen in September and October. It had hardly rained at all since September; nevertheless, nineteen of the acorns had germinated and sent a reddish, white-tipped
rootlet plunging into the ground. The rootlets, or radicles, as botanists call
them, were about ^{1}/$_8$ inch thick; one had extended almost 3 inches into the
hard, dry soil and needed to be dug out with a penknife. I opened one of
the acorns by slicing its thin shell. The nutmeat, or embryo, was creamy
yellow. It had a somewhat bitter taste, but not so bitter that I had to spit it
out. Boiling acorns in water leaches out the soluble tannins, much improving their flavor. Indians of many eastern tribes relied on acorns from the

white oak group as key foodstuffs. After treating the acorns to remove the tannins, they ground the nuts into a mealy flour and baked it into a hard, nutritious bread.

Deer, bears, squirrels, chipmunks, mice, and woodrats eat chestnut oak acorns. If they have a choice, deer select the less tannic, sweeter-tasting nuts of chestnut and white oaks over those of red, scarlet, and black oaks, which all belong to the red oak group, even though the acorns from the red oak species have a higher fat content. Bears gorge on acorns to build up fat for their winter hibernation. Our extensive oak forests often yield prolific mast crops; as a result, Pennsylvania's bears are among the largest, healthiest, and most reproductively successful black bears in North America. I often find areas of the forest floor where wild turkeys have used their large, clawed feet to rake away fallen leaves and expose the acorns of chestnut oak and other oak species. A turkey will swallow the acorns, even the larger ones, then let its gizzard—a muscular pouch in the digestive tract—crush and grind the nuts into digestible particles.

Although its acorns are low in tannin, the chestnut oak's bark has an extremely high tannin content. During the eighteenth and nineteenth centuries, when eastern forests were exploited by logging and allied industries, workers would fell chestnut oaks, then harvest the bark for its tannin, which was used to tan leather. Often they simply left the wood to rot, because white oak made better lumber. But when white oak became scarce, the loggers shifted to cutting chestnut oaks, whose wood possesses many of the same virtues.

The wood of *Quercus montana* weighs 47 pounds per cubic foot, dry weight. It has dark brown heartwood and lighter-colored sapwood. People have used it for flooring, furniture, boat building, barrels, pallets, and rough construction. Fairly durable in contact with the soil, it finds application as railroad ties, mine props, and fencing. Its density makes it a superb fuelwood; I probably burn more chestnut oak in my heating stove than any other species.

Quercus montana grows in mixture with many hardwoods and softwoods, including scarlet, black, and white oaks; pitch and Table Mountain pines; black-gum; black birch; and red maple. A 1930s study in Pennsylvania found that chestnut oak made slower diameter growth than red, black, scarlet, and white oaks on similar sites. Chestnut oak is fairly shade-tolerant, and its seedlings can survive overtopping by other trees; for this reason, chestnut oak can survive and ultimately become a dominant canopy tree in its preferred habitat of dry slopes and ridgetops. In such places, soils are usually very acidic. Beneath chestnut oaks, soil acidity is maintained by the breakdown of fallen oak twigs, bark, and leaves. Highbush and lowbush blueberries, and mountain laurel, all acid-loving shrubs, commonly cloak the ground beneath chestnut oaks.

After it has been sawed down, a chestnut oak will sprout prolifically and persistently from the stump. I cut down several chestnut oaks when adding a woodshed to my garage, and after five years, their stumps are still sending up sprouts—which are promptly browsed back by deer. Foresters estimate that 75 percent of chestnut oaks in the southern Appalachians came from stump sprouts rather than acorn reproduction; probably those numbers are also accurate for the Northeast. Because stump sprouts have a fully developed root system supplying them with nutrients, they grow much faster than seedlings that have arisen from acorns. In general, as trees grow older and larger, their ability to stump-sprout lessens.

Intense fires may sweep across the dry ridges and exposed sites inhabited by chestnut oaks. Many old trees in such areas have suffered wounds from fires, breaches in their bark that let in wood decay fungi. A decayed bole may become hollow, leaving a shell of a tree that is still alive and growing. Hollow chestnut oaks provide dens for squirrels, porcupines, raccoons, gray foxes, black bears, and cavity-nesting birds such as screech-owls, woodpeckers, black-capped chickadees, and white-breasted nuthatches.

Many insects eat the leaves of *Quercus montana*. June beetles sometimes strip entire trees. The larvae of the gypsy moth caterpillar can denude vast acreages.

Pennsylvania has an overabundance of oaks for two reasons. Oaks resprout quickly from the stump following logging, and the state's forests were almost completely logged off in the 1800s, with oaks growing back over large areas. Also, a chief competitor, American chestnut, was killed off by a fungal blight in the early twentieth century, and its place in the ecosystem was largely taken over by oaks.

In what is sometimes called an oak monoculture, trees are at a heightened risk of attack from pathogens and insects. The gypsy moth, an insect imported from Eurasia, has few natural predators in eastern forests, and it spread almost unchecked through our woodlands in the last decades of the twentieth century. Repeated gypsy moth defoliations killed many chestnut oaks, and other oaks as well. Three species in particular are now filling gaps opened up where chestnut oaks and other oaks died: black birch, red maple, and black-gum. Black birch and red maple produce copious seeds, which the wind disperses; black-gum spreads when birds eat its attractive, nutritious fruits, then deposit the seeds in their droppings. All three species can exist in the thin soils of mountain habitats where chestnut oaks thrive.

OTHER OAKS

RED OAK GROUP

Bear Oak *(Quercus ilicifolia)*. Widely known as scrub oak, this shrub or small tree forms extensive, in some cases almost impenetrable, thickets on rocky hillsides, sandy barrens, and mountain plateaus. Bear oak has a limited range, extending from Maine through southern New England and New York, and south to North Carolina. It grows in scattered areas throughout Pennsylvania, except in the far northern and western counties. Most specimens never get taller than 4 to 8 feet and have stem diameters of 1 to 3 inches; yet a few individuals become treelike, up to 20 feet tall. Bear oak often cloaks areas that have been swept by fire or logged repeatedly. Over time, taller species—scarlet oak, chestnut oak, red maple, aspen—may ascend above the bear oak and form a new forest.

The leaves are 2 to 5 inches long, with a wedge-shaped base; needlelike extensions of the veins tip the sharply angular outer lobes. The leaves are dark green and glossy above, pale and densely furred below, and have a leathery texture. They turn yellow and brown in autumn and often cling to the twigs into winter. The small, 1/2-inch-long, rounded acorns taste so bitter that they are said to be shunned by all wildlife except bears. Dense stands of this plant afford escape and resting habitat to black bears and other animals. A friend of mine had a deer camp in an area with many bear oak thickets; the bucks he bagged invariably had rubbed off all the fur on their shins from sneaking through the tangles.

State Game Lands 176, known as the Barrens, west of State College in Centre County, has extensive bear oak stands. The area supports a population of buck moths, rare black-and-white insects that, as adults, fly during the day in autumn—during buck season, which is apparently why they are so named. In spring and summer, the larvae eat the foliage of bear oaks. Ecologists believe buck moths evolved to fly and reproduce in the fall, because dry bear oak habitats often are swept by wildfires in spring before the trees put out foliage.

Shingle Oak *(Quercus imbricaria)*. Pennsylvania is at the eastern fringe of this species' range. Shingle oak occurs mainly in the Midwest, as far west as Michigan and Nebraska, and in pockets south to Louisiana and Alabama. In the Keystone State, shingle oak can be found in the southeastern counties, in rich, moist bottomlands along streams and in fertile uplands. Another name for the species is laurel oak, because the shiny, straplike leaves resemble those of mountain laurel. Shingle oak leaves lack the teeth and lobes of our other oaks; the red oak affiliation of this tree is shown by the single bristle tip at the end of each leaf blade.

Shingle oak is usually 50 to 60 feet tall at maturity, with some specimens achieving 100 feet. The acorns, which mature at the end of the second growing season, are only about 1/2 inch long, and rounded. Pioneers in the Midwest rived the wood into shingles for siding their houses. The Latin name *imbricaria* means "overlapping" and also refers to the use of this wood for shingles. In many forest stands, shingle oak mixes with post oak and black oak. It has been planted widely for hedges and windbreaks.

Blackjack Oak *(Quercus marilandica)*. Southeastern Pennsylvania is included in the rather large range of *Quercus marilandica,* which grows from Long Island and New Jersey south to the Florida Panhandle, and west to Iowa, Oklahoma, and Texas. Blackjack oak crops up on dry, wooded slopes and in the inhospitable habitats known as serpentine barrens, where it may form mixed stands with pitch pine, post oak, bear oak, and eastern red-cedar. Blackjack oak can grow to about 50 feet tall, although in the north of its range, it is usually more stunted, with a short and crooked trunk. The rough, thick bark is broken into squarish plates. The leaves are distinctive, the shape suggesting a child's kite: broadest across the middle, usually with three lobes. Thick and leathery, the blades have bristle tips. The species is also known as jack oak or barren oak. In the South, the part of its range where it grows largest, people use the wood of blackjack oak for fuel and lumber.

Willow Oak *(Quercus phellos)*. This southern tree ranges as far north as southeastern Pennsylvania and central New Jersey, growing in low, damp woods that may flood in springtime. Joseph Illick wrote in his *Pennsylvania Trees* that *Quercus phellos* is "usually found on wet sandy soil . . . and along swamps and streams," and occasionally "on higher areas where it may reach a fair size." He reported the species from Bucks, Chester, Delaware, Lancaster, and Philadelphia counties, a region where urban and suburban development have destroyed much natural habitat since Illick's era. The Pennsylvania Natural Diversity Inventory today lists willow oak as an endangered species in the Keystone State.

The shiny-topped, leathery leaves are 2 to 5 inches long and 3/8 to 3/4 inch wide. Each is tipped with a fine bristle. With their tapering knife-blade shape, they look much like the leaves of willows, also denizens of low, damp places. The acorns are rounded and about 1/2 inch long. People plant willow oak as a shade tree in the South, where the species is abundant.

Shumard Oak *(Quercus shumardii).* Shumard oak is similar to scarlet oak, except that Shumard oak has larger leaves: 6 to 8 inches in length, compared with 3 to 6 inches for scarlet oak. A large tree, Shumard oak grows to 90 feet tall, with a broad, rounded, open crown. In Pennsylvania, it has been reported from only a few south-central counties along the Maryland border. Because of its rarity in the commonwealth, *Quercus shumardii* is considered an endangered species in Pennsylvania. On a continental scale, it ranges south to Florida and west to Kansas, Oklahoma, and Texas. Its name honors Benjamin Franklin Shumard, a Lancaster, Pennsylvania, native who served as the state geologist of Texas in the mid-1800s.

The shiny leaves of Shumard oak usually have five to seven lobes; they turn an attractive scarlet or golden brown in autumn. The acorns are egg-shaped, and 3/4 to a little over 1 inch long. The wood, usually sold as red oak, is used for furniture, flooring, interior finish, veneer, and general construction.

WHITE OAK GROUP

Post Oak *(Quercus stellata).* A species of dry uplands, post oak ranges from southern Connecticut, New Jersey, and southeastern and south-central Pennsylvania south to Florida and west to Oklahoma and Texas. This small tree usually grows no taller than 60 feet, with a trunk 1 to 2 feet in diameter—although Joseph Illick, in *Pennsylvania Trees,* cites a post oak felled in 1912 near Mont Alto, Franklin County, that measured over 3 feet in diameter at breast height. The species name, *stellata,* refers to starlike formations of tiny hairs on the undersurfaces of the leaves; a magnifying lens is needed to verify this trait. The leathery-textured leaves have rounded lobes arranged in a shape often described as resembling a Maltese cross.

Post oak grows more readily than white oak on poor, rocky soils; it even thrives in the impoverished, severe environment of serpentine barrens. Its heavy, hard wood earns the species another common name, iron oak. Durable in contact with the soil, the wood is used for fence posts and railroad ties.

Bur Oak *(Quercus macrocarpa).* Bur oak is the northernmost American oak. It grows from New Brunswick across Quebec and Ontario to Manitoba and eastern Saskatchewan, south through parts of New England and New York to West Virginia, and from eastern Montana and Wyoming to Texas.

It makes its best growth in the deep soils of the Midwest. In Pennsylvania, bur oak occurs mainly in the south-central and southwestern counties. It thrives in dry to moist soils that are neutral or limestone-sweet and also does well as a planted specimen in cities. Its extensive root system helps it survive drought conditions.

The mature tree is 70 to 80 feet tall, with some specimens reaching a reported 170 feet. Individual trees can live more than four hundred years. Mature trees have stout, burly trunks and a broad canopy held up by thick, often crooked branches. Smaller branchlets bear corky, winged projections similar to those of sweet-gum. The bark is gray and deeply ridged; Joseph Illick in *Pennsylvania Trees* judged it "intermediate between [the] flaky bark of white oak and [the] very roughly ridged bark of chestnut oak." Bur oak bark is thick enough to withstand hot-burning grass fires in prairie settings. At about its midpoint, the leaf is divided—cut almost in half—by deep sinuses extending inward from each side; the upper half of the blade has shallower, more rounded lobes than the lower half. The acorns, up to 2 inches long, are the largest of our native oaks. They are clasped in deep cups whose shaggy outer fringes resemble the spiny burs or husks of American chestnut, perhaps another defense against fire. In a good year, a large bur oak can produce five thousand acorns.

Yellow Oak *(Quercus muhlenbergii)*. Yellow oak favors limestone uplands. It ranges from southern New England west to Iowa and Kansas, and south to Florida and Texas. Uncommon in Pennsylvania, yellow oak occurs in the southern half of the state. Its wavy-edged leaves resemble those of chestnut oak but have sharper-pointed marginal teeth. The bark is gray and flaky. Like the other white oaks, this tree produces sweet-tasting acorns favored by many wildlife species. The wood is exceedingly heavy: 54 pounds per cubic foot, dry weight. Strong, hard, and durable, it has been used for fence rails, railroad ties, fuel, and general construction. It checks, or cracks, badly when drying.

At maturity, yellow oak in the northern part of its range usually does not exceed 50 feet in height, although some specimens reach 80 feet, with a crown spread of 120 feet. An oak of this magnitude—the reigning state champion, as recognized by the Pennsylvania Forestry Association—stands near Oley in Berks County near Daniel Boone's birthplace. The tree is well over three centuries old, and it was standing when the pioneer Boone was born in 1734.

Yellow oak is sometimes called chinkapin oak. Sometimes spelled *chin-quapin,* this name refers to the leaves' resemblance to the foliage of chinkapins, small trees in the chestnut family. The word comes from the Algonquian Indian language.

AMERICAN ELM AND SLIPPERY ELM

Years ago, new to the technology of cutting wood and burning it in a heating stove, I chanced upon a half dozen dead, barkless trees in a grove on my landlord's farm. Most of the trees were about a foot in diameter. I received permission to cut them for firewood. I chainsawed their trunks into billets, then took up the splitting maul. Pound away as I might, I could not split the wood using the maul. After great effort, I finally sundered one billet by driving a steel wedge through it with a sledgehammer. I ended up cutting the other pieces lengthwise with my saw.

The dead trees were American elms *(Ulmus americana),* whose wood knits together tightly with spiraling, interlocking fibers. When I burned it, the dry, well-seasoned wood gave off heat—and odor. As I recall it, the smoke had a disagreeably acrid smell. Later I learned that country folk, in consideration of how its wood smells, refer to *Ulmus americana*—a stately and otherwise generally beloved tree—as "piss elm."

American elm grows from Nova Scotia to Saskatchewan and south to Florida and Texas: most of North America east of the Rocky Mountains. Few other trees have such an extensive range. Elms occur statewide in Pennsylvania; they are less common in the mountains than in the lowlands. Other vernacular names include white elm, gray elm, water elm, and soft elm.

American elms prefer rich, moist, well-drained soil in bottomlands and floodplains and along the banks of streams and lakes. They do not occur in single-species stands but mingle with other hardwoods, such as box-elder, eastern cottonwood, black ash, red maple, silver maple, hackberry, sycamore, and sweet-gum. In drier habitats—old fields, meadows, roadsides, hedgerows—elms mix with American beech, sugar maple, basswood, and other species. Elms colonize disturbed sites, such as mined areas and abandoned city blocks. Because of the American elm's pleasing shape, people have planted it in parks, cemeteries, and farmyards, and on campuses, town streets, and lawns.

As is true with most trees, should an elm grow in a woods setting, it will exhibit one form; should it flourish in full sunlight, it will take on another form. A woods-grown elm, competing for light with neighboring trees, sends up a long, straight trunk that divides into several equal-size branches 30 to 60 feet above the ground. If an elm grows in the open, its trunk usually divides 10 to 20 feet above ground level; each branch then subdivides again and again, with the outermost branches and twigs paralleling the ground or bowing down toward it. In many open-country specimens, the crown is broader than it is tall. The overall shape, beautiful and unique among trees, suggests a vase or a flowing fountain. The botanic explorer André Michaux judged the American elm "the most magnificent vegetable of the temperate zone."

In *A Natural History of Trees,* Donald Culross Peattie describes the quality of shade beneath an elm. "A big old specimen will have about a million leaves, or an acre of leaf surface, and will cast a pool of shadow one hundred feet in diameter," he wrote. "The leaves hang more or less all in one plane on the bough, and they make a pattern roughly like a lattice. Hence the dappling of shadow and light." That dappling pleases human sensibilities. Huge, stately elms seem to beckon people to gather beneath them—and, on occasion, to conduct momentous affairs there. It was beneath an elm in the Lenni Lenape village of Sachamexing, now a part of Philadelphia, that, in 1682, William Penn signed a treaty with the Native American tribe that was honored by both sides for many years, securing the future of Penn's New World colony. The Penn Treaty Elm blew down in a storm in 1810, but its image can be seen in several paintings hanging in the Pennsylvania Academy of Fine Arts in Philadelphia, and cuttings from the old tree have been transplanted to many places. At the time of its death, the Treaty Elm was 150 feet tall, with a 24-foot girth.

A mature elm can become 80 to 100 feet tall and have a diameter of 2 to 5 feet. Some individuals, such as the Treaty Elm, obviously grow even larger. Elms may develop enlarged buttresses at the base of the trunk, giving them a diameter of 8 to 11 feet at breast height. An old-growth specimen cut in Jefferson County, Pennsylvania, measured 140 feet tall and had a crown spread of 76 feet. At the sawmill, it yielded 8,820 board feet of lumber. (A board foot is a piece of wood 1 foot square by 1 inch thick.)

Elm bark is gray-brown, with long, irregular furrows between broad, flat ridges. The leaves alternate along the stem. They are 4 to 6 inches long, oval to oblong, with saw-toothed margins and a long, tapering point at the tip. The base is rounded and asymmetrical: larger on one side of the stem than the other. Many straight side veins run parallel on the leaf surface. The blade is thin, dark bluish green and usually hairless on its upper surface, paler and furred with soft hairs below. Elm leaves turn golden yellow in autumn. After the leaves have fallen, the massive trunks and limbs, ramifying into ever-smaller branches and zigzag twigs, stand etched against the sky; to my eye, elms are even more beautiful when bare than when clad with foliage.

Elms flower early in spring—late March and early April in Pennsylvania—two to three weeks before the trees' leaves emerge. The small flowers, clustered on inch-long, drooping stalks, contain both male and female parts. The wind moves pollen from the male to the female structures. A wet spring may hamper pollination, because the pollen-bearing anthers do not open when the atmosphere is saturated.

Mature American elms are becoming increasingly rare, as an Asian fungus has killed many trees. The illustration depicts the saw-toothed leaf and seeds, encased in a papery envelope.

Trees forty years old and older flower most abundantly and produce the greatest quantities of seeds. The disk-shaped fruit is a small samara about 1/2 inch across, consisting of a flat seed inside a thin, papery envelope. The fruits ripen quickly, in April and May, before the leaves are fully expanded. The lightweight samaras detach from their stems, and the wind scatters them up to 1/4 mile from the parent tree. Samaras that fall into moving water may be transported even farther.

Seeds landing on moist soil usually germinate within six to twelve days, although some lie dormant until the following spring. The seeds can send down rootlets into moist leaf litter, moss, and rotting logs and stumps. During their first year, seedlings grow best in partial shade—about one-third of full sunlight. Later the young trees thrive in full sun. Elms grow fast and can live a long time: 175 to 200 years, in some cases to 300 years. In heavy, wet soil, an elm's roots spread out and extend down only 3 or 4 feet; in drier soils, they may penetrate 5 to 10 feet. Elms can withstand flooding during winter and early spring, but they usually die if inundated during the growing season, in late spring and early summer. After falling, elm leaves break down quickly, improving the soil by liberating large quantities of potassium and calcium.

Elm wood is variously cited as weighing 35 to 41 pounds per cubic foot, dry weight. The heartwood is light brown; the sapwood is thick, and paler in color. The interlocking grain that I found so difficult to split makes elm useful for high-strength items like hockey sticks, mine props, and heavy-duty flooring. The wood tends to warp, so that elm finds few finish applications. Screws dig into it more securely than almost any other wood. Iroquois Indians used elm bark to sheath their canoes, apparently because they had limited access to good-quality paper birch. Writes John McPhee in *The Survival of the Bark Canoe,* regarding Iroquois canoe builders: "If they wanted to get across a river, they might—in one day—build an elm-bark canoe, and then forget it, leave it in the woods." In later times, wheelwrights favored the friction- and pressure-resistant wood of elm for the hubs of heavy wagons. Men who drove those wagons might peel an elm's bark and braid its inner fibers into strong, supple ox whips. Other past and current uses include rope twisted from the bark fibers, ship parts, barrel staves, caskets, boxes, crates, paneling, and furniture.

Many wild animals eat elm seeds, including bobwhite quail, ruffed grouse, wood ducks, rose-breasted grosbeaks, purple finches, squirrels, and opossums. Gray squirrels nibble on the flower buds and flowers. Cottontail rabbits, snowshoe hares, and white-tailed deer eat the twigs and leaves. Butterfly and moth caterpillars—including those of the beautiful mourning cloak butterfly—relish elm foliage. Elms even attract human foragers: in May, I look for morel mushrooms growing beneath dead elms. Elms, both living and dead, offer habitat to several wild species. Look for the pendulous, sack-shaped woven nests of Baltimore orioles in the dense foliage of outer branches. Red-headed woodpeckers chisel out nesting cavities in dead elms, of which all too many raise their barkless branches in the eastern woods these days.

In the 1920s, elms in Holland began dying from a fungal disease of Asian origin. The fungus *Ceratocystis ulmi* arrived in the United States in the 1930s, its spores carried by European elm bark beetles in English elm logs imported for the furniture industry. The beetles, scarcely bigger than a gnat, soon found American elms, which had no resistance to so-called Dutch elm disease. Foresters believe the fungus has wiped out over half of our native elms. Trees in forest, countryside, and urban settings have perished. It is now rare to find wild trees old and large enough to exhibit the distinctive vase-shaped form.

The European beetle and a related native elm beetle breed in infected elms, then fly to healthy trees to feed. I remember that the dead elms I cut for firewood had intricate channels like decorative engraving on the outer surface of their wood: brood galleries where the beetles had laid eggs. Evidence of such tunnels can also be seen on the inner bark that sloughs off from dead and dying elms. The fungus kills by producing toxins that plug up a tree's water-conducting sapwood. Leaves wilt and drop off, branches die, and eventually the entire tree succumbs. Death usually occurs within a single growing season.

The American elm seems not to be headed toward extinction. This past summer, I found several young elms growing amid roadside brush. The trees were about 25 feet tall. They looked healthy, although 100 yards away, a taller elm with a trunk about 6 inches in diameter stood dead and leafless. The ecologist Bernd Heinrich studied the elms near his Vermont home and reported on his findings in *The Trees in My Forest*. Heinrich discovered that small, roadside elms flower at a very young age. Of 540 live trees he inspected, only 47 had trunk diameters greater than 6 inches, yet many had flowered and produced seed. Heinrich suggests that elms that tend to reproduce early in life—before the fungus finds them—will be the ones to pass on their genes. The American elm of the future may be a small tree rather than a graceful, fountain-shaped giant.

Slippery Elm *(Ulmus rubra)*. Six species of elms occur in the eastern United States. Two are found in Pennsylvania: American elm and slippery elm. The latter is smaller than American elm, more raggedy looking, and not as symmetrical in form, with stout limbs ascending to a crown that is often broad and flat-topped. Most slippery elms grow 40 to 60 feet tall, with a trunk diameter of 1 to 2 1/2 feet. A few specimens attain 80 feet.

Slippery elm ranges from Maine to Florida and west to the Dakotas and Texas. It crops up locally throughout Pennsylvania, mainly in valleys, in moist floodplain woods, and along stream banks. It is rare or absent in the mountains. In southern Pennsylvania, slippery elm often grows on hillsides with limestone outcrops.

The bark is thick, rough, dark brown, and deeply furrowed. The leaves are 5 to 7 inches long, somewhat larger than those of American elm. If an elm leaf feels smooth or only slightly rough, it's an American elm; if it feels noticeably rough, it's a slippery elm—the opposite of what you'd expect from the slippery elm's name. The "slippery" appellation comes from the tree's inner bark, which is 1/8 to 1/4 inch thick, mucilaginous and slimy, and with a licorice taste. (You can detect the slipperiness by chewing on a twig.) People have used the bark for wound dressings and poultices; its mucilaginous quality will relieve a sore throat. Two other names for *Ulmus rubra* are red elm and moose elm.

The flowers of slippery elm cluster on short stalks. The resulting samaras look like those of American elm but are slightly larger. The heavy, hard wood, in contrast with that of American elm, is easy to split. Slippery elm wood resists rotting in contact with the soil, leading to its occasional use for fence posts and railroad ties.

HACKBERRY

The biggest hackberry I have ever seen was also the first hackberry I had ever seen, or at least noticed. It grew on a brushy, weedy, vine-tangled island in the Allegheny River south of Warren, Pennsylvania. It was the summer of 1988, and I was tagging along with Ted Grisez, an inveterate tree hunter who had found and registered more than a dozen state-record big trees, the largest of their species in Pennsylvania. For a minute or two, Grisez speculated hopefully that the hackberry we'd stumbled onto would be a new state record. It stood 91 feet tall—Grisez measured it with an optical device called a clinometer—and its trunk taped out at 125 inches in circumference, with a crown spread of 56 feet. Not a state champ, Grisez realized, but an impressive tree nonetheless.

The hackberry stood arrow-straight, claiming its share of the forest canopy among white ash, butternut, black walnut, and black maple trees. No limbs interrupted the hackberry's trunk for at least 60 feet. The crown was a great, verdant ball whose slightly drooping branches held out an array of elmlike, serrated leaves, which, because they were so far up, I was forced to examine using my binoculars. Close at hand was the tree's distinctive bark: pale brownish gray, adorned with wandering corky ridges and warty bumps.

Northern hackberry, *Celtis occidentalis,* belongs to the elm family. It ranges from southern New England and tidewater Virginia west to the Dakotas and south to Oklahoma and Georgia; it tends to be larger in the southern part of its range. On the Great Plains, it makes do with a scant 14 inches of moisture per year. A related species, southern or lowland hackberry, *Celtis laevigata,* often called sugarberry, flourishes in the South; some botanists believe *occidentalis* and *laevigata* hybridize where the two overlap. Dwarf hackberry, *Celtis tenuifolia,* is a southern species that extends north into southeastern and south-central Pennsylvania. A 15-foot-tall tree or shrub, it grows on shale banks, dry wooded hillsides, and limestone outcroppings.

Hackberry does best in the rich, moist soil of floodplains, valleys, and river islands. It does not grow in swampy soil. Hackberries ascend to bluffs, upland slopes, and limestone cliffs, usually growing as a single tree amid other hardwoods. According to the 1928 edition of Joseph Illick's *Pennsylvania Trees,* hackberry is a "rare tree" in Pennsylvania whose distribution is "occasional throughout the state." Illick noted that hackberries were particularly abundant along Conococheague Creek, a tributary of the Potomac River, in the Cumberland Valley.

Hackberry is usually a small to medium-size tree, 20 to 70 feet tall, with championship-caliber specimens soaring to 100 feet and higher. The usual trunk diameter is 1 to 2 feet. The Pennsylvania state record, a Montgomery County specimen, stood 106 feet tall, was 170 inches in circumference, and had an 81-foot crown spread when measured in 1990.

Growing in full sunlight, hackberry takes on a vase-shaped form similar to that of American elm. Hackberry tolerates shade fairly well and can survive in the forest understory as a small tree. Under good conditions, it springs up rapidly and can live for two hundred years or more. In floodplain forests, hackberry often grows with sycamore, eastern cottonwood, and box-elder, and it shares drier sites with basswood, American elm, and white ash. Hackberry sinks its roots deep—10 to 20 feet—letting it tap into groundwater during drought. With its thin bark, hackberry is damaged badly by fire, and such wounds open the tree to wood decay organisms. After hackberries are logged off, sprouts shoot up from the stumps of smaller trees, although not usually from larger ones. Fire-damaged seedlings and saplings also send up sprouts.

The tree's common name is thought to be a corruption of the

Corky, wartlike projections stud the grayish brown bark of the hackberry.

Scottish *hagberry,* which refers to a fruit-bearing cherry tree that grows in wetlands known as *hags.* Hackberry is also called sugarberry, hoop ash, beaverwood, nettletree, or bastard elm—the last two names because its leaves resemble those of nettles, common herbaceous plants of genus *Urtica,* and American elm. Hackberry leaves are 2 to 5 inches long and 1 1/2 to 2 1/2 inches wide, ovate with a sharp, tapering point at the end. They have toothed margins. Some leaves feel sandpapery on their shiny green upper surfaces, and all possess three prominent primary veins and undersides that are a paler green than their top surfaces. Most have uneven or asymmetrical bases, like the leaves of basswood. Hackberry leaves turn yellow in autumn.

In early May, about the time its leaves emerge, a hackberry puts out small, greenish flowers at the ends of slender, drooping stalks. The inconspicuous blossoms are about 1/8 inch across. The male flowers cluster at the base of the annual twig growth, and the female flowers stand singly at the base of the upper leaves on the same shoot. Wind carries pollen from male to female flowers.

By September, the female flower has developed into a mature fruit, a 1/4- to 1/2-inch spherical drupe, with purple skin and dry, sweet-tasting, orange-colored flesh. The flesh encloses a thick-walled nutlet with a single brown seed. Known as sugarberries, the fruits may hang on into winter, by which time they look like tiny, shriveled-up plums. Foragers report that the fruits taste like dates.

Some seeds fall to the ground; others get carried by streams and rivers and deposited on riverbanks and bottomlands. In a study conducted in Indiana, 34 percent of seeds germinated after being stored for a year in leaf litter, and another 20 percent germinated after being stored over two winters.

Many birds eat hackberry fruits: bobwhite quail, ring-necked pheasants, wild turkeys, woodpeckers, prairie chickens, crows, sapsuckers, flickers, robins, catbirds, brown thrashers, mockingbirds, and cedar waxwings. The birds scatter the seeds far and wide with their droppings. Fox squirrels and flying squirrels, gray foxes, opossums, raccoons, and skunks have all been spotted eating hackberries, and probably many small rodents consume the fruits and seeds as well.

A heavy wood, at 46 pounds per cubic foot, hackberry is considered to be moderately hard. Some mills market it mixed in with ash and elm. The sapwood is pale yellow to greenish yellow, the heartwood slightly darker. Since it is flexible, people have crafted hackberry into barrel hoops. Boxes, crates, hoe handles, and plywood are other products. Furniture makers use hackberry for solid parts in furniture, then hide its plain face beneath veneers of walnut, cherry, or mahogany.

RED MULBERRY

To observe frantic avian activity, stand in a mulberry grove when the fruit is ripening in early summer. Birds will be everywhere, gobbling down the sweet crop: grackles, starlings, cardinals, robins, catbirds, mockingbirds, thrushes, thrashers, orioles, waxwings, woodpeckers—even crows, clambering about clumsily on the springy boughs. The birds call stridently, scold one another, and go flapping through the dense foliage, trying to get at the luscious red to purple-black drupes.

The red mulberry *(Morus rubra)* ranges from Massachusetts and Minnesota south to Florida and Texas. Sometimes it is called black mulberry. It makes its straightest, tallest growth in damp coves and river valleys of the southern Appalachians, where it can become 70 feet tall and have a trunk 3 feet in diameter. Red mulberry is an uncommon tree in Pennsylvania. Here in the northern part of its range, it is often something of a shrub, although some individuals reach a height of 50 feet and have a trunk 12 to 18 inches in diameter. The current Pennsylvania state record specimen is 49 feet tall and stands on a house lot in Erie.

In Pennsylvania, red mulberry is found mainly in the southern half of the state, growing on rich, moist soil of lowlands and wooded slopes and keeping company with American elm, red maple, box-elder, and white ash. It is moderately tolerant of shade.

The mature tree has a short trunk that branches into a broad, dense, round-topped crown. Mulberry leaves are 3 to 5 inches long and almost as broad. They alternate on the twigs. The leaves have coarse, saw-toothed edges and prominent veins; they are dark green above, with a sandpapery texture, and soft hairs grow on their undersides. They come in several shapes, the most common of which is oval with a pointed tip. Particularly on sprouts and young twigs, leaves may develop one or several lobes. (The only other tree with this sort of irregular foliage is sassafras, whose leaves have smooth edges.) The bark is brownish, sometimes tinged with red, fissured into scaly plates. If damaged, the twigs exude a milky sap.

In May or June, red mulberry puts out clusters of tiny flowers, male and female flowers generally on separate trees, although occasionally on different branches of the same tree. The wind carries male pollen to the female flowers. The fruits, green at first, ripen by July. A mulberry is about an inch long; it looks like a cylindrical blackberry, composed of multiple thin-skinned fruitlets (each developed from a separate flower) whose sweet, juicy flesh surrounds a small seed.

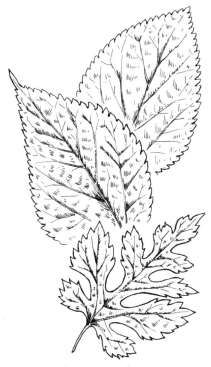

In red mulberry, some leaves are ovate while others have deep lobes. Both forms may occur on the same tree.

The fruits don't have to be fully ripe for birds to eat them, but in an unripe state, they are dangerous to humans, because they cause severe indigestion and contain hallucinogenic compounds. Gray and fox squirrels, woodchucks, foxes, skunks, opossums, and raccoons feast on mulberries, competing with the birds and with humans who pick the nutritious fruit to make juices and preserves. Through their droppings, birds and mammals disperse the seeds.

Because it is generally a small tree with a short trunk, people have not found a great many uses for mulberry wood. The wood resists rotting in contact with the soil, and so sometimes it is used for fence posts. It resembles black walnut when polished and has been fashioned into furniture and coffins. In olden days, Choctaw Indians in Louisiana wove cloaks out of the fibrous inner bark of stump sprouts that sprang up where mulberries had been cut down.

North America has five native and three naturalized trees belonging to the mulberry family, Moraceae. One other mulberry found in Pennsylvania and the Northeast is the white mulberry, *Morus alba.* (For more information on this species, see Common Introduced Trees.)

CUCUMBER-TREE

Although large and spectacular, the flowers of the cucumber-tree *(Magnolia acuminata)* are easy to overlook: they grow high on the branches, and their pale yellowish green petals scarcely differ from the color of the new leaves. In early May, I sought out a cucumber-tree along the township road; I had noticed its fruits littering the ground the previous autumn. Obtaining a flower was a bit more difficult, but finally, standing in the bed of my pickup truck and reaching up as far as I could with my tree trimmer, I managed to snip one off.

The flowers of the cucumber-tree stand upright and solitary at the ends of the branches. Each is 2 to 3 inches tall and shaped like a bell with the mouth pointed upward. Six large, succulent petals enclose pistils and stamens, the female and male reproductive parts, crowded together in a central, cone-shaped structure that looks like a pineapple and is the color of a not-quite-ripe banana. The blossom is at once intricate and primitive-looking, like something you might find in a tropical rain forest rather than in the Pennsylvania uplands.

In fact, cucumber-tree has a distinct southern connection. Also known as cucumber magnolia, it is classified with the magnolias, a group of trees and shrubs found mainly in southeastern North America and Central America. The name magnolia commemorates the French botanist Pierre Magnol, who died in 1715. The cucumber-tree is the hardiest and northernmost representative of its genus. Two other members of genus *Magnolia* are native to southern Pennsylvania: umbrella magnolia, *Magnolia tripetala,* and sweetbay magnolia, *Magnolia virginiana.* (For more information on these uncommon trees, see Odd Others.)

Cucumber-tree ranges from western New York and southern Ontario south and west to Arkansas, and in the Appalachian Mountains to northern Georgia, Alabama, and Mississippi. In Pennsylvania, it grows mainly in mountainous areas in the state's western half, scattered through the forest, never in pure stands. It favors rich woods and moist soils near streams but will also grow in drier habitats. In West Virginia and Pennsylvania, it does particularly well on limestone soils.

Cucumber-tree is closely related to tuliptree, *Liriodendron tulipifera,* and like the tuliptree, it is a fast-growing, light-hungry species. The tree matures in 80 to 120 years and seldom lives beyond 150 years. A full-grown specimen stands 60 to 80 feet tall, occasionally more than 100 feet, and is 3 to 4 feet in diameter. Cucumber-tree achieves its largest size in the southern Appalachians, particularly in the deep, damp soils of cove forests. Yet it can make impressive growth in the Keystone State. In *Pennsylvania Trees,* Joseph Illick notes that during the logging era around the turn of the twentieth century, "the largest log hauled out of the Hammersley Run of Potter County was a Cucumber. It was over 6 1/2 feet in diameter at the small end."

If it grows in the forest, a cucumber-tree will be symmetrical, straight, and tall; as it matures, the lower branches prune themselves away and the branch scars heal over, leaving a trunk uninterrupted by limbs for as many as 50 feet. If a cucumber-tree grows out in the open, it will assume a strongly pyramidal form, with limbs all along the trunk from ground level to the narrow top. Potential tree climbers take note: branches of the cucumber are weak and brittle, something worth considering if you are tempted to try for a bird's-eye view of those strangely beautiful flowers.

Dense hairs coat the young twigs and buds of this species. The leaves are large, 6 to 10 or more inches long and 3 to 6 inches broad, oblong with a pointed tip, and often with wavy edges. They are a rich yellow-green, paler and slightly hairy on their undersides, with a prominent midrib and veins. The leaves alternate along the twigs. The tree's bark is brown and tight, with shallow furrows and narrow, forking ridges; it looks something like the bark of white ash, only a bit more blotchy and flaking. The outer bark layer is rather loose and rubs off easily. The tree's root system spreads wide and deep, although usually a taproot is lacking.

The flowers of *Magnolia acuminata* close at night. They last two to four days. In *A Natural History of Trees,* Donald Culross Peattie writes that the blossoms are odorless; in the more modern *Field Guide to Eastern Trees,* George A. Petrides states that they have an unpleasant odor at close range. The specimen I clipped had a sweet, fresh scent, rather lemony, and not at all objectionable. As I stood beneath the tree looking up through binoculars, I saw flies, small bees, and a large yellow jacket, apparently attracted by the flowers' aroma, come and land in the pale cups. Beetles also visit the blossoms to get nectar. For the magnolias in general, beetles are important pollinators. In those insects, the sense of smell is more acute than the visual sense, and beetle-attracting flowers are generally plain white or dull-colored and give off a strong scent: fruity, spicy, or resembling fermented vegetation.

The green, immature fruit of Magnolia acuminata *looks like a cucumber, giving the cucumber-tree its common name.*

Its compound fruit—oblong, curved, knobby, and greenish—earns the cucumber-tree its name. Look for these miniature cucumbers on the ground following strong winds and thunderstorms. As summer progresses, the fruit turns a deep pinkish red. By September or October, it ripens into a red cylindrical mass 2 to 2 1/2 inches long, studded all over with pointed scarlet seeds "set on the surface like scanty grains of corn on a cob," observes Peattie. Each seed has a soft outer coating of fleshy, oily pulp. The seeds, ten to sixty per fruiting body, fall out of the small depressions in which they developed and hang suspended for a time from slender white threads 1 to 3 inches long. Why do they dangle exposed like that (Peattie calls it an "awkward machinery of distribution"), if not to attract foraging birds?

The fleshy fruits and seeds have a fat content of about 22 percent. Grackles and blackbirds are known to feed on the developing fruits. In my reading, I did not find accounts of other birds consuming the ripened seeds, but it seems likely that they would do so, given the berries' bright colors and food value. Black bears sometimes climb the trees to feed on the fruit. Cucumber-trees produce good seed crops every four to five years. Two *Magnolia acuminata* saplings are pushing up in the band of trees between the clearings for our house and barn; since no mature cucumber-trees grow on our land, I assume that birds ate the seeds some distance away and voided them here, with the young trees prospering in the narrow wooded zone exposed to sunlight on two sides.

In autumn, cucumber-trees' thin, translucent leaves turn a wan yellow, almost a tan. The first heavy frost blasts them. I have gone walking on frosty mornings, and as the sun began to mount in the sky, the frost on the leaves of the cucumbers started to melt and a breeze to stir; the leaves came plummeting down one after another, each making a soft but clearly audible thud when it hit the ground.

The wood of cucumber-tree is light at 29 pounds per cubic foot, dry weight. It is soft and brittle. Pale and bland looking, the wood shows little figure. It is very stable and does not warp when dried, or after it is used in applications such as interior house trim and parts of furniture that are rarely seen, such as drawer backs or cores. The wood takes paint well. It is similar to the wood of the closely related tuliptree, and the two are generally marketed together. People have used cucumber-tree wood for boxes, crates, slack cooperage (barrels not meant to hold liquids), and the slats of venetian blinds.

In the late 1700s and early 1800s, the French botanists André Michaux and his son François André Michaux collected and studied plants in eastern

North America. In 1802, as François botanized along the Juniata River in Bedford County, Pennsylvania, he wrote:

> The *magnolia acuminata* is very common in the environs; it is known in the country by the name of *cucumber tree*. The inhabitants of the remote parts of Pennsylvania, Virginia, and even the western countries pick the cones when green to infuse in whiskey, which gives it a pleasant bitter. This bitter is very much esteemed in the country as a preventive against intermittent fevers; but I have my doubts whether it would be so generally used if it had the same qualities when mixed with water.

TULIPTREE

One of Pennsylvania's largest tuliptrees *(Liriodendron tulipifera)* guards the entrance to Tyler Arboretum in Delaware County. The tree, as befitting its kind, stands utterly straight, its trunk clad with furrowed, pale gray bark. At ground level, its roots are thicker than a human's torso; in the crown high above, the leaves, with their distinctive notched tips, twist and twinkle in the breeze. When last measured in 1986, the tuliptree stood 136 feet tall; its trunk was 19 feet, 1 inch, in circumference; and its crown spread across 85 feet.

Viewing the tree one summer day, I was struck by the way it simply stood there, timeless and steadfast and removed, and it was no great stretch to imagine trees exactly like that one growing during the Cretaceous Period, more than sixty-five million years ago, when the Gulf of Mexico stretched north to join the Arctic Ocean, when tyrannosaurs preyed on triceratops dinosaurs, when the very first deciduous trees, including *Liriodendron tulipifera,* so the fossil record informs us, came to tower above the formerly dominant ferns and cycads.

Tuliptree is also widely known as tulip poplar or yellow poplar. However, it is unrelated to the poplars, which belong to the willow family. Taxonomists group tuliptree—sometimes simply called tulip—with that ancient sylvan tribe the magnolias. Tuliptrees grew in Europe and Asia before the glaciers of the Pleistocene extinguished it on those continents. Today the species' natural range is confined to eastern North America, from southern New England and the Great Lakes states to Florida and Louisiana. The only other member of its genus survives in China. *Liriodendron tulipifera* is common statewide in Pennsylvania, except in the extreme northern counties.

A long, straight, slightly tapering trunk distinguishes this woodland stalwart. Mature tuliptrees are 50 to 100 feet tall and have a trunk 2 to 3 feet in

diameter. The crown is rather narrow. In the woods, tuliptree often
does not have lateral branches for the
first 40 or 50 feet of its bole. The
bark on young trees is smooth; that
of older specimens is scored with
vertical furrows, similar to the bark of
the white ash but lacking the latter's
distinctive diamond-shaped fissures.
The bottoms of the fissures in tuliptree bark show white, a paleness
often visible from quite a distance.

The tuliptree leaf seems ancient
or primitive in appearance. It is 3 to
6 inches long and equally broad, with
a widened, squared-off tip indented
with a central notch, ahead of four
(sometimes six) short-pointed, paired
side lobes. The shape somewhat suggests a maple leaf; early English settlers likened it to an "old woman's
smock." The leaves alternate along
the stems. Thanks to their long, pliant stalks, they flutter whenever a
breath of air is moving. A shiny dark
green in summer, they turn bright
yellow in fall.

*Tall, straight, swift-growing tuliptree
produces valuable wood often used
for house trim. The inset shows
a cross section of the seed cluster,
containing stacked samaras.*

Tuliptrees thrive in deep, moist soils of valleys and low slopes, and also
in drier mountain habitats, where you can sometimes pick them out from
afar, with their whitish bark, standing taller than their neighbors and often
clustered around a spring seep or a streamcourse. On good sites where
sunlight is ample, seedlings can become 10 to 18 feet tall in five years. His-
torically, the tree made its best growth in the cove forests of the southern
Appalachians, where old-growth specimens approached 200 feet in height;
such mature trees were 250 to 300 or more years old. In the 1870s, the
naturalist Robert Ridgway documented many giant tuliptrees in the
Wabash River valley in Indiana. He measured the trunks of eighteen that
had been cut down by loggers: the trees averaged 143 feet in length and
6.2 feet in diameter.

Tuliptrees flower in May and June. The blossoms—which call to mind both the cultivated tulip and the water lily—open at the ends of the leaf-bearing twigs. The flower, not quite 2 inches deep, is composed of six thick, broad, yellow-green petals, each with a blush of orange at the base. Cupped within the petals, the male pollen-bearing structures fan out around a central overlapping cluster of female pistils, which contain the prospective seeds. A copious nectar flow attracts beetles, flies, and bees, which pollinate the blossoms. The bees include honeybees, and the tulip-tree is an important honey-producing plant. The Swedish scientist Peter Kalm, collector of many American plants in the 1700s, wrote that the tulip-tree's flowers "have no scent to delight the nose." Borne high up in the tree, the blossoms are rarely seen; the woodland walker is more apt to notice petals from the spent flowers lying on the ground.

In September or October, the fruit matures into a 3-inch, cone-shaped packet of winged seeds, or samaras. The long, flattened samaras detach and spin away on the wind, which may scatter them to a distance equaling five times the tree's height. When scientists monitored a North Carolina tulip-tree having a trunk diameter of 20 inches, they found that the tree produced 3,250 cones and 29,000 sound seeds in a single year. A study of nineteen southern Appalachian tuliptree stands revealed an average of 1.5 million seeds shed per acre. Recently in Maryland, I saw a pure and extremely dense stand of tuliptree saplings; it appeared they had risen from seed falling on abandoned farm fields. After releasing its seeds, the cone's core stands upright on the bare twig, often lasting well into winter. Seeds can stay viable in the forest litter for up to seven years. Squirrels, mice, and some songbirds—particularly cardinals and finches—eat tuliptree seeds.

More than forty insect species attack *Liriodendron tulipifera,* but few cause significant damage. Even the ravenous gypsy moth leaves tuliptree alone: I recall years when the oaks hereabouts were totally defoliated, when the only greenery left on the mountain clung to tuliptrees, flowering dogwoods, mountain laurel, and wild grape vines. Sapsuckers often drill into tuliptree bark, ringing the trunk with dense bands of their sap-collecting excavations.

Another name for tuliptree is canoewood. Several tribes of Native Americans made canoes from the tree, using fire, stone hatchets, or seashells to hollow out the trunk. The massive but lightweight dugouts could carry twenty paddlers and their provisions. It is said that Daniel Boone floated his family down the Ohio River, leaving Kentucky for the Spanish Territory in the late 1700s, in a 60-foot-long tuliptree canoe.

In the original forests of America, tuliptree was second in girth only to sycamore. From the southern colonies in 1709 came the report of John Lawson, surveyor general to the British lords proprietors of the Carolinas, of a hollow tuliptree "wherein a lusty Man had his Bed and Household Furniture, and liv'd in it, till his Labour got him a more fashionable Mansion." Settlers also used the lightweight, easily worked wood of the statuesque tuliptree for cabin logs, shingles, wainscoting, and well linings, since the wood imparts no taste to water. More recent applications include interior house trim, furniture, crates, toys, and paneling. The wood, weighing 26 pounds per cubic foot, is one of the lightest hardwoods. It is very stable when cured and is the top choice for drawer sides in cabinets and cases. The pulp is made into high-quality book paper.

Tuliptree has been a popular species with Europeans since they first met it. Thomas Jefferson particularly fancied the tree, planting it on the grounds of his summer home in Bedford County, Virginia, and sending quantities of the seeds to fellow horticulturists in France.

Tuliptree is an old friend to me. I like its regimental straightness; its familiar and easily recognized bark; its flowers glinting like candles on the boughs; the distinct and beautiful shape of the leaf, sometimes used as a repeating motif on local Amish quilts; the golden accent it brings to the autumn woods—and the sense that it is an ancient tree, a true forest elder.

PAWPAW

I smelled the strange essence before I could pick out the small, unfamiliar trees growing beneath tall red oaks and tuliptrees. A state forester led me along the south-facing slope of Conococheague Mountain in western Perry County. The fragrance as we approached the stand became sweet, full, and finally cloying.

The pawpaws *(Asimina triloba)* stood about 20 feet tall, their slender trunks supporting broad crowns. Large leaves sprouted from the tips of spindly, upraised branches. The leaves had a decidedly tropical aspect; they were dark green, 6 inches to almost a foot in length, with untoothed edges and a shape botanists describe as obovate-lanceolate: widening from the base and achieving their greatest breadth about three-quarters of the way to the tip, then quickly tapering to a point. The leaves, which drooped from their stems, reminded me somewhat of cucumber-tree leaves. Hidden among them, dangling heavily from their stems, were the fragrant pawpaws, paler and more yellowish green than the foliage. Some of the fruit were pear-shaped, while others curved like elongated kidneys.

Asimina triloba ranges from western New Jersey, southern Pennsylvania, and western New York, west through southern Ontario and Michigan, to eastern Nebraska. Pawpaws grow as far south as the Florida Panhandle and eastern Texas. The species is reputed to achieve its best growth in lowland forests of southern Indiana and Tennessee, along streams flowing into the Ohio River. In Pennsylvania, pawpaws are uncommon. They occur in the southern third of the state—"south of a line drawn from Pittsburgh through Harrisburg and Reading to Doylestown in Bucks County," wrote Joseph Illick in the 1928 *Pennsylvania Trees.*

The pawpaw belongs to Annonaceae, the custard apple family, whose members grow mainly in the tropics and include such exotics as soursop, cherimoya, custard apple, pond-apple, and ilana. The name pawpaw was bestowed by Spanish explorers, members of the 1541 DeSoto Expedition, who, seeing the green-skinned fruit on trees in the lower Mississippi Valley, mistook the plant for a similar species, the papaya, found in the Caribbean. Papaya is itself a transliteration of an Arawak Indian word. Other names for *Asimina triloba* are tall pawpaw, distinguishing it from several shrubby relatives in the Southeast; common pawpaw; Indian banana; false banana; jasmine; and fetid-shrub, because the crushed leaves emit a biting odor.

Pawpaws typically grow 6 to 20 feet tall, with unusually large specimens reaching 40 feet. The trunk's diameter rarely exceeds 12 inches. The bark is pale to dark brown, sometimes with grayish blotches; it is thin and has a warty texture. The alternate, simple leaves are dark green above and paler beneath. They turn yellow in autumn. Pawpaws grow in the understory of hardwood forests and rarely become established in pastures or fields. They favor deep, moist soil along streams and on low, fertile slopes. Although pawpaws sometimes form dense thickets, they usually occur as solitary specimens or in open groups, such as the small stand the forester showed me on Conococheague Mountain. There the pawpaws grew in a V surrounding and slightly downhill from a bench on the mountain's side, apparently in a band of soil collected below the level area. Pawpaw colonies usually expand by sending up sprouts from their root systems.

Pawpaws bloom in April and May, before the leaves emerge. The blossoms are 1 to 1½ inches in diameter, with three triangular brownish or purplish petals. Rutherford Platt in *Discover American Trees* likened the color to "well-done beefsteak" and noted that the hanging blooms are inconspicuous in the forest shadows. The flowers possess both male and female parts, and rely on odor to attract carrion-loving flies and beetles as agents of pollination. Reports the naturalist Janet Lembke in *Shake Them 'Simmons Down,* the odor wrinkles the nose "with a light but appalling smell"; it reminded Donald Culross Peattie of fermenting purple grapes. In each flower, the female parts, or pistils, mature earlier than the male stamens, so that a tree's female blossoms are unlikely to be pollinated by one of the tree's own male flowers. Scientists call this strategy protogyny, which translates roughly as "females first"; it is used by many plants, including apples and pears. In *Asimina triloba,* protogyny is not an efficient system: botanists believe that less than 1 percent of flowers ever produce fruit.

From the dozen or so pawpaw trees that the forester and I looked at, we managed to shake down about ten ripe and nearly ripe fruits. The pawpaw fruit is considered to be a berry, but it looks more substantial than that, at a bulbous 3 to 5 inches in length and weighing up to a pound. I had never eaten a pawpaw, but the odor beckoned. I peeled the skin from the softest of the batch. The flesh was as yellow as a ripe avocado. It had a consistency like custard or cooked sweet potato, and when I slurped it up, it tasted good, like banana but with a hint of something exotic—mango, maybe—and an overlying pleasant sweetness. Opossums, squirrels, raccoons, foxes, and birds eat the fruit. On the ground in the pawpaw patch, a pile of large, dark brown, lima-bean-shaped seeds showed where an animal had dined on a pawpaw and discarded the seeds. Some sources claim the seeds contain a powerful alkaloid that exerts a stupefying effect on the brains of mammals.

Pawpaw fruits are rich in carbohydrates, proteins, minerals, and vitamins C and A. They are considered more nutritious than apples, peaches, and grapes. Fruit growers and nurseries maintain and sell around nine domesticated varieties. The individual fruits have a short shelf life, blackening and becoming insipid after only a few days of ripeness. Better to find your pawpaws in the

The bulbous fruit of the pawpaw is 3 to 5 inches long and ripens in early autumn.

woods and eat them out of hand. Or, as the forager and writer Euell Gibbons recommended in *Stalking the Wild Asparagus,* take them home for baking or preparing into a custard-type pie.

Native Americans ate the fruits and wove fabrics and rope out of the trees' inner bark fibers. Some historians suggest that *Asimina triloba* was transplanted to the northern part of its current range by migrating Indians. John Lawson, in his 1709 *Natural History of Carolina,* wrote: "The Papau . . . bears an Apple about the Bigness of a Hen's Egg, yellow, soft, and as sweet as any thing can well be." He noted that Indians made "rare Puddings" of the fruit. The botanist John Bartram sent specimen trees to England in 1746.

Even if its fruit is too touchy to survive modern mass distribution, the pawpaw may yet prove valuable to our society. I noticed that the late-September leaves of the pawpaws on Conococheague Mountain showed remarkably little insect damage, while those of nearby oaks and maples were chewed to shreds. Natural insecticides made from pawpaw compounds—which are concentrated in the twigs, unripe fruits, roots, and seeds—repel some insect pests. Scientists also report that chemicals extracted from the pawpaw have shown promise in treating cancers in laboratory animals.

Pawpaw wood is yellow tinged with green. It is soft, weak, and, at only 25 pounds per cubic foot, one of the lightest of our woods—even lighter than tuliptree (26 pounds per cubic foot) and American basswood (28 pounds).

Those wishing to abet the pawpaw are advised to save the seeds from a particularly flavorful tree. Store them in a refrigerator for at least sixty days, mimicking winter conditions, before planting.

SASSAFRAS

Curious leaves adorn this small to medium-size tree. They come in three patterns: a simple egg-shaped form; a leaf like a mitten, with a lobe thumbing off to the left, or to the right; and a three-lobed variant, like a mitten fashioned by a knitter who absentmindedly added a thumb on each side. With the exception of red mulberry, no other tree native to Pennsylvania has such variable foliage. Leaves of all three types can show up on the same sassafras tree, the same branch—even the same twig. Younger trees generally have more lobed leaves than older specimens.

Sassafras albidum ranges from southwestern Maine to Florida in the east, and from southern Michigan to Texas in the west. Nearly statewide in

Pennsylvania, it is absent only from the extreme north-central part of the commonwealth. It springs up in young woods, fencerows, abandoned fields, clearings, burned-over areas, and forest edges. Sassafras is not a species of the deep woods, where trees with greater growth potential soon overtop it, shutting out the light and causing its demise.

In the Northeast, sassafras can be anything from a thicket-forming shrub to a tree 50 feet high and 2 feet or more in diameter. On a poor site—such as the rock-ribbed mountain bench where I live, where the soil depth is measured in fractions of an inch—a fully mature sassafras may have a trunk only 6 inches across. In the South, *Sassafras albidum* achieves a much greater stature: up to 80 feet tall, and 4 or even 6 feet across the trunk. According to foresters, the species grows largest in the Great

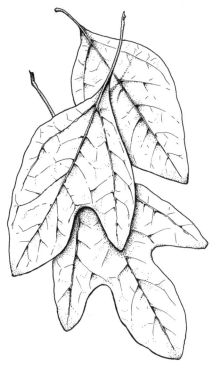

*Sassafras leaves come in three patterns:
single-lobed; double-lobed;
and obovate, having no lobes.*

Smoky Mountains, on rich, moist, well-drained, sandy loam.

The roots of sassafras run shallow, around 6 to 20 inches deep; broad-spreading, they branch freely to form a complex system. The short, stout trunk holds up a narrow, spreading crown. The bole is clad with gray-brown to reddish brown bark scored with deep, vertical fissures separated by flat ridges. Several field guides describe the branches of sassafras as "contorted"—wavy and twisting, not straight, and ending in sprays of twigs. The branches are brittle. The leaves are 4 to 6 inches long, smooth and yellow-green on their upper surfaces and a paler chalky green below. In autumn, they turn yellow, orange, rose, or red. The leaves on their long, slender stalks arise from graceful, upturned twigs; the twigs are covered with smooth, glossy green bark, which, scratched with penknife or thumbnail, gives off a nose-tickling, spicy scent, as does the crushed foliage. Chewed, the inner bark becomes gummy or mucilaginous in the mouth, like the twigs of slippery elm. Chewing the leaves stimulates salivation.

Sassafras puts out flowers in May. Male and female flowers resemble each other but grow on separate trees. The blossoms are greenish yellow and about 1/4 inch across; they hang in drooping clusters at the ends of the leafless twigs. Flies are the chief pollinators.

By autumn, the female flowers have developed into ripe fruits known as drupes. A drupe consists of a fleshy pulp surrounding a shiny brown seed. The fruit is elliptical in shape and about 1/2 inch long; dark blue and shiny, it sits at the end of a bright red, club-shaped stem, like a tiny, out-of-round golf ball perched on its tee. Everything about sassafras is colorful in September and October: the foliage, which catches the eyes of hungry birds; the sturdy stems; the fruits. Sassafras fruits have a high fat content, and are relished by bobwhite quail, wild turkey, pileated woodpecker, several flycatcher species (eastern phoebe, great-crested flycatcher, and eastern kingbird), red-eyed vireo, catbird, and others. Black bears pull down the branches and bite the fruits off, stems and all. Cottontail rabbits and white-tailed deer browse the twigs, and deer eat the leaves.

A number of insect species consume the foliage. Two common summertime feeders are the spectacular caterpillars of the spicebush swallowtail butterfly, bulky and green, with ferocious eyespots behind the head; and of the promethea moth, even fatter than the swallowtail larva, and studded with red bristles. The promethea larva often fashions its cocoon out of a sassafras leaf, curling the leaf lengthwise around its body and, using silk produced in its abdomen, firmly wrapping and anchoring leaf and cocoon to the stem. Gypsy moth caterpillars and Japanese beetles are two imported alien pests that have no difficulty digesting sassafras leaves.

Sassafras trees start bearing fruits at around age ten. Trees from twenty-five to fifty years of age produce the largest crops. Trees bear good crops every year or two. Wildlife that eat the fruits disperse the seeds in their droppings; fruits that remain uneaten fall from their stems in late autumn. Most seeds germinate the following spring, although they have the potential to stay viable for up to six years. The best place for a seed to end up is a patch of moist, rich, loamy soil covered with rotting leaf mulch, in the open or along the edge of a wooded tract where sunlight bathes the ground. Seedlings in forest settings show some shade tolerance, but need an opening in the leafy canopy to get the full sunlight they require for further growth. Sassafras reproduces itself more frequently and reliably by cloning, when an established tree sends up shoots from its root system. In full light, sprouts may climb as high as 12 feet in three years. The cloning habit leads to small thickets of sassafras.

Sassafras roots produce chemicals that may suppress the growth of nearby competing plants, a botanical strategy known as allelopathy. Other trees that commonly grow near sassafras include black locust, sweet-gum, bear oak, flowering dogwood, elms, ashes, eastern red-cedar, hickories, American beech, and tuliptree. In our home woods, sassafras stands with black-gum, red maple, and various oaks. Sassafras trees of all ages are highly susceptible to fire damage; fires and other injuries cause breaches in the bark, points of entry for wood decay fungi. Invasion by fungi leads to hollow trunks or limbs. Wild birds and mammals nest in the cavities of sassafras trees and shelter in these hidey-holes during bad weather.

The wood of *Sassafras albidum* is soft and brittle; like the leaves, twigs, and roots, it gives off a pleasant aromatic scent. A thin band of yellowish sapwood surrounds the orange-brown heartwood, which can show a pretty grain and figure. While curing, the wood shrinks less than any other North American hardwood. It is relatively light, at 31 pounds per cubic foot, dry weight. The wood does not rot readily in contact with the soil; in bygone days, people used it for fence posts and split it into fence rails. They also made buckets, small boats, and dugout canoes from sassafras. Today, artisans occasionally craft the wood into cabinetry and furniture. Its fragrance, like that of eastern red-cedar, is thought to repel clothing moths. Sassafras snaps and shoots off sparks, so some folks call it a poor fuel; when I can get it, I use the wood for kindling, since it splits fine and burns with a quick, hot flame.

The name "sassafras" apparently is a sixteenth-century Spanish adaptation of a word used by Florida Indians to describe the plant. Explorers in North America eagerly sought sassafras, because they thought it was a panacea, a cure-all for a host of ailments—everything from malaria to lameness to venereal disease. (People also thought that the smoke from tobacco, another New World plant, worked miracle cures.) Sassafras was the first cash crop shipped back to Europe by the earliest settlers. By 1622, the English Crown had obligated the colonists at Jamestown, Virginia, to annually ship 30 tons of sassafras back to Britain, where preparations from the bark and roots made a popular drink. Superstitious people crafted boxes from the wood for holding Bibles—it was supposed to ward off evil spirits—and some believed that a ship with enough sassafras in its hull would never wreck.

Over time, sassafras came to be regarded as less a wonder drug than a healthful tonic, traditional in springtime for thinning the blood, preparing the body to better withstand the coming heat of summer. Other names for sassafras include ague tree, chewing stick, cinnamonwood, and tea tree. Tea is usually brewed from chopped-up pieces of the smaller roots or bark from the larger ones. The active chemical ingredient of aromatic sassafras oil, present in every part of the plant, is known as safrole. Safrole has been used to flavor root beer, chewing gum, candy, toothpaste, medicine, perfumes, and soap. Dried leaves of sassafras, powdered fine, make a tasty thickener known as filé, mixed into stews and gumbos in Creole and southern cooking. Studies suggest that safrole may be a mild carcinogen if ingested in staggering dosages.

Taxonomists place *Sassafras albidum* in the laurel family, Lauraceae. The fossil record shows that sassafras trees once grew in Europe but were wiped out there during the ice ages. Sassafras is closely related to common spicebush, *Lindera benzoin,* a berry-producing shrub. Two other relatives are cinnamon, a tree native to India and Sri Lanka, and camphor laurel, common in China and Japan.

WITCH-HAZEL

In a 1952 article in *Pennsylvania Forests and Waters,* research forester A. B. Mickalitis pronounced witch-hazel "the most common shrub native to Pennsylvania" and noted that it was found in every county in the commonwealth. Witch-hazel *(Hamamelis virginiana)* sometimes grows large enough to be considered a small tree—albeit a straggling, many-trunked one. A specimen found in Potter County in 1984 had a trunk 16 inches in circumference (for a diameter of about 5 inches) and stood 42 feet tall; its crown spread out 28 feet horizontally. Another, reported from the Virginia Appalachians, had a trunk circumference of some 52 inches (one suspects that several stems had somehow grown together) and a 30-foot crown spread.

Witch-hazel ranges throughout the East, from Nova Scotia west across southern Quebec and Ontario to Wisconsin and Minnesota, and south to Florida and Texas. It grows along streams, in swamps, and on the banks of lakes and ponds. It prefers moist, rich soil but will also take root on drier, less fertile sites, including rocky slopes. A shade-tolerant plant, witch-hazel grows slowly in the understory of oak-hickory and mixed hardwood forests.

The trunk of witch-hazel is short or nonexistent, with the plant generally splitting into many spreading, crooked stems at or slightly above ground level, creating a clump of small trunks all emanating from the same root system. The smooth or scaly bark is light brown, sometimes mottled with pale blotches. A witch-hazel's crown is broad and open. In the woods around my house—on a dry, south-facing slope where chestnut oak and red maple are the most numerous tree species—the largest witch-hazels are about 20 feet tall by 18 feet wide, with the most robust stems 3 to 4 inches in diameter: pretty typical, in my experience, for specimens growing in Pennsylvania upland forests.

The witch-hazel leaf is oval, rounded or pointed at the tip, and has a blunt base that is divided into two unequal-size portions by the stem. The leaves alternate along the twigs. They measure 3 to 5 inches long and 2 to 3 inches wide, and have five to seven veins on each side of the midrib; their wavy edges are decorated with rounded teeth. The leaves are dark green above and pale green beneath, and in autumn they turn a green-tinged yellow. Witch-hazel has an interesting "naked" leaf bud. The bud is brown, and in it you can actually see the leaf that will form the following year.

An excellent time to look for witch-hazel is right after the deciduous trees drop their leaves—around the fourth week of October here in central Pennsylvania. Then, on sunny days, the witch-hazels stand out dazzlingly beneath the hardwoods, their bare outer branches spreading a haze of spidery yellow flowers. *Hamamelis virginiana* is the only Pennsylvania tree or shrub to blossom in autumn. It is also our only woody, deciduous plant that bears flowers and mature fruits at the same time.

Rounded flower buds begin forming in August. The flowers start to bloom in October, just before the witch-hazels drop their own leaves. About an inch in diameter, the blossoms contain both male and female parts. Each has four thin, ribbonlike petals, which twist and flare outward from a central cup. The flowers usually cluster in groups of three, their commingled petals creating a busy, snarled-thread appearance. The blossoms' faint fragrance and bright coloration attract pollinating insects.

On balmy Indian summer days, I have watched tiny gnats and larger wasps landing on witch-hazel flowers. John Eastman, in *The Book of Forest and Thicket,* suggests that these are likely to be fungus gnats and small parasitic wasps; Eastman also observed hover flies and tachinid flies visiting witch-hazel flowers. Since a witch-hazel holds its flowers for several weeks, it can usually count on a spell of warm autumn weather allowing insect pollinators to fly. If not, the flowers can self-pollinate. Pollen grains do not actually fertilize the flower's ovules until the following spring, and seeds begin developing at that time.

By early autumn, when a new wave of blossoms bursts forth, last year's flowers have become seed capsules: woody, rounded, yellowish brown vessels about 1/2 inch long. As they ripen, the capsules forcibly eject their seeds. In an entry dated October 22 in his book *Gone for the Day,* the Penn-

Witch-hazel is unusual in bearing flowers and fruit at the same time: the 1/2-inch-long seed capsules and ribbonlike yellow flowers decorate the branches in early autumn.

sylvania naturalist and wildlife artist Ned Smith writes of walking in the woods and hearing "the almost constant patter of [witch-hazel] seeds striking the ground or glancing off branches and trees." He explains the process: "The bony capsules split as they ripen, each exposing a pair of hard, slippery black seeds. While opening wider they shrink in diameter, exerting tremendous pressure upon their occupants, until the latter suddenly squirt from their chambers like apple seeds from between the fingers." Smith set up a group of ripe seed capsules at one end of a room, aiming them at the opposite wall. Overnight, all the seeds were expelled, and many of them bounced off the wall—a distance of 19 feet. Some sources report that witch-hazel can shoot its seeds 30 feet. The empty pods, with their flaring lips, cling to the branches throughout the year and are a good identifying mark in winter, when witch-hazels stand leafless and without flowers.

A witch-hazel in full sunlight will bear a heavier seed crop than one growing in the shade. The seeds look like 1/4-inch footballs; botanists believe that most of them remain dormant on the ground for two winters before germinating. Ruffed grouse scratch through the leaves beneath witch-hazels in search of the seeds, and also sometimes stuff their crops with the plants' cushiony flowers; wild turkeys, bobwhite quail, and squirrels eat the seeds as well. I see no reason why small rodents such as chipmunks and mice would turn up their noses at such fare. White-tailed deer browse the foliage and twigs of *Hamamelis virginiana*.

Winter-bloom and snapping-alder are two other names for witch-hazel, both pointing out distinctive characteristics of the plant. Why the tree is called witch-hazel is less certain. *Witch* may be a variant of the Anglo-Saxon *wych,* meaning "bending," or it may refer to the plant's weird habit of blooming in autumn, when all other trees look dead. *Hazel* denotes a resemblance to the hazels, nut-producing shrubs of the genus *Corylus.* Some gifted or clairvoyant folks claim they can find underground water by using a forked stick, preferably of witch-hazel, which dips in their hands when held above a subterranean flow. Siting a well using this technique is known as "water witching."

The twigs, leaves, and inner bark of witch-hazel possess mildly astringent properties; Native Americans made liniments and poultices from them. To this day, a lotion combining witch-hazel extract and alcohol is used to relieve minor skin abrasions and irritations like poison ivy. The wood of the witch-hazel is hard, close-grained, and, at 43 pounds per cubic foot, rather heavy. But since it exists mainly in spindling stems, it has not found practical application.

In Pennsylvania forests, I have hiked through areas where successive irruptions of leaf-eating gypsy moth caterpillars killed most of the oak trees. In some of those places, especially where high populations of deer stand ready to eat oak seedlings, witch-hazels dominate and spread. They can occupy a site for many years; the flexible shrubs are not vulnerable to wind-throw caused by storms, and *Hamamelis virginiana* has few insect pests and no deadly microorganism-caused diseases. In autumn, particularly when surrounding oaks fail to bear acorns, turkeys and grouse find important sustenance—as well as cover in which to shelter and rest—in witch-hazel thickets.

SWEET-GUM

The only place I have found sweet-gum *(Liquidambar styraciflua)* in the wild in Pennsylvania is Little Tinicum Island, a welt of sand in the Delaware River and a designated state forest natural area. "In the wild" may not be quite apt, since industrial Philadelphia and New Jersey hem in the river on both sides of Little Tinicum. The sweet-gums grew in a brushy forest that included silver maple, box-elder, red ash, black-gum, tuliptree, and several other species. It was October, and most of the trees had dropped their foliage—but not the sweet-gums. Their leaves blazed with color: brilliant red, fiery orange, glistening maroon, glowing purple, some leaves blending several or even all of those colors into a background of summery green.

Sweet-gum grows mainly in the Southeast. It ranges from southern Connecticut to Florida, and from southern Ohio, Indiana, and Illinois to Oklahoma, Texas, and the Gulf coast states. The species also occurs in Mexico and Central America. In North America, the deep gumbo soils of the Mississippi River valley produce the largest specimens; in the past, loggers there cut down old-growth trees 140 feet tall, with trunks 4 to 5 feet across. In the Northeast and the Appalachians, *Liquidambar styraciflua* is smaller, around 20 to 50 feet tall, in some cases 75 feet. In Pennsylvania, botanists consider the species rare; our native sweet-gums grow mainly in damp coastal plain woods of five southeastern counties: Bucks, Chester, Montgomery, Philadelphia, and Delaware. People have planted sweet-gums outside their natural range. I nurtured three seedlings in our meadow here in central Pennsylvania, and twenty years later they are 35 feet tall.

My trees display the corky, flangelike ridges or wings along the outer twigs that characterize this species. (Bur oak and hackberry are two other northeastern trees having this trait.) The star-shaped leaves, 3 to 5 inches long, alternate on the twigs. The leaves look something like maple leaves, with each of the five (occasionally seven) lobes ending in a drawn-out, pointed tip. Fine teeth line the margins, and the leafstalks are long and rounded. The thick, leathery leaves shine a bright green above, with paler undersurfaces; crushed between the fingers, they release a spicy, resinous scent. The bark on mature sweet-gums is grayish brown, deeply furrowed and ridged, sometimes as thick as 1 1/2 inches. Younger trees have thinner, dark gray bark.

Although sweet-gum prefers rich, deep soil, it will grow on a range of soils and sites. It does not tolerate shade well. It generally develops a straight trunk and a conical crown. Sweet-gum seeds itself onto logged-over land, clearings, and old fields. Saw one down, and it will sprout vigorously from the stump or root system.

Sweet-gum flowers in the spring, when the new leaves are just emerging; in Pennsylvania, this is usually in late April. A tree puts out clusters of male flowers, along with solitary female flowers in the axils of the upper leaves. The flowers of both sexes are globe-shaped and green; sensitive to cold, they may be damaged by late frost. Over summer, the fertilized female flowers develop into prickly brown balls 1 to 1½ inches in diameter, laden with seed-bearing fruits. As do the seeds of maples, those of the sweet-gum have papery wings: they look like miniature tadpoles with big tails. The wind disperses them, and most fall to earth within 200 feet of the parent tree. Sweet-gums start bearing seeds when twenty to thirty years old. Most trees produce some seeds every year and bumper crops about every third year. The seedheads often dangle in the trees in the winter, after the seeds have fallen.

A few animals eat the seeds, including these birds: goldfinch, purple finch, yellow-shafted flicker, yellow-bellied sapsucker, black-capped chickadee, white-throated sparrow, eastern towhee, Carolina wren, mallard, bobwhite quail, and wild turkey. Chipmunks, squirrels, and mice forage for the seeds. Sapsuckers excavate feeding wells in sweet-gum bark. Mice and rabbits nibble on seedlings, and beavers cut and eat the bark and smaller twigs.

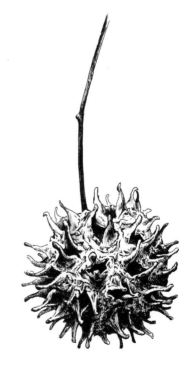

At various times during the twentieth century, sweet-gum has been a major commercial hardwood in the Southeast, second in production only to the oaks, with most of the logging conducted in Louisiana and Mississippi. At 37 pounds per cubic foot, the wood is fairly heavy. The heartwood is pink or ruddy, the sapwood pale. Some uses of sweet-gum are plebeian: boxes, crates, barrels, railroad ties, plywood, paper pulp. The grain is attractive, and the wood also finds application in inte-

The prickly fruits of sweet-gum contain many small winged seeds.

rior finish work and as a veneer for furniture and cabinets. In an odd twist, sweet-gum has been exported to Europe, stained and used as a veneer to dress up chairs and tables, and sent back to this country as antique mahogany, rosewood, or Circassian walnut.

If its bark is breached, a sweet-gum will seal the wound with thick sap that hardens and weathers to a sticky golden or brown gum. The tree's common name stems from this sweet-smelling repair agent. *Liquidambar,* the name assigned to the sweet-gum's genus by Linnaeus, describes the aroma of the substance and its resemblance to amber. The first reference to the tree in the New World came from the journals of Don Bernal Díaz Castillo; he wrote of the ceremonial meeting, in 1519, between the Spanish conquistador Cortés and the Aztec emperor Montezuma II, who smoked sweet-gum resin mixed with tobacco in a highly ornate pipe. The fragrance reminded Castillo of incense used in Spanish churches—incense made from the aromatic gum of a Middle Eastern tree also in the *Liquidambar* genus.

Pioneers in the southeastern colonies used the "liquid amber" as a chewing gum, an antiseptic, and a base for homemade medicines. During the Civil War, doctors in the Confederate forces treated dysentery with it. In more modern times, people have tapped the trees for the gum, employing it in the manufacture of salves, adhesives, perfuming powders, soaps, and tobacco flavoring.

Sweet-gum is a hardy tree, seemingly not very palatable to insects, and resistant to most diseases. Its defenses have been forged in the furnace of evolution: twenty extinct species of sweet-gum have been identified from fossils worldwide. Paleobotanists consider *Liquidambar styraciflua* an ancient species, along with tuliptree and the magnolias, remnants of the primitive deciduous forest that emerged during the Cretaceous Period between 135 million and 65 million years before the present, a span during which dinosaurs disappeared and flowering plants began to develop.

SYCAMORE

To the sycamore *(Platanus occidentalis)* goes the title of the most massive tree in eastern North America. In the 1700s, George Washington, and then twenty years later, botanist André Michaux, each measured the same old-growth sycamore on an island in the Ohio River. It was 40 feet, 4 inches, around the trunk, or about 13 feet in diameter. The age of that mammoth is not recorded, but sycamores can live for five or six centuries.

Today great sycamores still stand rooted in the land, perhaps not quite as gargantuan as that Ohio specimen, but giant trees nonetheless. Consider the one near Licking Creek, Franklin County, on the farm of Lester Risser: at 1 1/2 feet above the ground, it is 31 feet in circumference; above that height, it divides into four stems, each the size of a rightful tree; its uttermost twigs reach 106 feet into the air; and its canopy stretches across 122 feet. People have measured sycamores 168 feet tall. Most are probably 70 to 100 feet in height, and the average trunk diameter is 3 feet.

Platanus occidentalis ranges from southern Maine and Ontario west to eastern Nebraska, and south to northern Florida and eastern Texas, with scattered specimens in the mountains of Mexico. Sycamores occur in every state east of the Great Plains except Minnesota. The tree achieves its greatest size in the alluvial soils of the Ohio and Mississippi river drainages. In Pennsylvania, sycamore is statewide and common in all regions except the extreme north-central. It thrives in deep, moist, well-drained soils but also can grow on drier sites. In the wild, look for sycamores along streams, rivers, lakes, and in old fields in areas with a reliable supply of groundwater. Sycamores grow singly or in small groups, rarely in extensive pure stands.

On stream banks and small islands, sycamores often shade out and replace pioneering shrubby trees such as alders and the smaller willows, especially after the soils that collect on those sites have been stabilized by the shrubby trees' roots and risen to become well-drained. Sycamores grow rapidly and sometimes reach 70 feet after only twenty years. In its favored bottomland habitat, *Platanus occidentalis* keeps company with American elm, green ash, silver maple, black walnut, hackberry, eastern cottonwood, black willow, and river birch.

The most striking characteristic of a mature sycamore is its bark: brown at the base of the trunk, and

The dappled, peeling bark of sycamore is a good identification mark for the tree, which usually grows along rivers and streams. Wood ducks nest in cavities in the trunks of older specimens.

above that, mottled with patches of white, lemon, tan, and pale green. The crazy-quilt colors show through where flat, irregularly shaped scraps of the outer bark have fallen off, or exfoliated. The upper bole and branches are often a smooth, grayish white: a sycamore standing in a foggy bottom looks like a forest specter raising its arms in the air. The bark of very young trees is thin and smooth; the flaking commences when the tree is about four years old. As a sycamore ages, its crown becomes deep and broad, composed of many wide-spreading, crooked branches.

Sycamore leaves look much like maple leaves. They are large and coarse, usually 4 to 10 inches long and 6 to 8 inches across, bright green above, and pale green and covered with fine hairs on the underside. The hairs are light and sharp, and when they fall off as the leaf matures, they irritate the lungs of some people. The leaves have three to nine lobes and prominent veins, and are toothed along the margin. In autumn, they turn dull yellow or tan before falling. I like to sit by a slow stream in late October and watch the sycamore leaves float past; sodden ones can just be glimpsed ghosting along underwater.

A sycamore's sturdy, spreading root system makes it fairly wind-firm, able to resist strong blasts without toppling. If young sycamores are cut down, they sprout from the stump. Slips or cuttings from vigorous stems send out roots and may grow into new trees. My favorite story about this sort of reproduction concerns the Rodman Sycamore near Bristol in Bucks County. When William Rodman was a young man, around 1745, he plucked up a little sycamore to use as a riding whip. Finishing his ride, he stuck it into the ground next to a spring. The tree supposed to have grown from that riding crop became a leviathan with a girth of 29 feet, 4 inches; a storm felled it in 1984, 239 years after it was planted.

In May, along with the leaves, sycamores send forth flowers. Each tree produces both male and female blossoms, borne on separate stalks. Female flowers are yellowish green, male flowers are dark red, and neither is at all conspicuous. The wind pollinates the female blossoms, which, by October, mature into ball-shaped composite fruits about an inch in diameter, dangling from slender stalks. A fruit is made up of many closely packed achenes: one-seeded, thin-walled nutlets about 3/4 inch long. The fruits break up during winter or the following spring; wind scatters the nutlets, which have small tufts of hair that act as parachutes. Seeds are also carried away by running water, to be washed up on stream banks, mudflats, and sandbars. Seeds and seedlings need direct sunlight to germinate and grow.

The seeds are not highly sought after by animals. Purple finches and goldfinches eat some, as do squirrels. Far more important to wildlife are the trunk cavities that develop in mature sycamores. Squirrels, opossums, and raccoons shelter in and nest inside these nooks. Bats and swarms of honeybees house themselves in the holes. Owls and woodpeckers nest there. Several times I've been startled by a wood duck launching into flight out of a cavity in a sycamore, where the species often nests; soon after hatching, the ducklings jump out and float down like tiny balls of cotton, to a relatively soft landing on water or earth 20 or more feet below.

Never have I witnessed a spectacle like the one John James Audubon saw while traveling through the wilds of Kentucky in the early nineteenth century. One evening, the bird artist watched thousands of chimney swifts—he called them "swallows"—pouring themselves into a hollow sycamore. "I remained," he wrote, "my head leaning on the tree, listening to the roaring noise made within by the birds as they settled and arranged themselves, until it was quite dark." He likened the rushing sound to "a large wheel revolving under a powerful stream."

Early settlers took advantage of the sycamore's propensity to become hollow with age. The pioneers might stable livestock in the heart of a monster tree, or take up house-keeping inside the great trunk until a cabin could be built. Saw off a section of hollow trunk, nail a bottom onto it, and you've got yourself a cask. Tubs, troughs, cisterns, and containers of all sorts were fashioned out of hollow portions of sycamores. Sound logs were sawn into cart wheels: the wood is extremely tough, its interlocking fibers preventing it from splitting. Native Americans made dugout canoes from sycamores; one such vessel is said to have been 65 feet long and capable of carrying 9,000 pounds.

Sycamore wood weighs about 34 pounds per cubic foot. The sapwood is white or yellow, and the heartwood is light brown to reddish brown. In recent times, people have used sycamore for food containers, furniture, fence posts, railroad ties, pallets, broom handles, butcher blocks, barber poles, flooring, paper pulp, and plywood. Sycamore is widely planted as a shade tree. But *Platanus occidentalis* can get too big to comfortably stand between sidewalk and street; thus the sycamore seen in an urban setting may well be a cultivated variety or a hybrid London planetree, slightly smaller than our native species. The planetree has the added advantage of resisting anthracnose, a fungal disease that kills the leaves and twigs of sycamores. Sycamores can tolerate pollution and compacted soil, adding to their popularity as city trees.

Sycamore goes by several names: buttonwood and buttonball, on account of its round fruit; American planetree; water beech; and whitewood. The name sycamore might seem to have an Indian ring to it, but the word can be traced back through Latin and Greek; it describes a kind of fig tree. Our native species may have gotten its title from colonists who noted a resemblance between its leaves and those of sycamore maple, an unrelated tree in England.

HAWTHORNS

Hawthorns (*Crataegus* species), also called thornapples, are large shrubs that sometimes achieve the size and spread of small trees. It's not certain how many species exist in North America. Some taxonomists name around a hundred; others cite a thousand or more. Hawthorns hybridize readily, blending their leaf shapes and flowering and fruiting characteristics, making positive identification of many species impossible for amateur naturalists and extremely difficult even for professionals. In *The Vascular Flora of Pennsylvania,* Ann Rhoads and William Klein chose to map the ranges of various hawthorns "at the level of broad species complexes."

Key identification marks for the group are their long, slender, sharp-tipped thorns; their leaves, variable in shape but generally small, oval, saw-toothed, and often with distinct side lobes; their clusters of fingertip-size apples that are usually red but in some species ripen to orange, yellow, or dark blue to almost black; and their preferred habitats of woods edges, old fields, and fencerows. People have also planted hawthorns widely as ornamentals and hedges.

Hawthorns are closely related to mountain-ash, shadbush, crabapples, apples, cherries, and plums. The genus *Crataegus* has the center of its distribution in eastern North America. Some botanists theorize that the vast numbers of hawthorn species arose after Europeans settled the continent, cutting old-growth forests and converting land to agriculture. Uncountable acres of new open habitat let hawthorns spread widely and hybridize freely.

As handsome as hawthorn fruits appear, they don't seem overly attractive to wildlife. Because their fat content is low (1 to 2 percent, by weight), they do not provide much caloric value. Ruffed grouse, cedar waxwings, and fox sparrows eat the fruits, and perhaps other birds as well. Hawthorns are of greater value to wildlife as cover: predator-proof habitats in which to breed and rest. Many songbirds build their nests in the crowns of these dense, thorny plants. Of course, hawthorns did not evolve their thorns to protect birds' nests. The plants grow clustered together, and their inter-

The thorns of the hawthorns deter animals from browsing on the trees' foliage.

meshed branches form a phalanx of spiky armor to deter mammals, such as deer, from eating the shrubs' foliage.

I have long been fascinated by the names given to some of the hawthorn species: Brainerd's hawthorn, *Crataegus brainerdii,* honors its discoverer, Ezra Brainerd, a Vermont botanist and president of Middlebury College. Pear hawthorn, *Crataegus calpodendron,* puts forth pear-shaped fruit. Biltmore hawthorn, *Crataegus intricata,* is named for an estate in North Carolina where early studies of hawthorns were conducted. Downy hawthorn, *Crataegus mollis,* has leaves densely covered by white hairs; it is one of the largest hawthorns, occasionally reaching 40 feet in height. Washington hawthorn, *Crataegus phaenopyrum,* was introduced in the early nineteenth century into Pennsylvania from the Washington, D.C., area as a hedge plant. Frosted hawthorn, *Crataegus pruinosa,* produces fruit cloaked with a glaucous bloom, like a plum's.

Two of the most common—and most treelike—hawthorns in Pennsylvania are cockspur hawthorn and red-fruited hawthorn.

Cockspur Hawthorn *(Crataegus crus-galli).* Both the common and the species names refer to the sharp spines bristling from this small tree. Cockspur hawthorn ranges from southern Canada to northern Florida and west to Iowa and Texas. In Pennsylvania, it is most abundant in the eastern and southern regions, spotty and local elsewhere. *Crataegus crus-galli* thrives on limestone soil and often grows in extensive thickets. When naturalists fight their way into these fastnesses, they pay for their temerity with numerous scratches and punctures.

A broad, exceedingly thorny plant, cockspur hawthorn can grow 25 to 30 feet tall, with a trunk diameter of 10 to 12 inches. The short trunk usually divides into several stout, spreading branches that form a dense, flattish crown whose width can equal or exceed the tree's height. The dark gray or brownish bark is stippled with small scales, and spines project from trunk and branches. The reddish brown spines or thorns are long, slender, and needle-sharp. The alternate, simple leaves are spoon-shaped or narrowly elliptical, broadening from a narrow base to become widest beyond their middle portion. They have saw-toothed margins, usually are not lobed, and grow 1 to 3 inches long. Thick and leathery, they glint a shiny dark green above, and their pale undersurfaces have conspicuous veins. In autumn, the leaves turn orange or red.

Cockspur hawthorn flowers in late May or June, after its leaves have emerged. With their five white petals, the flowers look like miniature apple blossoms. They are about 2/3 inch in diameter and, like the flowers of all hawthorns, include both male and female reproductive structures. Their fruit ripens in August and September and often hangs on into winter. The tiny apples are about 1/4 inch long, greenish to dark dull red, and grouped in drooping clusters. Each hard, dry fruit has a thin pulp and one or two nutlets.

Crataegus crus-galli has been planted and groomed as a hedge since colonial days. The wood is hard and dense, weighing 45 pounds per cubic foot. People have used it for fence posts and tool handles and burned it as fuel. The long spines made pins for closing the mouths of cloth sacks.

Red-fruited Hawthorn *(Crataegus coccinea).* Although red-fruited hawthorn can grow 30 feet tall, it rarely exceeds 20 feet. The maximum trunk diameter is 10 to 12 inches. The trunk is short, giving way to spreading, crooked branches that support a flat, broad crown.

The species ranges from southern Canada south through New York and Pennsylvania to North Carolina; it grows west to Minnesota and Iowa. In Pennsylvania, red-fruited hawthorn is statewide. It grows in open woods and fields and along road edges and stream banks. Joseph Illick, in *Pennsylvania Trees,* cited "rocky woods and old pastures with sandy or gravelly soil" as primary habitats; he considered red-fruited hawthorn to be less common in southwestern and northern Pennsylvania than in other parts of the state.

The bark is variously described as red-brown and scaly, and light brown to ashy gray and roughened by shallow fissures and small scales. The stiff, rounded twigs sprout wicked thorns about 2 inches long; the thorns are straight, whereas those of most thornapples are curved. The leaves are 1 to 5 inches in length, broadly oval in shape, with pointed tips and rounded bases. Their margins are deeply toothed. Four or five lobes often project on each side of the blade from midleaf outward. The flowers open around June, when the leaves are almost fully developed. They are white and between 1/2 and 1 inch in diameter. Their odor, said to be unpleasant to human sensibilities, does not put off insect pollinators. The brilliant red fruit is about 1/2 inch in diameter and elliptical in shape; dry and mealy at first, it becomes more succulent as it ripens from August through September.

Also known as scarlet hawthorn, *Crataegus coccinea* was one of three North American hawthorns first described by Linnaeus in 1753, from specimens sent to Uppsala, the university where he taught in Sweden. Illick described the wood as heavier and more valuable than that of cockspur hawthorn and reported its use in the early twentieth century for making canes, napkin rings, engraving blocks, and rulers.

MOUNTAIN-ASH

Here and there on the long mountain ridges near my home, boulder fields interrupt the woods. The sun beats down on those dry, severe places, where rattlesnakes bask on the pale jumbled slabs, where ravens croak as they glide past overhead, and where the views stretch for miles across the staid agricultural lowlands of Pennsylvania's Ridge and Valley physiographic province. Geologists refer to these rocky mini-wildernesses as talus slopes. White pines and occasionally Table Mountain pines stand as green sentinels on the hogback ridges; and amid the boulders, or on the edge of the surrounding oak-and-maple woods, small mountain-ash trees raise their meager stems toward the sun.

American mountain-ash *(Sorbus americana),* also called American rowan, is hardly an impressive tree, but it offers color and interest in all seasons. Its leaves appear in May and are soon followed by flat-topped sprays of creamy white flowers that almost match the old bone color of the exposed quartzite rocks. In summer, when heat waves shimmer above the boulders, the deep yellow-green leaves stand out in verdant splendor. By autumn, when the leaves turn golden yellow, the flowers have become bright red fruits. If birds don't eat them, the fruits hang on the branches into winter, contrasting vividly with the somber hues of bare trees, stormy skies, and snow filling the gaps between the rocks.

American mountain-ash is unrelated to the ash trees of genus *Fraxinus,* which are common in Penn's Woods. Mountain-ash can be a shrub with several stems rising from the same root system, or a small tree, rarely topping 20 feet, with an 8- to 12-inch trunk diameter. The biggest mountain-ashes rise to 50 or 60 feet tall and have a 2-foot trunk diameter; the reigning national champion is in West Virginia. *Sorbus americana* ranges from Newfoundland west to Manitoba and Minnesota, throughout much of New England, and south in the Appalachians to North Carolina. In Pennsylvania, it grows in the mountains, mainly in the south-central, north-central, and northeastern regions.

The compound leaves are 6 to 10 inches in length, each composed of thirteen to seventeen leaflets; the leaflets are 2 to 4 inches long and up to an inch in width, lance-shaped and with toothed margins. They grow outward from a central stem, or rachis. The twigs are stout, grayish to reddish brown, hairy when young, and marked by large leaf scars; the short trunk ends in a narrow, straggling crown. The thin, light gray bark varies from smooth to slightly scaly.

I have often met with mountain-ash in its rocky ridgetop setting, and I've encountered it along the edges of bogs and swamps. It also grows in cool, moist woods openings and along the banks of lakes and streams. Mountain-ash favors acidic soil. It occurs singly or in small groups, along with other shrubs and trees that prefer the additional light that bathes the forest's edge. *Sorbus americana* is slow-growing and fairly short-lived. Moderately shade-tolerant, it can hang on for a time after taller trees rob it of direct sunlight.

In spring, up to a hundred pale blossoms open on each upward-facing flower panicle; often a mountain-ash will put out several such inflorescences, each 3 to 5 inches across. An individual flower is 1/8 to 1/4 inch in diameter and has five petals. The flowers contain both male and female reproductive organs. They attract insects that inadvertently transfer pollen from the male to the female structures. In *The Trees in My Forest,* which sets down observations made on his wooded land in Maine, the ecologist Bernd Heinrich writes concerning the long-horned beetles of family Lepturinae: "There are

Cedar waxwings feed on the fruits of the mountain ash.

250 different species of this relatively small group. . . . In the spring dozens of different ones crawl and feed in the flowers of the mountain ash nearby, undoubtedly pollinating them. By taking part in the life cycle of these trees they ensure plenty of red berries that feed migrant flocks of cedar and Bohemian waxwings in the fall."

Each berry is technically a pome: a miniature apple about the size of a pea. The fruit's pulp is bitter, and it has a low fat content, perhaps explaining why the pomes are not a favored treat for birds. However, since the fruits persist into winter, foraging birds often get around to feeding on them after they have cleaned up other foods. In addition to waxwings, the following birds eat mountain-ash fruits: ruffed grouse, yellow-bellied flycatcher, thrushes, and grosbeaks. Sometimes the fruits ferment on the stem, and the birds get an alcoholic jolt from consuming them. Martens and fishers are also reported to eat the fruit, and moose browse on the foliage, twigs, and inner bark.

The wood weighs 34 pounds per cubic foot, and I have found not a single reference to any commercial, practical, or even whimsical use. In my mind, the tree is singularly valuable because it enlivens those bare-bones ridges near my home, and because it contributes such pretty white flowers and cheery red pomes.

CRABAPPLE

Some autumns here in the valley, fallen crabapples lie so abundantly beneath the shrubby trees that they make the footing treacherous, there on the damp streamside land that was once pasture and now is gradually reverting to forest. It's like walking on marbles or ball bearings, as I hunt through the thickets in search of the ruffed grouse and woodcock that sometimes can be found there. In other years, I pass by dozens of crabapple trees without finding more than a handful of the small, pale green fruits. It depends, I would imagine, on the kind of spring we had, whether the bees did their job of pollination or rain kept them inactive, whether late frost nipped the trees' showy flowers.

The range of American crabapple *(Malus coronaria)* centers on southern Michigan, Indiana, and Ohio; it extends east across Pennsylvania, south in the Appalachians to North Carolina, west to Arkansas, and north to parts of New York and southern Ontario. In the mid-1700s, Peter Kalm, a pupil of the great classifier Linnaeus, traveled in Pennsylvania, New York, New Jersey, and southern Canada, collecting plants to take back to Sweden; he reported that wild crabapples were plentiful in William Penn's colony. Today the American crabapple is found throughout Pennsylvania, with the possible exception of the state's northeast corner.

Crabapples grow in rich, moist soil of old fields, fencerows, and woods edges. A mature tree can reach 25 to 30 feet tall, with a trunk 6 to 14 inches in diameter. The short, stout trunk usually forks within a foot or two of the ground, dividing and broadening into a crown of slender, crooked branches, which gives the tree a fairly open, round-topped form. Many crabapples are hunched and shrubby. The twigs, after they are a year old, sprout stubby spurs and sharp spines. Exploring in crabapple thickets, I have driven those spines through my cap and into the top of my head. In general, the thorns on crabapples are not as profuse as those of the hawthorns, shrubs and small trees that are closely related to *Malus coronaria.* Crabapple and hawthorn, along with serviceberry, apple, plum, cherry, and mountain-ash, are members of Rosaceae, the rose family.

The outermost bark layers of American crabapple are gray and scaly; vertical cracks often reveal reddish brown inner layers. The leaves are about 1^1/2 inches wide by 2 to 5 inches long. Usually they are oval or elliptical, with rounded bases, pointed tips, and toothed margins. Leaves on young twigs may have triangular lobes and coarser teeth. The leaves are dark green above and paler green below. Leaf-bearing twigs do not stand opposite each other, but alternate along the stem. American crabapples leaf out later in the spring than domesticated apple trees, and they drop their leaves earlier in autumn. When I visited a thicket on August 31 to obtain foliage specimens, I found that about a quarter of the trees' leaves had already turned yellow, and some had fallen. It was a drought year, and the lack of soil moisture may have contributed to the early color change and leaf fall.

Crabapples bloom in spring after the leaves are almost fully developed, around May or June in Pennsylvania. The five-petaled flowers are pink or white, about 1 1/2 inches across, and look much like the blossoms of domesticated apples trees, although the crabs' flowers are usually pinker and more colorful. The flowers appear in clusters; their perfume draws in pollinating insects. Crabapple used to be called the garlandtree for its comely blossoms, which were woven into garlands for the May queens who reigned over vernal celebrations of an earlier age.

The fruits ripen around October. Yellowish green and fragrant, the apples are about an inch in diameter, or a bit larger, and hang on long, slender stems. Beneath the waxy outer skin lies pale flesh that is heavily loaded with malic acid, which gives the fruits an extremely sour taste. Why the name crabapple? According to the *Oxford English Dictionary*, it may derive from *skrabba*, a Norse word for the fruit of the wild apple tree. Or it may come from *crab*, as

Deer, raccoons, foxes, birds, and other wildlife eat the fruits of American crabapple, which may hang on the branches into winter.

used to describe a nasty person: "A fruit externally promising," says the *OED*, but "crabbed and ill-conditioned in quality."

In times past, the fruit was used for cider, perhaps of an inferior sort: the eighteenth-century French botanist and explorer André Michaux wrote that he pitied Americans for never having tasted cider made from fine Normandy apples. If enough sugar is added, crabapples make a lovely orange-red jelly; ample natural pectin in the fruit ensures that the preparation will set. Foragers also transform the hard miniature pomes into spiced fruit, sweet butters, and chutney.

At least some of the year's fruit crop remains hanging on the branches through winter, and I often find crabapples that have fallen and become impaled on thorns lower down in the tree. Even on the ground, the apples may not rot until the following spring. Deer, raccoons, skunks, foxes, and birds feed on them. I have not found evidence of grouse eating crabapples, but the birds certainly hide beneath the tangled, overarching limbs, and when they flush, they tend to do so from the far side of the concealing trees—so that I hear them but fail to see them. Songbirds of many species nest and roost in the crowded, leafy crowns. On my late-August foliage-collecting trip, I spotted black-capped chickadees preening the bark of crabapple limbs, seeking insect prey. A pair of small flycatchers perched in one crab and made short forays to catch insects fluttering past. And a band of a half dozen warblers fed actively among the foliage and twigs of several of the trees.

The trunk of the crabapple is too small to provide much useful wood. The heartwood is brown to light red, the sapwood thick and yellow. Dried, the wood weighs 44 pounds per cubic foot. Although it is dense and hard, carvers can work with it, and people have fashioned it into tool handles and woodenware. A friend gave me a cane made from a knobbly, burl-tipped stem, and I have known people to make hiking sticks from the ruddy wood. Orchardists sometimes graft cultivated apples onto the hardy, disease-resistant rootstock and trunk.

SHADBUSH

Three times a year, this small, unobtrusive tree strongly states its presence. In April, its gauzy blossoms are some of the first arboreal flowers to brighten the winter-drab woods. In June and July, its early-ripening fruit attracts many wild foragers—and a few human ones, as well. And in October, its bright yellow-to-red foliage becomes part of the grand and colorful mosaic that is the eastern deciduous forest.

Shadbush *(Amelanchier arborea),* also known as juneberry, generally grows 10 to 25 feet high and has a trunk 6 to 12 inches in diameter—"a tall, gangly shrub, reaching up for sunlight," is how the naturalist Hal Borland described shadbush. Specimens on excellent sites can become 40 feet tall or taller and have a 2-foot trunk diameter. Three such trees, all in northern Pennsylvania—in McKean, Clarion, and Clinton counties—are currently recognized as cochampions in the Big Tree Program sponsored by the Pennsylvania Forestry Association; they range in height from 42 to 64 feet.

Amelanchier arborea occurs from Nova Scotia west to Minnesota and south to Florida and Oklahoma. A fairly common tree in the Northeast, it is statewide in Pennsylvania and most abundant in the mountains. Don't search for groves of this species: it usually stands as a solitary tree in the forest understory, or as a clump of several individuals. Look for it in dry and moist habitats along the borders of woods and the edges of woods roads, in thickets, on stream banks, and on cliffs. On our land, a few shadbush trees are scattered in among red maples, chestnut oaks, and red oaks. Botanists have long puzzled over whether there are many different shadbush species or a range of variable and hybridized forms best regarded as a single species. Shadbush belongs to the family Rosaceae, which includes hawthorns, plums, apples, cherries, and mountain-ashes.

Shadbush possesses alternate leaves: arranged along the twig not opposite each other, but staggered back and forth, one on the left, the next a bit farther along on the right, and so on. The leaves, around 3 inches long, have saw-toothed edges and sharp-pointed tips; sometimes they show a heart-shaped base. They are dull green above and paler beneath. The trunk is usually straight and slender, with little taper—although the specimens in our woods, straining to get sunlight, twist and turn as they ascend. The bark is gray and fairly smooth; with age, it develops shallow furrows and low, narrow ridges running vertically on the trunk, taking on a marbled appearance as gray and black areas interlace. The crown is shallow and narrow, with numerous fine sprays of branchlets. In winter, the bark is a good identification mark, as are the dormant leaf buds: long and pointed, shaped much like those of the American beech, often two-toned red and green, and covered with numerous overlapping scales.

Early settlers bestowed the name shadbush, and also shadblow: when the tree's flowers burst forth in April, people knew it was time to go to rivers and streams and set nets for the shad swimming up from the Atlantic to spawn. The flowers are white, about 1 1/4 inches across, and airy looking with their five thin blades. They hang in drooping clusters. They produce a sweet nectar, a perfume easily enjoyed by standing downwind of the tree on a breezy day. The flowers are perfect, equipped with both male and female parts. Insects, mainly small wild bees, pollinate them. Some trees bear great masses of the showy blooms, which appear before the leaves come out.

Shadbush lives up to its alternate name, Juneberry, by yielding berries in June, as well as in July in Pennsylvania. The fruits look like tiny apples about 1/4 or 1/3 inch across. A rich maroon or purple color, sometimes they have a whitish bloom on the surface. Their insides are stocked with many small, rather soft seeds. Fruits from some trees are dry and bland; other trees bear juicy, sweet pomes.

While working in the woods in McKean County many years ago, I happened onto a shadbush that a bear had worked over. The bruin's claw marks cross-hatched the 15-foot tree, and the bear had broken many branches, and pulled them inward to its perch, to get at every last fruit. Birds flock to ripe shadbushes: gray catbird, brown thrasher, mockingbird, robin, thrushes, cedar waxwing, towhee, titmouse, blue jay, crow, woodpeckers, flicker, wild turkey, ring-necked pheasant, ruffed grouse—the list goes on and on. In addition to bears, mammals ranging from chipmunks to foxes relish the fruit. Both mammals and birds disperse the trees' seeds in their droppings. Deer, elk, moose, rabbits, and snowshoe hares browse on twigs and foliage.

Native Americans of many tribes ate the berries and blended the dried fruits into venison and bear meat in making pemmican. The fruits are excellent as preserves and as pie filling; Juneberry pie is said to taste like sweet cherry. The central Pennsylvania forager Euell Gibbons wrote in *Stalking the Wild Asparagus,* "I'm sure that God put Juneberries on earth for the use of man, as well as for the bears, raccoons and birds. Let's get our share!" I applaud his sentiment but usually find that the wildlife have beaten me to the punch.

An old rural name for the plant is serviceberry, sometimes rendered "sarviss." Sarviss is thought to be the original form, derived from *sorbus,* a

Latin taxonomic name for the related mountain-ash. A more colorful story holds that "service" refers to memorial services that circuit preachers performed in spring, around the time of the shadbushes' blossoming, to commemorate settlers who had died during the preceding winter.

Shadbush grows slowly and lays down hard, strong, close-grained wood. At 49 pounds per cubic foot, it is one of the densest of the eastern hardwoods. The wood, dark brown and often tinged with red, tends to develops checks, or cracks, and to warp badly as it cures. Indians fashioned it into lance shafts, and settlers used it for tool handles. According to *Native Trees of Canada,* published by the Forestry Branch of the Canadian government, the wood is "sold in small quantities as 'lancewood' for fishing rods." Shadbush and several related species are used for ornamental plantings and as grafting stock for pears and quince shrubs.

Other *Amelanchier* Species. Most taxonomists recognize several shadbush relatives in Pennsylvania and the Northeast. These small trees and shrubs have white flowers in early spring that develop into edible fruits by summer. The following descriptions represent recent thinking on the different species, as presented in *The Plants of Pennsylvania,* by Ann Fowler Rhoads and Timothy A. Block, and in *A Field Guide to Eastern Trees,* by George A. Petrides:

Smooth shadbush, *Amelanchier laevis,* occurs in rocky woods and thickets and on roadside banks throughout Pennsylvania. It is an erect shrub or a tree up to 40 feet tall.

Mountain juneberry, *Amelanchier bartramiana,* also called oblong-fruited serviceberry, grows to a shrubby 6-foot height. A rare plant, it inhabits sphagnum bogs and peaty thickets in Pennsylvania's northeastern and north-central counties.

Oblongleaf juneberry, *Amelanchier canadensis,* is a coastal plain species. In Pennsylvania, it is limited to the southeastern counties, where, depending on site conditions, it may become a small tree 25 feet tall.

Low juneberry, *Amelanchier humilis,* is a rare colonial shrub that prefers dry, open sites and bluffs.

BLACK CHERRY

My college roommate's father was a farmer in Sugar Valley in southern Clinton County. Noah Shreckengast cut black cherry trees on his mountain land and stacked the boards in his barn to cure. He died before he could build the new house he envisioned, which would have been paneled with cherry. Some years later, I bought the boards and hired a master woodworker to craft them into a bed, a blanket chest, and kitchen cabinets. Those furnishings are the crowning touches in our home, their dovetailed notches exact, the wood aged to a deep, glowing red that grows richer and more beautiful with each passing year.

Along with black walnut, black cherry *(Prunus serotina)* is one of the preeminent hardwoods in Pennsylvania and the Northeast. *Prunus serotina,* wild black cherry, is the largest tree among the North American cherry species. It ranges from Nova Scotia to Florida in the east, and in the west from Minnesota south through eastern Kansas to Texas, with a closely related race in Mexico and Central America. Black cherry is statewide in Pennsylvania; the tallest, straightest trees—which yield the most valuable lumber—come from even-aged stands in the northern tier of counties, including the Allegheny

The bark of a mature black cherry breaks up into small irregular plates with brittle edges. The illustration also shows typical leaves and fruit.

Plateau. Black cherry thrives on rich, moist soils of bottomlands and slopes. It also grows on dry, rocky sites that are poorer in nutrients.

Forest-grown trees have narrow, irregular crowns. Often they are quite straight, with a long trunk clear of branches for half its length. A tree on a good site can top 100 feet in height, but demand for cherry wood is so great that few trees achieve such stature. A typical mature specimen stands 60 to 75 feet tall, with a trunk diameter of 2 to 3 feet. In old-growth stands in the Tionesta Scenic Area of the Allegheny National Forest in northwestern Pennsylvania, foresters have documented black cherries over 130 feet tall.

The bark on young trees is smooth, glossy, and reddish brown, with whitish horizontal lenticels. As a tree ages, its bark thickens and becomes dark gray, breaking up into small, irregular plates whose brittle edges jut out from the trunk. The simple, alternate leaves are lance-shaped with small marginal teeth and pointed tips. They are 2 to 5 inches long. Their upper surfaces are dark glossy green; the undersurfaces are light green, and small hairs may coat the midrib on the bottom side, especially near the leaf base. The leaves turn reddish or yellow in autumn.

In May or June, after the leaves have pushed forth, multiple flowers bloom on a drooping stem, called a raceme, about the length of a human's finger. The individual flowers are white, 1/4 inch in diameter, and fragrant. Insects pollinate them; many forest-dwelling solitary bee species visit black cherry for the flowers' nectar. Over summer, the blossoms develop into pea-size cherries. The fruits are dark red, turning purple-black as they ripen, from August 15 through early September on the Allegheny Plateau. Ripening dates are earlier to the south, later to the north. The cherries consist of a thin pulp with a hard pit. The pulp has a slightly bitter taste and is mouth-puckering sour, although the fruit, with sugar added, makes an excellent jelly. Most trees fruit abundantly every third or fourth year. After falling, the seeds remain viable in the leaf litter for up to two years.

I have never figured out an easy way of gaining access to good quantities of black cherries, but birds and other wild creatures certainly have. No less than seventy bird species are known to feed on black cherries. Ruffed grouse and wild turkeys pick fallen cherries off the ground; woodpeckers, thrushes, cedar waxwings, grosbeaks, and others home in on cherry-laden tree crowns. In autumn, I have spotted robins flying haphazardly, gaining a perch with much awkward wing flapping, and sitting perched or on the ground in an apparent stupor, having intoxicated themselves by eating over-ripe, fermented cherries. Birds disperse cherry pits in their droppings or by regurgitating them. A pit that has gone through a bird's digestive system has an improved likelihood of germinating.

Black bears and raccoons claw their way into trees, sometimes breaking branches in their eagerness to get at the fruit. Foxes, chipmunks, mice, rabbits, and squirrels eat fallen cherries. Voles gnaw on cherry bark in winter, and cottontails nibble on the seedlings. Deer browse the leaves and twigs, even though they contain bitter-tasting cyanide compounds. In areas with too many deer, their browsing may destroy black cherry seedlings, but deer cannot subsist solely on black cherry browse. Cherry foliage can poison domestic livestock.

Black cherry often grows mixed in with oaks, maples, white ash, American elm, yellow birch, and basswood. Young cherry trees are fast-growing, and they thrive along the sunlit edges of forests and in small openings where large trees have fallen. They also grow, albeit more slowly, in the shady understory of mature woodlands. As cherry trees age, they become less tolerant of shade. Cherries have roots that spread rather than go deep, and strong winds sometimes fell the trees. Cherries often lift their crowns above the general canopy in mixed-species stands, making them vulnerable to storm breakage. Wildfires and logging stimulate trees to send up new shoots from the base of the trunk and from the stump. Black cherries can live 150 to 200 years, with some old-growth specimens exceeding 250 years.

Eastern tent caterpillars often build their weblike communal nests in the forks and crotches of black cherries. They represent one of more than two hundred species of butterfly and moth caterpillars that feed primarily on the foliage of *Prunus serotina*. Tiger swallowtail caterpillars shelter in silk-spun nests inside folded-up cherry leaves. Cecropia moth larvae anchor their brown, bag-shaped cocoons to cherry twigs. Gypsy moths, which evolved in Eurasia, refuse to eat cherry foliage even when their populations peak and the caterpillars go starving.

Early settlers used to mix juice from black cherries with rum or brandy to make a drink known as cherry bounce. The tree's bark and leaves contain hydrocyanic (prussic) acid, used in modern cough medicines.

The wood is considered weak—not recommended for structural framing members—and medium hard. It weighs 35 pounds per cubic foot. Cherry has been used for tool handles and the casings of scientific instruments and spirit levels: the wood is stable and, once cured, unlikely to warp. It has a fine, even texture, usually without much figure or obvious grain, but sometimes—as on a friend's recently laid floor—marked with a striking grain pattern, a glowing quilted aspect, or bird's-eye speckles. The wood can be polished to a fine luster. Black cherry is in high demand for use as interior trim, cabinetry, and furniture. In today's market, a large veneer-quality tree can fetch several thousand dollars.

The legendary pioneer Daniel Boone is said to have fashioned a series of black cherry caskets for his eventual ultimate rest. As an elderly man, he occasionally slept in one at night. He gave them away to friends, all but the last one.

PIN CHERRY

Pin cherry *(Prunus pensylvanica)*—also known as fire cherry or bird cherry—is one of twenty-seven species of native trees that I have found on our thirty acres of woodland, just downslope from the long, high bluff known as the Allegheny Front. Several of these small trees sprouted on our property around 1980, when the largely oak forest surrounding our land was logged in the wake of a gypsy moth irruption. Along with numerous aspens, a large number of pin cherries sprang up on the cleared land, and also on the sun-drenched edges of our woods. Now, two decades later, the short-lived pin cherries have reached full size and are starting to die off—no doubt having left behind seeds that will sprout should another round of cutting or caterpillar devastation hit the woods.

Recently I checked on one of our pin cherries. The tree was about 35 feet tall; its diameter at breast height was 8 inches. The tree had the slick, papery, mahogany brown bark characteristic of the species: bark that shows to its best advantage in the low, angled light of winter, when it gleams like hammered bronze. According to several sources, as the tree matures, the bark may become gray and also break up or fissure into scaly plates. Prominent lenticels mark the trunks of younger trees.

Pin cherry is a small tree or a large shrub. At maturity, it generally stands no taller than 40 feet, with a typical maximum trunk diameter of 1 foot. Often the trunk divides into two or more stems. The branches are horizontal or ascending, usually forming a narrow crown, although on a good site the boughs may "elbow out a great deal of room for this swift-growing invader," says Donald Culross Peattie in *A Natural History of Trees*. The leaves are 2 to 5 inches long, broadly lance-shaped, long-pointed, and finely saw-toothed along their margins. They are a shining green, with a smooth texture on both the upper and lower surfaces. The twigs are redder than the branches and have several buds clustered at their tips.

Pin cherry ranges from Newfoundland to British Columbia and south in the Appalachian Mountains to Tennessee and Georgia. It is found up to elevations of 6,000 feet in the southern Appalachians, the region where it achieves its greatest size; the currently recognized national champion is in Sevier County, Tennessee, an 85-footer with a circumference of 71 inches. In Pennsylvania, *Prunus pensylvanica* is most common in the central mountains and scarce in the state's southeast and southwest corners. According to Joseph Illick in *Pennsylvania Trees,* pin cherry is rare or absent southeast of a line drawn from Easton to Harrisburg to Chambersburg. Illick notes that in the wake of widespread clear-cut logging in the early twentieth century, pin cherry often formed "almost impenetrable thickets in lumbered areas" of northern Pennsylvania, with three thousand to five thousand saplings per acre. The largest pin cherry Illick ever found was 14½ inches in diameter at breast height.

Pin cherry grows on a wide variety of sites, from dry, sandy soil to wet loam. It invades clearings, roadsides, burned areas, woodlands flattened by high winds, spoil banks caused by coal mining, fencerows, and abandoned fields. When growing in a dense thicket, pin cherry forms a closed canopy in three to seven years and reaches maturity in twenty to forty years. Often it stands alongside quaking and bigtooth aspens; paper and yellow birches; striped, red, and sugar maples; various oaks; and American mountain-ash. *Prunus pensylvanica* stabilizes newly exposed soil and prevents erosion while providing cover and light shade for the seedlings of other species destined to rise above the short-lived pin cherries and become the next generation of forest trees. Pin cherry needs direct sunlight and dies if it is shaded over.

The leaves emerge in April and early May. The white flowers expand along with the foliage; they are clustered together on umbels, structures in which a number of stalks arise from a common point. (Black cherry, *Prunus serotina,* and chokecherry, *Prunus virginiana,* have their flowers on racemes, which are shared, elongated stems.) Pin cherries can fruit as early as two years after sprouting, although larger quantities of fruits are not produced until the tree is four years of age or older. A West Virginia study found that a typical tree with a 4½-inch trunk diameter bore about ⅔ quart of cherries per year. Forest scientists have estimated that fifteen-year-old pin cherries growing in a pure stand can produce over a million fruits per acre.

The cherries ripen in July and August. They are red, rounded, and about ¼ inch in diameter, their thin skin covering juicy, sour flesh and an oblong stone. Many birds and mammals eat pin cherries. Black bears usually pull the limbs toward their mouths, sometimes breaking them, and gobble down leaves, twigs, and fruits. A bruin may straddle a smaller tree and walk forward, riding the tree down and bringing its crown to mouth level. Beavers eat pin cherry bark, and deer browse the twigs and foliage.

The droppings of bears and other wild animals spread pin cherry seeds throughout the land. Botanists believe the seeds can stay viable for 50 to 150 years, buried in the forest floor. As the years pass, their tough coats become more permeable to water and oxygen. If fire, logging, or some other event wipes out mature trees, the pin cherry seeds germinate, perhaps signaled by temperature fluctuations caused by the sudden removal of shade.

Seedlings grow rapidly in full light. When a seedling reaches a height of about 3 feet, it begins sending out lateral roots. In West Virginia, foresters examined the root systems of wind-toppled twenty-five-year-old pin cherries and found that they were confined to the top 2 feet of soil. New shoots can arise from pieces of torn-off root left in the ground after a storm has knocked a tree over.

Many microorganisms may invade pin cherry during its lifetime of roughly thirty-five years. They include molds, mildews, and rusts. The fungus *Fomes pomaceus* causes trunk rot in many northeastern pin cherries. A multitude of insects feed on the leaves, including the well-known eastern tent caterpillar and the graphically named uglynest caterpillar, a leaf-rolling species that constructs dense nests throughout a tree's foliage.

Fruit growers sometimes graft domestic sour cherry cuttings onto pin cherry rootstocks, one of the few uses that people have found for *Prunus pensylvanica*. The soft, weak wood is occasionally chip-harvested for fiber and fuel, and some trees go for paper pulp. I have burnt it on occasion in my woodstove.

A close relative is chokecherry, *Prunus virginiana*. It is mainly a shrub, although rarely—in rich, deep soil, particularly in the southern Appalachians—it becomes a scraggly tree. Growing in thickets, clearings, rocky woods, fencerows, abandoned fields, and roadside banks, it is statewide in Pennsylvania and most abundant in the western counties. Its name comes from the mouth-puckering astringency of its cherries, borne in long, drooping clusters. Many wild animals eat the fruits, which ripen from August to September. Among of the best-tasting and most beautiful wild preserves I've ever enjoyed was the clear, claret-colored chokecherry jelly made by my old friend and fellow forager, Clinton "Dob" Studholme of Centre Hall.

HONEY-LOCUST

Needle-sharp thorns guard the trunk and branches of the honey-locust. This distinctively armored tree bears feathery compound leaves and odd, straplike fruits, some of which hang on the branches all winter. As a boy, sledding on a golf course near my home, I was careful to steer clear of the thorny honey-locusts, whose foot-long, twisted brown pods rattled in the wind on those brisk winter days, when we ran our sleds time and again down the high-banked, snow-covered greens.

Also known as sweet locust or thorny locust, *Gleditsia triacanthos* is primarily a midwestern tree. Its range extends from central Pennsylvania south and west to Alabama, Texas, and eastern South Dakota. Honey-locust has been widely planted and is now naturalized throughout the Northeast, in rural areas, towns, and cities. Although honey-locusts do best in moist bottomlands, they also grow in the uplands. They thrive on limestone soils. The largest specimens have been reported from stream valleys in southern Indiana and Illinois: trees up to 140 feet tall, with trunks 4 to 6 feet in diameter. Most Pennsylvania honey-locusts are 40 to 50 feet tall, with a 1- to 2-foot trunk diameter. In the Keystone State, honey-locusts are found mainly in the southern counties.

The mature tree typically has a short trunk; a broad, open crown; and spreading branches that droop at their ends. The roots divide abundantly and, in good soil, may penetrate 20 feet below the ground. On young trees, the bark is smooth, with many conspicuous lenticels; on older trees, the bark is grayish brown to almost black, marked with a few vertical fissures, which divide thick, slablike ridges with projecting edges. The trunk is studded with thorn clusters that resemble spiny sea urchins. Horticulturists have developed thornless honey-locusts, and some of those varieties have established themselves in the wild.

The formidable spines are 2 to 8 inches long and end in needle-sharp points. As they begin growing, they are bright green; later they change to bright red; and when mature, they are a shiny chestnut brown. Many of the thorns branch, with smaller thorns angling out to the side. Since the thorns arise from the tree's wood, they cannot easily be pulled off. Notes Donald Culross Peattie in *A Natural History of Trees*, "Sometimes the thorns bear leaves, proving that they are modified branches."

The tree's real leaves are 6 to 15 inches long, compounded of twenty or so leaflets, each $3/8$ to $1 1/4$ inches long, and often with a slightly wavy edge. Unlike the black locust, the leaf of the honey-locust has no terminal leaflet. Sometimes a leaf will compound a second time, with one or more additional compound leaves branching off partway along the shaft of the original leaf. Honey-locust leaves turn yellow in autumn and drop off early in the season.

In spring, after their leaves emerge in mid to late May, the trees put out small, greenish flowers, with both male and female blossoms appearing on the same tree, generally on different branches. Insects pollinate the flowers. The resulting fruits are flat, mahogany-colored pods 6 to 16 inches long, which often become twisted as they ripen by mid-October. The pods fall off the tree unopened. They contain many oval, brownish seeds in a sweet-tasting pulp. Cattle and hogs relish the pods, as do squirrels, deer, opossums, birds, and other wildlife. The seeds are spread about in the animals' droppings.

Honey-locust seeds have tough, impermeable coats that keep them viable for months or years. Individual seeds become permeable after varying amounts of time, so that a single year's crop can yield seedlings for several years. If a seed passes through an animal's digestive system, it is more apt to sprout than one remaining uneaten. Seedlings establish themselves in open settings or beneath gaps in the forest canopy. Because they have fairly thin bark, the young trees are easily damaged by fire.

Honey-locust is a hardy tree that can tolerate soil salinity and drought. The wood is dense, hard, and durable, much like that of black locust. People use it for fence posts, railroad ties, and rough lumber. The Cherokee Indians in Tennessee made bows out of honey-locust. No doubt they found many things to do with the thorns, as did the European settlers, who used them for carding wool and pinning shut the mouths of sacks.

REDBUD

I know of just one redbud *(Cercis canadensis)* near my home in the Bald Eagle Valley of central Pennsylvania. In April it bravely puts forth flowers, standing in solitary splendor in the woods just off the township road, where it seems to be natural and not an ornamental planting. But if I drive south and cross broad Nittany Valley, then take the road through the notch in Tussey Mountain and descend into Stone Valley, I find redbuds in abundance. They dot the hills and rim the fields, particularly on south-facing slopes. Stone Valley lies south of an imaginary line drawn across the middle of the state from east to west: below this line redbud is common, north of the line it is rare to nonexistent.

The heart-shaped leaf of eastern redbud is 2 to 6 inches long and equally broad.

For a fortnight in spring—in late March, April, or early May, depending on the year—redbud is easily the most beautiful plant in the landscape. As its name implies, it puts out bright reddish flowers. In Stone Valley last spring, I proved to my satisfaction that the flowers are technically "violet-purple"—this according to a quaint, tattered, exhaustive little manual of my father's, *Color Standards and Color Nomenclature,* by Robert Ridgway, published in 1912, with 1,115 1/2-by-1-inch color panels that somebody painstakingly glued onto its fifty-three plates. My father, a mycologist, used the book to identify and describe mushrooms. I associate my father also with the redbud, because he planted one in our backyard.

Eastern redbud grows 15 to 20 feet tall, with a few Pennsylvania specimens reaching 30 feet, and others, mainly in southern states, rising to 50 feet. The tree ranges from southern Pennsylvania to Florida, and from eastern Nebraska to Mexico. Despite its Latin species name, *Cercis canadensis* is rare in Canada, where a few specimens are confined to southernmost Ontario bordering Lake Erie. The redbud's trunk is 8 to 12 inches in diameter, rarely 18 inches. Usually the trunk is short, dividing into several stout, spreading branches. The bark is dark gray or brown, grooved, sometimes with curling plates. Redbud has distinctive leaves: heart-shaped, 2 to 6 inches long and equally broad or even broader, not toothed, dull green above and paler green below, with five to seven conspicuous veins radiating up and out from where the stem meets the blade. The leaves look like those of American basswood, except the redbud leaves are smaller and lack the basswoods' serrated edges. In autumn, they turn yellow.

Cercis canadensis flourishes in open light, on dry to moist, rich soils, including those derived from limestone rock. A short-lived tree, it grows slowly and becomes less tolerant of shade as it matures. Redbuds crop up along the banks of streams, in rich bottomlands, in ravines, on abandoned farms, on field edges, and as understory trees in forests that are not too shady.

They do not survive on poorly aerated soils and die if their roots are flooded too frequently. The crown takes on a narrow and upright form in the woods and becomes flat-topped and spreading in the open. In *The Book of Forest and Thicket,* John Eastman writes, "Under full summer sunlight, leaves in the upper crown often fold, thus reducing the amount of radiation received."

The flowers appear before the leaves in spring. A study in Indiana found that redbuds needed thirty days of temperatures averaging more than 50 degrees Fahrenheit before they would flower. Redbuds have the curious property of sending out blooms all along their twigs and branches—in some cases, even from buds on the trunk. Four to eight flowers cluster at the ends of slender stalks. An individual blossom is about 1/2 inch long and looks like a pea flower, with five slightly unequal petals. Redbud flowers are perfect, or bisexual, having both female and male parts; thus they can self-pollinate, which seems to be the case with the redbud along our road: even though there are no other redbuds in the vicinity, the tree produces fruit in most years.

Insects pollinate the flowers, including butterflies and especially honeybees; beekeepers in some regions consider redbud to be an important nectar-producing plant. The fertilized flowers develop into pods with dry, leathery wrappers. The pods are 2 to 3 inches long by 1/2 inch wide, and each contains four to ten brown, hard, flattened, beanlike seeds about 1/4 inch in length. In some years, by July and August, the redbuds are loaded with pods. The pods split open along one edge to release the seeds; the pods fall in late autumn or winter, or they hang on until the following spring. Seeds usually remain dormant on the ground for several years before sprouting.

People have watched wildlife feeding on redbud seeds—ring-necked pheasants, bobwhite quail, cardinals, and rose-breasted grosbeaks, as well as deer and gray squirrels—but the seeds do not seem to be an important or a highly sought-after food. Human foragers sometimes add the flowers to salads or fry them, and the young seedpods are also edible.

The wood of the redbud is not highly regarded. It is heavy, at 40 pounds per cubic foot, close-grained, dark brown with a paler sapwood, and judged hard but weak. In none of my references could I find a commercial or even an arcane application, other than a dye made from the red roots.

However, no practical use is required of a tree that shows us so prettily and emphatically that spring is just around the bend.

BLACK LOCUST

Eric Sloane, in *A Reverence for Wood,* observed that the eminently useful black locust "looks like a dying tree, even at its best, during the summer." True, the locust leafs out late in the spring, several weeks after other trees have sent forth their foliage. The trunk of an open-country specimen divides low to the ground into crooked, skeletal-looking stems, which hold up a sparse and irregularly shaped crown. The leaves themselves have a fragile, fernlike appearance. True, as well, that winds and wet snow may damage the limbs and the brittle, zigzag twigs of this fast-growing, short-lived species, and many insects attack it. Yet the locust is a survivor, tough and adaptable.

At maturity, black locust *(Robinia pseudoacacia)* is a medium-size tree, generally 30 to 40 feet tall in Pennsylvania, with a trunk 1 to 1 1/2 feet in diameter. On good sites, such as moist limestone soil, a locust can reach 80 feet or taller, with a trunk 2 to 4 feet across. In an even-aged stand, black locust may grow quite straight, with a single trunk free from branches for three-quarters of its length. The bark is pale grayish brown to reddish brown, deeply furrowed, often with high, rounded ridges, and an inch or more thick.

Robinia pseudoacacia grows on many different soil types. It seeds itself on rocky slopes and has been planted on disturbed sites such as strip-mined land. Look for it in abandoned fields, forest edges, fencerows, roadside thickets, and regenerating clear-cuts. The species' natural range centers on the Appalachian Mountains, from central Pennsylvania and southern Ohio south to northern Alabama; black locust also shows up in the Ozark and Ouachita Mountains of Missouri, Arkansas, and Oklahoma. People have planted it widely throughout North America, Europe, and Asia.

Black locust leaves are alternate, sprouting from one side of the twig, then the other; and they are compound, consisting of a central stem feather-edged with numerous small leaflets. The overall leaf is 6 to 12 inches long. The leaflets grow on short stalks. They are ovate; 1 to 2 inches long; have entire, not notched, edges; and stand opposite one another save for the single leaflet at the tip: thus their number (seven to nineteen) is invariably odd. The leaflets are bluish green above and paler below. They droop and fold up at night, and expand again in the light of day. At the base of the leaf stem on the twig stand a pair of stout spines 1/4 to 1/2 inch long.

The flower clusters open in late May or early June, after the leaves have emerged. They hang down in drooping spikes 4 to 8 inches long. Each individual flower is five-petaled, creamy white, and a bit less than an inch in length, and looks much like the blossom of the pea plant. The fragrant nectar attracts hordes of bees. A friend and I used to keep honeybee colonies, and in years when the black locusts flowered heavily, we would make a special harvest of the resulting honey: clear as water, light-tasting, indescribably sweet.

After the bees pollinate them, the flowers develop and become flat pods 2 to 4 inches long and 1/2 inch wide; inside the papery walls of each pod lie four to eight small seeds. The pods ripen by fall and sometimes hang in the trees through winter. Black locusts generally bear heavy seed crops yearly or at two-year intervals, with trees fifteen to forty years of age producing the greatest quantities of seeds. A locust seed has a hard, tough coating. A few birds and small mammals eat the seeds, which are not considered an important wildlife food.

Black locusts propagate more frequently by cloning, sending up shoots from their roots, than from the dispersal of their seeds. The trees' roots—yellow and said to have a disagreeable odor—are dense and broad-spreading; they produce many sprouts, which form thickets of smaller, genetically identical clones. Nitrogen-fixing bacteria in the root nodules help fertilize and enrich the soil. After I made my house clearing in the woods, a black locust sprouted, apparently from a seed, on a dirt pile near my garage. The tree pushed upward at a terrific rate, so that by the time I cut it while doing some landscaping a decade later, I was able to get a nice fence post, plus some firewood, from its trunk. I still haven't banished that weedy tree: each year its roots send up new sprouts in the lawn and garden where the trunk once stood.

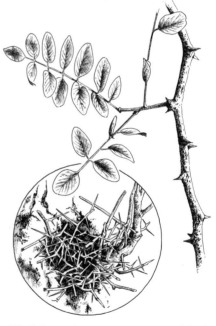

Black locust wood is very heavy, at 52 pounds per cubic foot. Hard and strong, it is stiffer than hickory and more durable than white oak. Its fuel value is among the highest of any American tree: a cord of black locust contains as much heat energy as a ton of anthracite coal; the wood

Black locust has an airy compound leaf and prickles on its twigs. The inset shows a thorn cluster on the trunk of the closely related honey-locust.

burns cleanly, with a blue flame. Because it lasts for years in contact with the soil, black locust is the top choice for a post: a locust post has held up our mailbox for twenty years, and will probably outlast my tenure on the place. The heartwood is an attractive yellowish brown to cherry red color, surrounded by a narrow band of greenish or yellowish sapwood. People have fashioned the tough wood into trunnels ("tree-nails") for holding together the wooden frames of ships, insulator pins on telegraph and telephone poles, ladder rungs, buggy hubs, and policemen's billy clubs. Other uses include mine timbers, railroad ties, boxes, crates, and stakes.

Early colonists in Jamestown, Virginia, cut locust corner posts for their dwellings. Those same settlers named the tree for its supposed resemblance to an Old World species, the carob, *Ceratonia siliqua,* also known as locust; one wonders if the settlers had ever actually laid eyes on *Ceratonia siliqua,* which grows in the Mediterranean region. Other names for black locust are honey locust, yellow locust, white locust, common locust, and false acacia.

Black locusts seldom live longer than a hundred years. According to J. C. Huntley, writing in *Silvics of North America,* "Black locust is severely damaged by insects and disease, probably more than any other eastern hardwood species." Two of its many insect pests are the locust leafminer and the locust borer, both beetle larvae. The leafminer defoliates trees, which can cause death during times of drought. Locust borers chew feeding tunnels in the wood; later, heart rot fungi enter through the holes.

Black locust needs abundant sunlight to thrive. A pioneer species, it quickly grows in light-flooded openings and old fields, then dwindles as taller, more shade-tolerant trees catch up to it and overtop it. Dense stands of locust provide escape and resting cover for wildlife. Deer browse on the young growth, and birds—including downy and hairy woodpeckers and yellow-shafted flickers—nest in the cavities that often develop in overmature trees.

Paleobotanists theorize that the last continental glaciation, around eighteen thousand years ago, almost extinguished *Robinia pseudoacacia.* The species' range contracted to a small area in the valleys of the southern Appalachians. Since that time—on its own and abetted by tree-planting humans—that consummate survivor, the black locust, has made an impressive comeback.

HOLLY

A cold rain fell as I walked along the banks of the Susquehanna in York County. The rain dimpled the broad, slow-moving river. Clouds obscured the wooded and rocky slopes that rose steeply from the dark water. The Indian Steps Museum—an old mansion housing a collection of artifacts found in the vicinity—stood closed for the winter, gloomy and shuttered, its gutters spouting rain. On the museum's deserted grounds, deciduous trees were bare of leaves, their essential shapes revealed: straight, massive tuliptrees; crookedly branching black walnuts; expansive, leaning silver maples.

I was searching for a smaller tree, one that would be green despite the season: American holly *(Ilex opaca)*, the only broad-leaved evergreen native to Pennsylvania and the Northeast.

Most of our other evergreens—pine, hemlock, spruce, fir—are needle-leaved trees. The holly's leaves are egg-shaped, 2 to 4 inches long, their scalloped edges armed with sharp prickles: the familiar green used for Christmas decorations. Individual leaves remain on a holly for two or three years before falling, and the tree perpetually wears a green cloak.

The holly for which I was searching suddenly loomed up in the mist, a tall, near-perfect pyramid, its dark leaves glistening, brilliant red berries scattered in small clusters among the foliage. It was the record holly for Pennsylvania, the largest of its species known in the state.

Ducking beneath the dripping boughs, I bent and picked up a fallen leaf and several berries. The leaf felt thick and leathery. Its edges, in addition to being scalloped and spiny, were slightly rolled under. A central rib stood out prominently on the leaf's underside, a paler shade of green than its lustrous upper surface. The berries were pea-size or a bit smaller, not quite the flaming red of barberry fruits, but a strong, beautiful scarlet nonetheless.

The natural range of American holly extends from New Jersey south to Florida and west to southeastern Missouri, Arkansas, and Texas. According to literature published by the U.S. Forest Service, "American holly grows best and reaches its greatest development in Alabama and in southern Arkansas, Louisiana, and east Texas, on well drained, moist soils." In the South, holly regularly grows as tall as 50 feet and may even reach 100 feet. Writes Donald Culross Peattie in *A Natural History of Trees,* "Sometimes it is scattered in with Pines, Magnolias, Hickory, Sweet Gum, and Sassafras; again, the traveler in the South may find himself in a beautiful little forest of pure Holly." Holly was a favorite of George Washington, who sowed its berries and transplanted small sprouts from the woods to beautify his estate, Mount Vernon, in Fairfax County, Virginia.

More than a dozen species of holly are recognized in the United States. About half of the species are evergreen and half are deciduous, dropping their leaves in winter. All produce red berries. Five species are native to Pennsylvania. Other than American holly, all are shrubs that grow mainly in swamps, bogs, shoresides, and other damp places. Deciduous plants, they drop their leaves and stand bare over winter. English holly, *Ilex aquifolium,* is the only other evergreen holly in the Northeast. It grows to 50 feet tall and has a smaller leaf than American holly. This popular European species is often planted in hedges, yards, and formal gardens.

In Pennsylvania, American holly is found mainly in the southeastern quarter of the state, although horticulturists have planted it throughout the commonwealth. It is generally a shrub here on the northern edge of its range. The holly at Indian Steps Museum has been judged the largest of its tribe in Pennsylvania since at least the 1940s, according to "Hollies in Pennsylvania," an article by H. Gleason Mattoon in *Forest Leaves,* a publication of the state forestry association. The 1948 article claimed the Indian Steps holly was over three hundred years old.

While sheltering beneath the tree, I examined its bark, a pale greenish gray with a surface neither furrowed nor scaly, but much roughened by small bumps and warts. At breast height, the trunk was about 2 feet in diameter. Coming out into the rain again, I backed off and gave the holly a good, long look. Through the leaves, I could see that the trunk forked partway up. When last measured in 1991, the holly stood 65 feet tall and had a 35-foot crown spread. I doubted that it had increased in size much in the succeeding decade: hollies grow very slowly in the shaded habitat that they prefer.

American hollies are either male or female, and the berries on this tree signified that it was female. Some botanists suggest that there are three or four male hollies for every female tree. The berries persist into winter, and many birds feed on them: ruffed grouse, bobwhite quail, wild turkey, and various songbirds, particularly the thrushes (bluebird, robin, hermit thrush, gray-cheeked thrush, and wood thrush), as well as the gray catbird, northern mockingbird, brown thrasher, eastern towhee, cedar waxwing, yellow-bellied sapsucker, and pileated woodpecker. The birds scatter the trees' seeds in their droppings. Bears, raccoons, skunks, foxes, and small rodents occasionally eat the fruit, and deer sometimes browse the trees' leaves. The dense foliage of American hollies provides resting and nesting cover for small birds year-round.

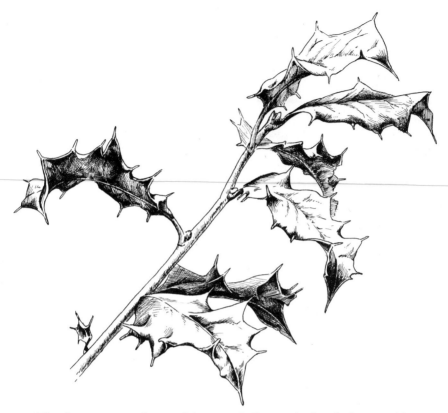

The glossy evergreen leaves of American holly are edged with sharp prickles.

American holly flowers from April to June. The small blossoms are pale greenish or white. *Pennsylvania Trees,* by Joseph Illick, quotes a Dr. H. Justin Ruddy of Millersville, who reported American hollies growing abundantly along the Susquehanna "below McCall's Ferry, Lancaster County. About every twentieth tree on the islands and banks is an American Holly. Formerly many large trees occurred there, some reaching a height of 50 ft. and a diameter of 12 inches or more. When these large trees bloomed they filled the whole canyon-like valley for miles with perfume."

In the past, at Christmastime, professional pickers would cut or break off the green boughs of hollies and sell them to stores, which in turn offered them to shoppers. Illick cited a wreath in a rural Lancaster County school in 1916 over 50 feet long and made from holly gathered locally. Unregulated picking damaged many hollies. Today the American holly is classified as a threatened species in Pennsylvania, and it is illegal to remove its foliage.

American holly has never been an important commercial lumber tree in the Northeast, but holly is cut for its wood in parts of the South. The heartwood and sapwood are both chalky white in color, and the heartwood particularly is said to resemble ivory. The wood is heavy and hard, its growth rings practically indistinguishable. It cuts smoothly and readily takes dyes and stains. Holly has been used for furniture parts and cabinet inlays, knife handles, scroll work, measuring scales and rules, and in musical instruments: piano keys, violin pegs, and fingerboards are often holly, dyed black in some instances to resemble ebony.

American holly remains common in New Jersey, Delaware, and Maryland, growing as an understory tree in coastal floodplain forests. Today in Pennsylvania, botanists have documented it in Bucks, Dauphin, Chester, Lancaster, Lebanon, and York counties. Hollies still grow on islands in the lower Susquehanna and in wooded ravines leading down to the river. People can view holly at Kelly's Run Natural Area, on the opposite side of the Susquehanna from the Indian Steps Museum, on lands owned by Pennsylvania Power and Light Company. Holly also grows at Susquehannock State Park in Lancaster County.

It can be difficult to tell whether a holly found growing in Pennsylvania is a native tree—or if it is native to some other part of the species' range and was propagated in a nursery, planted as shrubbery, and then seeded into the wild by birds. Botanists are checking historical records and trying to document where native holly still exists in Pennsylvania. Sites with native plants receive special protection from the state Department of Conservation and Natural Resources.

John Kunsman, a botanist for the Nature Conservancy, is a modern-day holly hunter. Over the telephone, he told me that American holly may in fact be extending its natural range. "I was driving on the turnpike around Harrisburg last month and spotted a holly growing out of the rocks in a roadcut," Kunsman said. "Did it come from a native source or from a tree in somebody's backyard? It wasn't too far from the Susquehanna, so it may well have been a native plant."

BOX-ELDER

Box-elder *(Acer negundo),* or ash-leaved maple, is a small to medium-size tree that grows in floodplains and on the edges of streams, lakes, and swamps. In 1928, according to Joseph Illick, chief forester for Pennsylvania and the author of *Pennsylvania Trees,* box-elder was "rare and local" in the commonwealth, most abundant in the eastern and southern sections. Today it has become common and widespread throughout Pennsylvania and many other states, both because people have planted it in urban and rural settings, and because the tree, a prolific seeder, has spread on its own.

The current accepted name, box-elder, is cobbled together and, as George Petrides notes in his *Field Guide to Eastern Trees,* "fails to indicate proper taxonomic relationships." It seems that *box* refers to the fact that *Acer negundo* is often planted to create a hedge, as is a popular unrelated species, Eurasian boxwood. It's also possible that the link comes from the tree's whitish wood, which resembles that of Eurasian boxwood. *Elder* stresses the similarity between box-elder's foliage and the leaves of elderberry, a common North American shrub. Ash-leaved maple is probably a better, if less frequently used, name. *Acer negundo* is indeed a maple, which can be inferred from its opposite leaves and paired winged fruits, also called samaras or keys. And its toothed compound leaves do suggest those of ash trees.

Box-elder ranges from coast to coast and from Canada to Guatemala, making it the most widespread of the maples. The species' range centers on the bottomland hardwood forests of the lower Ohio and Mississippi river valleys, where it grows along with silver maple, eastern cottonwood, sycamore, hackberry, and several willow species. *Acer negundo* has been naturalized in the Northeast, New England, southern Canada, and the Pacific Northwest. It thrives in moist, fertile soils, yet it is hardy enough to grow in drier, poorer habitats, including disturbed sites such as spoil banks, old factory yards, and vacant lots in cities. Across its extensive range, it withstands extremes of temperature, drought, wind, and dust. Floods can choke its roots for a month without killing it.

Tough though it may be, box-elder is short-lived, at least for a tree, with an average life span of sixty years; individuals rarely achieve a full century. Box-elder grows rapidly, especially during its first fifteen to twenty years, making it a popular choice for landscape planners wanting quick shade for parks and city streets, or a farmer needing a windbreak or a shade planting in a pasture or around a livestock or poultry barn. Some people in the East consider box-elder little more than an invasive weed tree. Lately, sensitized to the species, I have noticed box-elders in settings as various as the yard of a townhouse along a busy street, where my son takes music lessons; behind the barn of a friend, who had no idea where the tree came from; and growing in junglelike luxuriance along the banks of Pine Creek in rural Lycoming County.

Box-elder can become as tall as 70 feet, with a 3-foot-diameter trunk, although 50 feet in height and 2 feet in breadth are probably more usual. The short, tapering trunk supports a bushy crown that is deep, broad, and rounded. The bark, thick and seldom scaly, has many narrow ridges, broken up by fissures that become furrows as the tree ages. The roots spread wide but remain shallow. Storms and snow often knock off the brittle branches and twigs, which litter the ground beneath the tree.

Box-elder is the only maple that has compound leaves. Each leaf is 4 to 10 inches long and consists of three to five leaflets, 2 to 4 inches in length, ovate or elliptical and long-pointed at the tip, with coarsely toothed edges. The dense foliage is light green in summer and turns a dull yellow in autumn.

Flowers, male or female, grow on separate trees. The small yellow-green blossoms cluster on slender, drooping stalks; they appear in April in Pennsylvania, before or along with the leaves. By summer's end, they have ripened into clusters of paired samaras, each 1 to 1½ inches long, with a curving wing and a plump, nutlike seed. Winter winds gradually strip the samaras from their twigs, distributing them continuously until spring. At least some of the fruits usually hang on through the winter; squirrels and birds, especially pine and evening grosbeaks, feed on the nutritious morsels.

The seeds need full sunlight to sprout and grow; botanists judge box-elder to be less shade-tolerant than other maples. If a young, vigorous tree is cut down or otherwise damaged, it can send up shoots from the stump or root system.

The wood of box-elder weighs only 27 pounds per cubic foot. Pale sapwood and heartwood blend together and are nearly indistinguishable. Box-elder is not, and never has been, an important lumber tree, even in the heart of its natural range around the Ohio and Mississippi river valleys. People have used the soft, weak wood for paper pulp and fashioned it into barrels, woodenware, and, one source reports dismissively, "cheap furniture" and "easily broken toys." Woodworkers like its figuring, often invested with green and pink highlights, and use it for turning bowls. The Crow Indians of the Great Plains tapped the trees and boiled the sap to make sugar, even though box-elder sap has a much lower sugar content than that of sugar maple, and an acidic taste to boot. Box-elder is also called Manitoba maple, sugar ash, or—again the object of insult, judged wanting in comparison with the grander *Acer* species—bastard maple.

RED MAPLE

Whatever the season, red maple *(Acer rubrum)* shows its namesake color, vividly or with subtlety and restraint. In winter, the buds and twig tips are a rich wine red. As winter gives way to spring, the swelling buds form a red haze on the hilltops. Soon the flowers open, adding crimson to the faintly greening landscape. The leaves unfurl ruddily in April and May; when they assume their summer green, the leafstalks remain touched with red, keeping faith with the distinguishing hue of *Acer rubrum*. And in autumn, the leaves become scarlet, some of the brightest foliage in the woods.

Red maple is a medium-size tree. When mature at seventy to eighty years, it is normally 50 to 60 feet tall, with a trunk 1 to 2 feet in diameter. On an excellent site, red maple can become 100 feet tall and 3 to 4 feet in diameter. *Acer rubrum* grows from Nova Scotia west to Manitoba and Minnesota, and south to Florida and Texas: throughout essentially all of eastern North America. In various parts of its range, this species is known as scarlet maple, swamp maple, water maple, soft maple, or white maple. Red maple is most common in New England, the Mid-Atlantic states, and the Upper Midwest. It is statewide in Pennsylvania, where its numbers are increasing as it takes the place of oaks killed after repeated defoliations by gypsy moth larvae or cut down for timber products.

As with all the maples, red maple has opposite leaves—directly across from each other on the twigs. The leaves are 2 to 6 inches long, and nearly as broad. They generally have three (sometimes five) lobes, with the notches between the lobes relatively shallow. Coarse teeth rim the leaf margins. The leaves are light green above and paler green, occasionally silvery, below. The bark on a young red maple is thin and smooth, often a pale gray color similar to that of American beech. As red maple ages, its bark darkens and breaks up into rough, shaggy ridges that may peel away in long plates.

Red maple is one of the first trees to flower in the spring—March or April in our central Pennsylvania woods, earlier during warm springs, and later when winter is reluctant to loosen its grip, with flowering completed by the time the leaf buds open in early May. I've seen red maples blooming

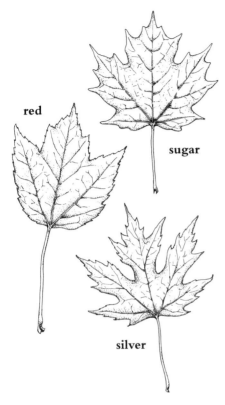

red

sugar

silver

*Typical leaves of sugar maple, top;
red maples, middle; and silver maple,
bottom. Within a given species, leaf
shape can vary slightly from one
individual tree to another,
and even on the same tree.*

in south Florida swamps as early as
December, their trunks and limbs
bedecked with air plants and lichens,
and sharing the muck with such
exotic trees as poisonwood, strangler
fig, and gumbo-limbo.

Most flowers grow on branches
in the well-lit crowns of the trees,
but one can usually find blossoms at
eye level, often on smaller specimens
at the edges of clearings. Red maples
have both male and female flowers.
The male flowers are airy, pollen-
bearing clusters of yellow and pink;
the female flowers, destined to
become the fruits, are larger and
more substantial, hanging at the ends
of slender, deep red stems. Some
trees have only male flowers, some
have only female flowers, and a few
present flowers of both sexes on separate branches.

The wind, and perhaps a few
wild, solitary bees, pollinate red
maple flowers. Pollination is timed
to take place before the emergence
of leaves, which might shield the
flowers from the wind and obstruct
the successful transfer of pollen. Fer-
tilized female flowers ripen into winged fruits, called keys or samaras, 1/2 to
1 inch long, attached in opposing pairs at the ends of the drooping stems. At
first the fruits are bright red; later they fade to brown. A samara consists of a
small seed and a thin, papery wing. Red maple produces the lightest seeds of
all the maples. In May and June, the seeds flash through the air and flutter to
the ground. Most germinate within a week, although some, particularly
those landing in shady places, lie dormant for a year and sprout the following spring.

Red maples grow "on a wider range of soil types, textures, moisture,
pH, and elevation than any other forest [tree] species in North America,"

assert Russell S. Walters and Harry W. Yawney in their chapter on *Acer rubrum* in the U.S. Forest Service's *Silvics of North America*. Of all the maples, red maple shows the greatest tolerance of different climatic conditions. In Pennsylvania, I have found red maples thriving in chilly peat bogs, on river islands, and on hot, dry, rocky ridges. In Pennsylvania, West Virginia, and Ohio, red maples have seeded themselves onto strip-mine spoil banks. An ideal habitat is a moderately well-drained, moist site at a low or intermediate elevation.

In wetlands, red maples produce short taproots and long, well-developed lateral roots. Where the soil is dry, the taproot is longer while the laterals remain short. Generally, the root system is horizontal and in the top 10 inches of soil. Temporary flooding does little harm to red maples: in one study, sixty days of flooding slowed tree growth, but only slightly; in another investigation, red maple root systems recovered rapidly after saturated bottomland soils dried out again. Red maples can weather drought by halting their growth, then resuming it when moist conditions return.

With their thin bark, red maples are severely damaged by fire, and even a moderate blaze can kill a mature tree—although not its roots, which are likely to send up many vigorous sprouts. Red maples also sprout from the stump after they are cut down. Connected to a complete root system, the sprouts grow faster than seedlings.

Red maple is moderately tolerant of shade—more so than pioneer species like the aspen and pin cherry, less so than slower-growing trees such as sugar maple and American beech. Red maple can be a dominant tree in the canopy on some sites. In a typical northern hardwood forest—a common silvic type in northern Pennsylvania, New York, and New England—sugar maples usually start to replace red maples after about eighty years.

Red maples seldom live longer than 150 years, and most die long before that age. Red maples wound easily, from their own branches dying and self-pruning or breaking under a load of ice or wet snow; from other trees battering against their crowns during winds or falling into them; from woodpeckers drilling for insects, and sapsuckers and squirrels breaching the bark to start the flow of sweet sap. In *Acer rubrum,* such wounds do not heal readily: a large area of cambium usually dies back before new growth can seal off the breach. Many different species of fungi invade red maple through wounds. The result is often heart rot, followed by a wind-snapped trunk or a fallen tree.

A couple of springs ago, in the woods below our pasture, I found where a pair of black-capped chickadees had picked out the rotten wood from a maple stub—the pale punk, lying on the leaves beneath the snag, caught my eye. The birds had built their nest in the open-topped cavity. A suite of hole nesters take advantage of red maple's propensity to become hollow, and many other birds nest in the tree's branches. Prairie warblers in particular nest in bushy, young red maples.

I have seen porcupines perched in red maples, eating the bright flowers in spring; they also relish the bark. Deer browse on twigs, leaves, and sprouts. In Pennsylvania, elk eat the buds, foliage, twigs, and bark of red maple. Red maples produce huge quantities of seeds: a crop nearly every year, and a bumper crop every two years or so. Trees with trunks only 8 inches in diameter can bear up to ninety thousand seeds. Songbirds, squirrels, and mice gorge on the seeds, and the rodents store them for winter food. Horses have been poisoned by eating fallen red maple leaves.

Humans put red maple to many and varied uses. We plant it to shade our houses and streets, cut it for lumber, fashion it into furniture, plywood, flooring, kitchenware, and clothespins. The wood is fairly soft and not particularly strong, and it weighs about 38 pounds per cubic foot when dry. A craftsman friend of mine builds award-winning rocking chairs. He makes the frame, rockers, armrests, headboard, and seat out of red maple, which he buys from mills under the designation soft maple (as opposed to hard maple, which is sugar maple, *Acer saccharum*). He shaves the back-cushioning ribs from black walnut. The contrast between the two woods is stunning: the walnut a deep, lustrous brown, the maple bone white. My friend picks through maple boards to find ones with a tiger-striped grain pattern. I see such figuring from time to time in the red maple I split for the woodstove; usually I set those billets aside to enjoy for a while, picking them up and turning the wood back and forth to catch the light, so that the grain winks light and dark, like flames dancing.

In autumn, red maples light up the hills and the mountainsides and flare up along the edges of the swamps, in hues grading from yellow-orange to deep red. Weather and soil moisture affect the colors' brilliance each year, and soil chemistry may have an impact: researchers suggest that the more acidic the soil, the deeper the red coloration. The scientists believe that most of the trees turning orange are females, with the males displaying that particularly combustible red.

SUGAR MAPLE AND BLACK MAPLE

In a woods not far from home, during a magical week in mid–October, the resident sugar maples *(Acer saccharum)* all go yellow at once. Yellow light suffuses down from overhead, yellow light glows upward from the ground, yellow angles in from the sides and drifts downward as more leaves let go. Hiking this patch of forest is like being caught in a yellow snowstorm.

Sugar maple leaves also turn vivid orange and brilliant red. They form the primary colors of autumn in New England and elsewhere in the East. *Acer saccharum* ranges from Nova Scotia to Manitoba, Minnesota, and Missouri, and south in the Appalachian Mountains to North Carolina and Tennessee. Statewide in Pennsylvania, it is most common in the northern, western, and eastern sectors. Sugar maple grows in moist woods, ravines, bottomlands, and on wooded slopes—often on the cooler, north-facing aspects, especially in the southern part of the commonwealth. It does best on rich, well-drained soil but can manage on thin, nutrient-poor ground. It does not grow in swampy or extremely dry settings. People have planted sugar maples in cemeteries, parks, farmyards, lawns, and lining town streets, where the trees' dense foliage casts a deep, cooling shade.

Sugar maple grows in pure stands and also in mixture with black cherry, basswood, yellow birch, American beech, red oak, eastern hemlock, and many other species. It is more common among northern hardwoods than in oak-hickory woods. Also known as rock maple or hard maple, *Acer saccharum* achieves its largest size in central New England, New York, northern Pennsylvania, and the Great Lakes region. An old-growth tree can reach 120 feet in height and have a trunk 5 feet in diameter. Most mature maples are smaller than that, at 40 to 70 feet high, with a trunk 2 to 3 feet across at breast height. Growing in the open, a sugar maple sends up a short trunk supporting stout, erect branches that form a round-topped crown. In a woods setting, the tree grows a long, straight trunk and a shallow crown; often such a tree will self-prune or shed its lower branches for over half its overall height.

The gray-brown bark splits into deep channels separated by long, irregular vertical plates or flakes, which often come loose along one side. On mature trunks, black chevrons like upside-down Vs mark the points of attachment for branches and scars where the boughs formerly grew.

The sugar maple leaf has a clean geometric shape. Canadians have chosen it as the emblem for their national flag. Think of a hand with the fingers splayed: the leaves are generally five-lobed, with each intervening notch U-shaped at the base. (The notches in the red maple's leaf, which has a similar shape, end in Vs.) Like the red maple leaf, the sugar maple has toothed margins, but the teeth are fewer and not as sharp. The leaves are generally 3 to 5 inches in length, and as wide as they are long, or slightly wider. They are dark green above and pale green below. The undersides may be glaucous, covered with a whitish waxy bloom. On some leaves, the veins are hairy.

Trees generally do not flower until they are more than twenty years old. The flowers bloom just before and as the leaves are unfurling—in April or May, depending on the latitude. The greenish yellow male and female flowers occur in separate clusters, scattered along the twigs and at the twig ends. In some trees, certain limbs send forth only male flowers, and other limbs produce only female flowers. Male flowers often greatly outnumber the female ones. Botanists long believed that sugar maple flowers were pollinated solely by insects. Wild solitary bees do feed on the nectar and incidentally pollinate the blossoms; however, recent studies have shown that wind can also bring about pollination when insects are excluded from the flowers.

Over summer, the female flowers develop into paired samaras. A samara consists of a small, seed-carrying vessel attached to a papery wing about 1/2 to 1 inch long by 1/3 inch wide; the overall length is 1 inch to 1 1/4 inches. The fruits ripen around September and begin falling just before the leaves let go. The twinned samaras come twirling down; winds can carry them 100 yards or farther. Usually only one of a pair carries a viable seed. Large, mature trees can produce huge numbers of samaras. In a Michigan study conducted during a good seed year, an estimated seventy thousand samaras per acre landed in the center of a ten-acre clearcut. Bumper crops arrive every two to five years—a pulsing of seed production that often leads to even-aged stands of sugar maple.

Seeds overwinter in the leaf litter. If the weather warms and gets dry too fast in spring, the seeds fail to germinate. Seeds contain considerable energy, enough to let their roots penetrate through heavy leaf litter and reach the mineral soil beneath. In spring, the seeds often germinate and their paired leaves start photosynthesizing before all the snow has melted in the woods.

In the dense shade of a mature woodland, sugar maple seedlings grow a tiny bit each year, starved for sunlight—waiting. In *The Trees in My Forest,* the ecologist Bernd Heinrich describes how he homed in on a hole in the leaf canopy created by a mature tree falling. On the sun-bathed ground grew a near-solid mat of sugar maple seedlings, averaging 4 to 5 inches tall. Heinrich pulled up seventy-one seedlings in a 4-square-foot plot. "[This] density of nearly eighteen seedlings per square foot covered an area of some five hundred feet," he writes, "and, in total, the 'hole' where the tree had fallen must have contained more than ten thousand seedlings." Probably only one of the seedlings would survive to replace the fallen tree; some were dead already. Heinrich cut their thin stems with a razor blade and counted their annual growth rings under a microscope. "In the sample of thirty-five that I examined," he wrote, "the growth rings indicated ages of six to ten years."

Sugar maples can live in dim light; they actually conduct their maximum photosynthetic activity under about 25 percent of full sunlight. Among the larger broad-leaved trees, only American beech is as shade-tolerant as sugar maple. Young sugar maples are easily killed by fire, but wildfires are uncommon in sugar maple stands because of the high moisture content of the leaf litter.

The roots of *Acer saccharum* go somewhat deeper than those of other maples. Strong, wide-spreading lateral roots branch extensively; they can reach out to twice the diameter of the tree's crown. The roots release a chemical that may slow the growth of yellow birch, a frequent competitor. After about 150 years, the upward growth of sugar maples ceases or becomes negligible. Mature trees often live for two hundred years, and some reach four hundred years.

Sugar maple samaras sometimes hang on their stalks into winter; evening grosbeaks, which migrate south into the Northeast during some years, feed avidly on the seeds, as do nuthatches and finches. Red, gray, and flying squirrels, chipmunks, and mice hoard and eat the seeds. Deer and rabbits browse on sugar maple buds and vegetation; porcupines feed on bark and on new spring leaves. John Eastman, in *The Book of Forest and Thicket,* reports that red squirrels gnaw wounds in trees, "creating a regular sap flow that evaporates on the bark. The squirrels then make the rounds of these flows, licking up the sweet deposits." Yellow-bellied sapsuckers peck feeding wells into the bark of sugar maples. On warm days, gnats and flies are attracted to the sugary sap, and migrating birds—warblers, flycatchers, hummingbirds—nab the nutritious insects.

Syrup and sugar made from the sap of *Acer saccharum* were the only sweeteners available to the original human inhabitants of North America. Members of the Iroquois and Chippewa tribes collected the sap in vessels, then concentrated it by letting it freeze and removing the ice to get rid of excess water. They also boiled the sap in small batches by filling elm-bark containers and troughs hollowed into logs, and putting fire-heated rocks in with the sap to steam off the water. European settlers adopted and advanced the sugar-making technology. No other type of sugar was available during

the colonial era, and maple success-
fully competed in price with cane
sugar until the second half of the
nineteenth century.

Today people collect sugar maple
sap by drilling holes through the bark
into a tree's sapwood, then inserting a
hollow tap, or spile, which guides the
sap into a lidded bucket or a network
of plastic tubing that carries the liquid
to a central collection point. The
sucrose that makes sap sweet was
manufactured by the previous year's
leaves and stored in horizontal cells
in the trunk. Sugar content varies
among trees, ranging from 2 to 7
percent; early sap flows usually have
the highest sugar content. Across

Sugar maple sap, collected in buckets
during late winter and early
spring, is later boiled down
to make syrup and sugar.

southern Canada, New England,
New York, northern Pennsylvania
and Ohio, and the Great Lakes states,
maple sugarers go to work in February and March. Some are backyard

hobbyists who make enough syrup for their own needs. At a modern commercial operation near Johnson, Vermont, 80 miles of plastic tubing conduct
sap from 12,000 taps, and 120,000 gallons of sap yield 3,000 gallons of maple
syrup. From Virginia south—because there is little of the freeze-thaw weather
that stimulates heavy sap production, and because trees shift rapidly from dormancy to leafing out in spring—sap is not collected for syrup.

Warm, sunny days followed by chill nights spur a tree to convert to
sugar the carbohydrates stored in the stem wood. Sugar maple has small
bubbles of carbon dioxide in its sap. As the day warms, these bubbles
expand, forcing the sap out of the tapholes. Tapping removes 10 to 12 gallons per taphole during the sugaring season. Around 40 gallons of sap, on
average, yield a gallon of syrup. A season's tapping can drain off 15 percent
of a tree's carbohydrate reserves, but some sugarbushes—the traditional
name for a stand of maples used for sugar production—boast trees that have
been tapped for 175 years with no loss in vigor or in the quantity or quality of sap produced.

Maple syrup is nothing short of ambrosial. I enjoy it best on wild blueberry pancakes and admit to taking a teaspoonful, neat, every now and then.

Sugar maple's value extends beyond nourishing wildlife and people. The wood is hard, tough, and close-grained, the heartwood a warm tawny color, the sapwood—which is frequently 3 to 4 inches thick—white with a reddish tinge. The wood polishes to a bright gleam. It weighs 43 pounds per cubic foot, dry weight. Products made from sugar maple are legion and include boxes, crates, clothespins, shoe lasts, toys, veneers, rulers, railroad ties, bowling lanes, gymnasium floors, rolling pins, cutting blocks, knife racks, tool handles, bowls, and house trim. Hard-maple flooring in a Philadelphia store withstood foot traffic longer than did a marble floor laid at the same time. Recently, a Canadian company has started making baseball bats out of sugar maple. Major league sluggers claim the resilient wood propels the ball farther than white ash, the orthodox choice for bats, and doesn't crack as easily.

Sugar maple is in demand for fine furniture and cabinetry, particularly the decorative types known as curly maple, quilted maple, and bird's-eye maple. In these variants, it is believed, fungal growth causes changes in the structure of the wood fibers, yielding wavy figures, ripples, and dots like the eyes of birds.

Sugar maple makes an excellent firewood. It smells good when you split it. It burns hot, lasts a long time, doesn't throw off sparks, and emits a pretty-colored flame. Little ash residue is left.

Acer saccharum cannot tolerate polluted air; for city plantings, the imported Norway maple, *Acer platanoides,* does better. (For more information on Norway maple, see Common Introduced Trees.) Salt, used to melt the ice on paved roads, can kill sugar maples. Far more dangerous to the species as a whole is the ongoing problem of acid rain and snow, which ecologists term acid deposition. Across the northeastern United States and southern Canada, the health of sugar maples has declined markedly in the last half century, and acid deposition, caused by power plant and industrial emissions farther west, may be the culprit. The acid leaches out key elements from the soil, including magnesium, potassium, and phosphorus. It may kill or disable mycorrhizal fungi, microorganisms that mingle with the roots of trees and improve their ability to take in nutrients and water.

Scientists, foresters, and maple sugar producers report thinner foliage, dying branches, and decreasing growth rates in sugar maples. Trees that are under stress change colors and drop their leaves early. They are also more likely to die from drought, insect defoliation, and wood rot fungi. According to Charles Little in *The Dying of the Trees,* sap from pollution-hit sugar maples "contains aluminum, manganese, iron, sodium, and barium, while healthy elements such as calcium and potassium are absent."

Sugar maples are fairly resistant to insects, but recent irruptions of pear thrips—a flea-size pest that feeds on the leaf buds—has killed many trees. Some scientists warn that global warming may banish the cool-adapted sugar maple from parts of the Northeast, including much of New England, during the twenty-first century.

Black Maple *(Acer nigrum)*. Some taxonomists classify black maple as a separate species; others believe it is simply an ecotype, or physiological race, of *Acer saccharum*. The leaves of black maple are 5 to 6 inches long and dark green; their undersurfaces are velvety. They have three lobes rather than the five typical of sugar maple. Rutherford Platt, in *Discover American Trees,* notes that black maple leaves suggest "sketches of sugar maple leaves simplified, with clean, straight edges, no fancy teeth."

Black maple ranges from southern Canada and scattered sites in New England west to South Dakota, Iowa, and Kansas, and south to North Carolina, Tennessee, and Arkansas. Black maple thrives in warmer, drier habitats than sugar maple and is more abundant west of the Allegheny Mountains than east of that range; west of the Mississippi, *Acer nigrum* becomes more common than sugar maple. In Pennsylvania, black maple occurs in the eastern, the central, and especially the western regions.

Scientists believe black maple developed during an earlier warm and droughty, or exothermic, climatic era. In the Northeast, black maple hybridizes readily with sugar maple. The growth habits, wood, and sap of black maple differ little or not at all from those of sugar maple.

SILVER MAPLE

A great silver maple *(Acer saccharinum)* grows beside a stone farmhouse in the hamlet of Baileyville, in western Centre County, near where I live. I visited the tree on a crisp September day. I hooked my tape measure to a ridge of bark and unscrolled it around the trunk: circumference, 22 feet. Had two friends been with me, the three of us could not have touched fingertips around the trunk. About 10 feet up, the bole divided into four upward-slanting limbs, each thicker than most trees hereabouts. A black cherry seedling sprouted from the leaf mold accumulated in the pocket created by the four divergent stems.

High in the silver maple, dead branches and scanty foliage signaled that the tree was approaching the end of its days. Across the road grew a smaller silver maple, perhaps a scion of the old one. Its greenery was full and lush. In both trees, the wind pushed the leaves this way and that, their upper surfaces dark green, their bellies pale, the trees' crowns riffling as the zephyrs passed through them. Half of one tree would turn quicksilver, then green, then back to shimmering silver again.

I plucked a leaf from a low branch of the younger maple. Arborists describe the foliage of *Acer saccharinum* as having a cutleaf shape. Prominent sinuses—notches, to the layperson—angle in deeply from the margins toward the center. The leaf's main central lobe is narrower at its base than farther toward its tip, a key identification feature for this species. This central lobe is itself divided into three lobes. The intricate leaves are doubly sawtoothed: the marginal teeth sport their own smaller serrations. Leaves of the silver maple grow 2 to 10 inches in length and are nearly as wide as they are long. On the one that I picked, the vegetative or photosynthetic portion, known as the blade, measured 4 inches long; the free stalk, or petiole, was a generous 3½ inches. In addition to being long, silver maple leafstalks are supple and slightly flattened, like the leaves of aspens and cottonwoods, letting them spin and sway even in a light breeze.

Most silver maples grow 40 to 60 feet in height; folks who have measured the Centre County specimen peg it at 80 feet tall. The usual mature trunk diameter is around 3 feet; that of our local giant is 7 feet. The bark is smooth and gray on young trees; older trees have brownish gray bark furrowed into thin flakes that remain fastened to the trunk at the center while curling away from it at both ends. The twigs when broken or crushed emit a pungent, rather unpleasant odor.

On a typical silver maple, the trunk is short, dividing into lateral branches that fork freely, forming a broad crown. On many trees, the lower side branches droop, then curve upward at their tips. Some call the silver maple's crown ragged and do not consider it aesthetically pleasing; and perhaps it cannot compare with the symmetrical fountain shape of an American elm, or the horizontal robustness of a field-grown white oak. But gazing at the Baileyville specimen, I found myself siding with Donald Culross Peattie, who, in *A Natural History of Trees,* extolled the "dignity and lively grace" of *Acer saccharinum.*

Silver maple occurs from New Brunswick west to Minnesota and south to northwestern Florida and eastern Oklahoma. The Ohio Valley is the center of the species' range, where deep, fertile, damp soils along rivers and streams provide an ideal growing substrate. The species is found throughout Pennsylvania, mainly on the banks of watercourses. Silver maples grow on flat and gently sloping land, but not on slopes or at high elevations in the mountains. Swamp borders, river islands, and lake edges support silver maples, and many have been planted as shade trees in cities and towns. Other names for the species are river maple, swamp maple, white maple (because of the wide, pale sapwood), and soft maple.

Sycamore is a frequent companion of silver maple in the streamside habitats, as are elms, red maple, basswood, hackberry, river birch, and other lowland species. Silver maple is the fastest growing of all the maples, achieving full stature in less than a century.

It is perhaps the earliest of our trees to flower. In March or April, well before the leaves emerge, separate sprays of male and female flowers appear—both sexes on the same tree, or one sex only on a single tree. The greenish or reddish flowers are about 1/4 inch long and situated too high in the tree to be easily seen. The wind pollinates the female flowers. The resulting samaras hang in pairs; they ripen quickly, becoming light brown. They are the largest samaras of any maple: 1 1/2 to 3 inches. They consist of an oblong seed that may exceed 1/2 inch in length, attached to a thin, papery vane. The samaras twirl down during a two- to three-week period, around May in Pennsylvania, just as the tree's leaves are expanding.

When hard frosts damage the flowers, seeds may be few; usually, though, silver maples bear prolific seed crops annually. Grosbeaks and squirrels eat the seeds. Those that land on suitable soil germinate quickly. Growth is most rapid during a tree's first fifty years, when it may add 1/2 inch of trunk diameter per year. The root system spreads and usually remains quite shallow. Silver maples can withstand temporary flooding, but fire easily kills them. The branches are brittle and apt to break during wind and ice storms, opening portals for fungal spores to enter and spread disease. Individual trees rarely live beyond 125 years.

The wood weighs 33 pounds per cubic foot. Pale, almost white sapwood surrounds the light brown heartwood. A bit softer than red maple, and somewhat brittle, the wood has been used for cheap furniture, packing crates, and paper pulp. Silver maple sap, although sweet, contains less sugar than that of sugar maple; nevertheless, syrup can be made from it. According to Hal Borland in *A Countryman's Woods,* sugar from silver maple includes enough tannic acid to turn a cup of tea black.

In autumn, the leaves of most silver maples become a wan yellow, often with a hint of green—sober dress, compared with the fiery foliage of the upland maples. Peattie wrote that the "orange and scarlet tints are quite absent," but a photograph in *The Audubon Society Field Guide to North American Trees,* by Elbert L. Little, shows a silver maple leaf that's a bright orange-yellow.

STRIPED MAPLE

Of all the trees in the forest, which has the handsomest bark? Perhaps paper birch, with its pale, shreddy wrapper, a white beacon in the woods. Or sycamore, patched and dappled like the hide of some great, mute animal. Or shagbark hickory, whose whiskery plates suggest age and wisdom. I like the bark of all those species—and another, belonging to a less impressive tree than the large specimens just mentioned: striped maple, named for its streaked, particolored bark.

Both trunk and branches of striped maple *(Acer pensylvanicum)* are an overall bright olive green, interrupted with vertical stripes of paler green, each stripe brightening to white at the center. The stripes occur on young stems and limbs and where the tree's expanding girth has split the outer bark. As a striped maple ages, the background color of its bark becomes a pale brownish gray, and the greenish white stripes may show mahogany-colored edges. Small warts and horizontal ridges are scattered across the smooth-textured surface. On old trees, the bark is darker and rougher, with less-prominent stripes.

Acer pensylvanicum ranges from Nova Scotia west to Michigan's Upper Peninsula, throughout upland New England and New York, and south in the Appalachians to Georgia. This small, slender tree has a trunk that generally divides within a few feet of the ground into several limbs, whose side branches zigzag out to spread their leaves over a broad area. Striped maple grows in cool, rocky woods, particularly on shaded mountain slopes and in damp ravines. It is statewide in Pennsylvania, except for the extreme southeast. In *Pennsylvania Trees,* Joseph Illick reported striped maple to be "very common in Mifflin, Centre, Blair, and Huntingdon counties." In Huntingdon County, he wrote, locals called it "seven bark" (seven colors in that intricate pattern?), whereas Potter Countians knew it as "streaked maple." These days, some taxonomists want us to call it moosewood.

Another name is goosefoot maple, because of the way the leaf is shaped: three pointed lobes and a rounded base, like the foot of a big goose seen in outline. Most leaves are 5 to 7 inches long. Fine teeth serrate the margin, and three prominent veins extend upward from the base, one centering each lobe. Some leaves are lightly haired on the undersurfaces, which are paler than the upper sides and may also show a tint of rust-brown. In autumn, the leaves turn a rich golden yellow; next year's leaf buds are about 2/5 inch long.

In the Northeast, a mature striped maple may grow to 20 to 30 feet, with a trunk diameter of 6 to 12 inches. Most individuals are stunted, subsisting in the limited light of the forest understory, where they reach only 10 to 15 feet tall. Really big specimens—such as the current Pennsylvania state record, on Cove Mountain in Lycoming County—can be 50 feet tall. The largest striped maple presently known in North America is 77 feet tall and has a trunk 50 inches in circumference; it grows in an arboretum in Nassau County, New York. In the wild, striped maple achieves its greatest stature and girth in the Great Smoky Mountains of Tennessee and North Carolina.

In Pennsylvania, *Acer pensylvanicum* flowers in late April and early May, after the tree's leaves have fully expanded. The flowers are borne at the twig ends in narrow clusters dangling on slender, drooping stalks. Some authorities deem striped maple's flowers inconspicuous, but the keenly observant Donald Culross Peattie termed them a "brilliant canary yellow" in *A Natural History of Trees.*

The sex expression of striped maple is both variable and changing. Some trees put out male and female flowers. Other trees produce only female flowers, and still others bear only male flowers; the same tree may be male one year, female the next. In a Massachusetts study, scientists found that 4 percent of trees were monoecious, putting forth both male and

Buck deer often rub their antlers on the trunks of striped maple. The shape of the leaf earns the tree its nickname "goosefoot maple."

female flowers, and 96 percent were dioecious, either male or female; of the latter, there were eight female trees for every male. Trees producing female flowers often were less healthy than those making male flowers. Perhaps the less vigorous trees' "strategy" was to produce a smaller number of female seeds, each of which presumably had a higher likelihood of becoming a tree, compared with the huge numbers of male pollen grains, even less likely to fertilize a female flower.

Striped maples fruit each year. Large, productive trees can yield several thousand fruits, which are typical for maples: paired samaras, or keys, joined at the seed, with a thin, wind-catching wing attached to each seed and flaring out away from each other. The fruits ripen in September and October, fall off, and disperse in October and November. If a samara lands on crusted snow, the wind may blow it several miles from the parent tree.

In forest shade, striped maple spreads out its branches and arranges its leaves to capture stray shafts of sunlight—sunflecks, in the parlance of tree scientists—that come flickering down through the canopy as breezes shift the leaves of taller trees overhead. *Acer pensylvanicum* has no need for deep roots to anchor itself, because the hardwoods towering above it blunt the wind and provide protection against storm damage. Its shallow, spreading root system lets a striped maple take in soil moisture and nutrients efficiently. The tree may gain as little as 12 inches of height in ten years. It can survive for a hundred years, completing its entire life cycle in the forest understory.

Striped maple also prospers in small openings, and if logging or some other disturbance fells its taller neighbors, striped maple responds quickly to the increased light by putting out leaves and growing vigorously upward. When other trees are wiped out in forest stands that include abundant striped maples, *Acer pensylvanicum* can become the dominant tree, shading out other hardwood species for years.

The pale wood of striped maple weighs 33 pounds per cubic foot. It is soft and weak. Because the trunk is generally spindly, loggers find no use for it. Cabinetmakers sometimes inlay it into darker woods. In the 1700s, colonial farmers fed both the green and dried leaves to cattle, and in the spring, they turned their horses and cows into the woods to eat the young shoots.

Moose, woodland caribou, and white-tailed deer browse the twigs, buds, and leaves. Cottontail rabbits and beavers eat the bark, especially in winter. A study in Maine found that ruffed grouse eat the seeds, and it would not be surprising if rodents also consume them. Buck deer seem to seek out striped maples for polishing the velvet off their antlers prior to the autumnal breeding season. I walked my woods the other day, and every striped maple I came to, nine in all, displayed healed-over buck rubs, as those scarrings are known.

BUCKEYES

Three trees in genus *Aesculus,* known as buckeyes, grow in Pennsylvania. Two native species—Ohio buckeye and yellow buckeye—occur naturally in the western counties and have been planted in other places and in some instances have "escaped," as the botanists put it, into the wild. Horsechestnut, an imported species, has been widely planted as a shade tree in Pennsylvania and throughout the East, and the casual naturalist is probably more apt to encounter it than the two natives. (See Common Introduced Trees for an account of horse-chestnut, *Aesculus hippocastanum.*) Overall, these three trees are not particularly common, and the likeliest places to see them are parks, campuses, and arboretums.

Buckeyes have opposite, compound leaves whose large, toothed leaflets fan out from the tip of a long, single stem, resembling the spokes of a wheel or the outspread fingers of a hand. No other group of North American trees exhibits this arrangement. In all three *Aesculus* species, the compound leaves range in overall length from 4 to about 15 inches.

The species can be distinguished by differences in the number of leaflets per leaf; the color of the pith, the soft material inside the twigs; the smell caused by breaking the twigs; the structure of the flowers; and characteristics of the terminal buds and fruit husks.

Ohio Buckeye *(Aesculus glabra).* Ohio buckeye is native to a handful of counties in western Pennsylvania, the species' current eastern limit. It ranges across Ohio, west to eastern Kansas, and south to Tennessee, Alabama, and Texas. Ohio buckeye thrives in openings along stream banks in moist woods and bottomlands. It is also called fetid buckeye or stinking buckeye, because the twigs and foliage, when broken or crushed, release a foul smell. A smallish tree, Ohio buckeye grows 30 to 70 feet tall, usually around 40 feet, with a trunk 1 to 2 feet in diameter.

This species gets the jump on spring by leafing out and beginning its shoot growth in late April, when its lowland neighbors—hackberry, American elm, box-elder, sycamore, sugar maple, American beech, and various

hickories and oaks—remain winter-
bare. The compound leaves have
five leaflets. At the other end of the
growing season, Ohio buckeye is one
of the earliest trees to drop its leaves
in autumn.

Pale yellow flowers emerge after
the leaves in late April and early May.
The flowers stand at the ends of the
branches in upright clusters, or pan-
icles, 4 to 6 inches long. The pani-
cles consist of both bisexual and male
flowers. Insects pollinate the flowers,
and ruby-throated hummingbirds
take nectar from them. Over summer, fertilized flowers develop into
fruits that consist of one to three
large seeds housed in a rounded,

*The large toothed leaves of Ohio
buckeye fan out like the spokes of
a wheel or the fingers of a hand.*

leathery, slightly spiny husk. The seeds are the namesake buckeyes, so dubbed
by early settlers because they resemble the eye of a deer: dark brown, gleaming, and possessing a large, pale scar of attachment suggesting an eye's iris.

The seeds fall in September and October. They bounce and roll away
from the tree, squirrels carry them off and bury them, and sometimes they
fall into streams and rivers, later to wash up on floodplains; they lie dormant
over winter and germinate the following spring. A study in Ohio found
that fox squirrels fed on the seeds in fall, winter, and spring. Observers have
also spotted fox squirrels eating the sugary pith of the terminal twigs.

Because the foliage, twigs, and seeds of Ohio buckeye contain a narcotic alkaloid that is poisonous to livestock, farmers have eradicated the tree
in some regions. Native Americans were aware of the plant's narcotic properties and used the mashed seeds and branches to stun fish so they could be
caught easily. The pale wood is lightweight, at 28 pounds per cubic foot,
soft, and easily worked with hand tools. It has been fashioned into furniture, crates, food containers, musical instruments, and artificial limbs. Ohio
buckeye is the state tree of Ohio, which is also known as the Buckeye State.

Yellow Buckeye *(Aesculus octandra).* Yellow buckeye is larger than Ohio
buckeye. It grows to 90 feet tall, with a trunk diameter of 3 feet. Its range is
more limited: the uplands of southwestern Pennsylvania, down the Ohio

River valley through much of West Virginia, to southern Indiana and Illinois, and in the Appalachian Mountain chain in western Virginia, western North Carolina, eastern Kentucky, and eastern Tennessee. *Aesculus octandra* grows best in moist humus in river bottoms; it also thrives in deep mountain valleys, or coves, and on north-facing slopes, particularly in the Great Smoky Mountains of North Carolina and Tennessee, where it attains its greatest size. Its attractive form and foliage make yellow buckeye a popular shade tree.

The compound leaf has five leaflets, and the twigs do not smell foul when broken. Yellow buckeye flowers in April or May in Pennsylvania, after the leaves have emerged. The 4- to 7-inch-long flower clusters are made up of many small, yellowish green flowers, each about 1 1/4 inches long. The resulting oblong fruits are 2 to 3 inches in length, pale brown, and smooth, not spiny like those of Ohio buckeye. They mature in early autumn; when their husks part, each releases one to three large, shiny seeds. The seeds contain a toxin, aesculin, that causes vomiting, stupor, and paralysis in people and livestock, although some sources have reported cattle and hogs eating the seeds safely. Native Americans roasted the seeds, mashed them, and soaked them in water to leach away the toxic element, producing a nutritious paste.

Yellow buckeye, also known as big buckeye or sweet buckeye, has the softest wood of all American hardwoods. It has been used for crates, boxes, woodenware, and paper pulp. The foliage of this tree turns a clear yellow in autumn.

BASSWOOD

Put yourself in the shoes of a colonist, a settler in North America in the late 1600s, perhaps in the Massachusetts Bay Colony, established by Puritans from England. Walking in the woods, you chance upon a tree— with a face carved into it. Eyes bulging, thick and twisted lips set in a sneer, a grotesque, startling image as white as bone. The tree is a basswood, a species whose pale outer sapwood is so soft that it can easily be carved with a knife. The Iroquois made masks in this way, working on the living trunk, then splitting off the finished false face and hollowing it out from behind. The Iroquois were at home in the eastern woods and used trees to make all manner of objects, from baskets to bandages to ceremonial masks. The English, on the other hand, feared the forest and saw it as a savage, hostile wilderness—although they, too, learned to use the diverse products it so generously supplied.

American basswood *(Tilia americana)* grows throughout much of eastern and central North America, from Maine to Minnesota and south to North Carolina and Arkansas, including southern Canada and all of New England, New York, and Pennsylvania; Michigan, Indiana, and Ohio stand at the approximate geographic center of the species' current range. Basswood does best on rich, well-drained loamy soils, often along streams; it also grows on dry, stony sites. At one time the species was found in nearly pure stands, but today it is scattered through the woods. In Pennsylvania, basswood grows statewide, frequently in the company of red oak, white ash, American elm, sugar maple, red maple, American beech, tuliptree, and yellow birch. Its other names include lime tree, whitewood, bee-tree, whistlewood, and American linden. Basswood is a close relative of the lindens of Europe, renowned as shade trees, and our species is often planted to cast its cool, deep shade on city streets.

Basswood is fairly shade-tolerant, and it grows faster than most other tree species. On good sites, it can reach 120 feet, with a trunk diameter of more than 4 feet. The largest bass-wood known in the United States as of 2000 was in Pottstown, Pennsylvania; it stood 94 feet tall and was 292 inches (more than 24 feet) around the trunk, with a 100-foot crown spread. A basswood can live for two hundred years, and some even achieve three hundred years. Basswood often grows as a cluster of trunks developed from sprouts around an old, logged-off stump; lesser stems may surround a central, dominant one. The roots of bass-wood run deep and wide, making the tree quite wind-firm.

The leaves are some of the largest on our deciduous trees—5 to 10 inches long—and heart-shaped, with a lopsided or uneven base. The leaf margin has distinct, sharp-looking teeth; the leaf tip is drawn out into an acute point; and the slender stem,

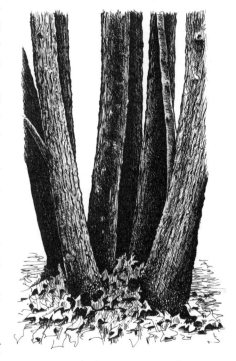

Basswood often grows as a clump of trunks sprouted from a single root system.

or petiole, is several inches in length—about a third as long as the leaf blade. The leaves are a dark dull green above, with pale, shining undersides. A subspecies of *Tilia americana* known as white basswood—variety *heterophylla,* which some taxonomists consider a separate species, found in the Appalachians from New York to Alabama—has leaves whose silvery white undersurfaces are cloaked with fine hairs. Berry pickers used to cover berry-filled baskets with big basswood leaves to protect the fruit from the sun. The leaves turn a wan yellow in autumn; when they fall, they enrich the soil with calcium, magnesium, nitrogen, phosphorus, and potassium.

The bark of young basswoods is thin, dark green, and shiny; that of mature trees is grayish brown, with deep furrows running up and down the trunk, forming ridges that are themselves divided by transverse secondary furrows. The bark, although thick and firm, is easily cut. The tree's inner bark possesses tough bast fibers that Native Americans wove into cordage and nets, and it's likely that the tree's common name evolved from "bastwood." The inner bark also had medical applications: the Indians boiled it, then used the liquid to soothe burned skin.

Six to eight weeks after leafing out, basswood trees flower; in Pennsylvania, this occurs about June. The pretty, five-parted flowers are about 1/2 inch long and creamy yellow, and it's hard to see them, up among those expansive leaves. It is easier to detect them by smell: their copious, powerfully sweet nectar tolls in bees, flies, butterflies, moths, and other nectar-feeding pollinating insects. Another clue to the presence of a flowering basswood is the loud buzzing of honeybees in its crown. (Basswood nectar makes a pale, strong-tasting honey prized by beekeepers and connoisseurs.) The flowers last for two to three weeks. Five to forty blossoms hang down in a cluster; the stem bearing these flowers connects to a green bract, a slender, winglike structure that acts as a communal parachute when the fruits finally fall.

Basswoods begin to flower and produce seed at around fifteen years. Most trees bear ample seed crops almost every year. One hot, humid, gnat-ridden August day, I was hiking up Beech Bottom Hollow in Clinton County on my way to a stand of old-growth hemlocks at Forrest Dutlinger Natural Area. Striding along on an old logging grade, my feet skidded on something round and hard. Scattered all over the trail were little green spheres, about the size of peas and ball-bearing hard. I trained my binoculars overhead: in the tops of tall basswood trees hung many more such fruits. Apparently a crown-thrashing storm had passed through the hollow, knocking down thousands of the immature nutlets.

Under normal conditions, the fruits ripen and drop from the tree in autumn, sometimes hanging on until winter or early spring. Slowed down by their parachutes, the nutlike fruits generally drift within a distance of one to two tree heights from their point of origin. Each fruit contains one or two seeds; the seeds have a tough coating and can lie dormant up to four years before germinating. Basswood seeds form part of the mast, or nut crop, of the eastern forest. Biologists report bobwhite quail, chipmunks, squirrels, and mice eating basswood seeds, and I suspect that ruffed grouse and wild turkeys might also pick them up. Rabbits and white-tailed deer nip off twigs and seedlings. Porcupines dine on the lush summer leaves and on basswood bark.

The wood of *Tilia americana* is a pale tan color, the thick, creamy white sapwood merging gradually into the somewhat darker heartwood. The wood seasons quickly and weighs a mere 28 pounds per cubic foot when dry. Native Americans hollowed canoes out of basswood logs. I used to keep bees, and in the spring my partner and I would place small frames made of thin basswood in our hives for the workers to fill with comb and honey. We tried to capture the nectar flow from black locust trees, as there weren't many basswoods where we kept our hives, even though our apiary was set near a village called Linden Hall; the resulting honey was almost as clear as water and wonderfully sweet. These days, round plastic sections are supplanting the traditional basswood frames for comb honey.

Because the dried wood is light, odorless, and tasteless, people have used basswood for packaging food, including vegetables and berries, weighing the negligible little boxes along with the produce they contain. According to Eric Sloane in *A Reverence for Wood,* in the 1800s strips of basswood were "made into thin 'scaleboards' and bent into all sorts of clever shapes, forming boxes with lids and some even made in once piece." Basswood has seen use as carriage stock, lightness being a virtue in a horse-drawn conveyance, as well as interior trim, drawer sides, cores of furniture components (subsequently covered with veneers of more lustrous wood), excelsior, crates, yardsticks, kitchenware, picture frames, models, toys, and whistles, which are made from the twigs. A knife easily cuts the soft wood across the grain, making it a favorite for whittling. As I write this chapter, a master woodworker I know has been commissioned by a nearby city to help build an old-fashioned carousel; he is on the lookout for basswood blocks to carve into merry-go-round horses.

BLACK-GUM

Some trees yield cross-grained wood, and black-gum is one of them. Its lumber is twisted and contorted, the grain spiraling irregularly up the trunk rather than running straight, like a series of progressively larger cylinders, as is the case with most other trees. Whether heavy or light in weight, cross-grained wood is tough, almost impossible to split even if you use a maul and wedges. In bygone days, a man said to be cross-grained was difficult to deal with, contrary. Because of its cross-grained aspect, black-gum *(Nyssa sylvatica)* was largely shunned by our wood-using pioneer ancestors. It is an important tree for wildlife, and a species increasing in Pennsylvania today.

Black-gum ranges from southwestern Maine and southern New England west to Michigan and Wisconsin; southward, it reaches Florida's Lake Okeechobee, eastern Texas, and northern Mexico. The species is abundant on the Atlantic coastal plain and in the Ohio River valley. In Pennsylvania, it is common in the eastern, central, and southern parts; local in the west; and rare in the extreme north-central counties. Black-gum grows in a variety of settings, including damp soil along streams, burnt-over areas, logged-off woods, abandoned fields, dry mountain slopes, rocky ridges, and the edges of bogs and swamps.

At maturity, a typical black-gum is 40 to 60 feet tall, with a trunk 1 to 2 feet in diameter. Exceptionally large individuals can be 125 feet tall and 5 feet in diameter. The trunk of the black-gum is fairly straight—although in central Pennsylvania, where I live, the black-gums seem to be highly susceptible to ice damage, with many losing the leading stem and ending up with unsightly crowns of scraggly sprouts that surround the remnant dead wood. Such a tree is said to be "stag-headed" because the dead wood and numerous uprights look like a deer's antlers. An undamaged crown is dense and conical, or sometimes flat-topped. The tree has crooked branches that gently zigzag back and forth. High branches usually ascend, while low branches droop toward the ground, and branches in the middle of the tree extend out horizontally, yielding an attractive, easily recognized winter silhouette.

Young trees—which particularly show the horizontal side-branching habit—are clad in grayish bark. As a tree ages, its bark darkens to almost black and breaks up into thick, scaly, squarish or many-sided blocks: "alligator bark" this checkered pattern is called, for its resemblance to the reptiles' rough, ridged skin.

The leaves look tropical: glossy green and simple in outline, suggesting the evergreen leaves that many southern hardwoods hold onto year-round.

A black-gum leaf is a smooth oval, lacking marginal teeth or lobes; thus *Nyssa sylvatica* can be listed with flowering dogwood, the magnolias, paw-paw, persimmon, and the unlobed form of sassafras as the only Pennsylvania native trees to possess such undifferentiated foliage. (Those trees are all considered primarily southern species that have extended their ranges into Pennsylvania and the Northeast since the last ice age, around ten thousand years ago.) The leaves of black-gum are 2 to 5 inches long and end in a pointed tip. They have a firm, leathery texture. The leaves grow crowded on short twigs that project from the sides of the branches.

In autumn, black-gum leaves turn color early, when the leaves of most other forest trees remain green. Guidebooks usually describe the fall foliage as scarlet; in fact, black-gum sets forth a range of attention-grabbing colors. Many black-gums grow in the woods around our house, including one, 15 feet from my office window, that I instructed the bulldozer operator to work around, at great pains and no little expense, when he dug the foundation for our addition. By the middle of September, our black-gums are turning a spectrum of radiant colors: lemon yellow, peach, mustard, orange, orange-red, maroon, scarlet. In many leaves, the colors burn along the central stalk and radiating ribs, while the rest of the blade remains a lush green. The bright colors attract resident and migrating birds, which eat the trees' fruit and help spread the seeds.

In May in Pennsylvania, black-gums put out dense, many-flowered, 1/2-inch-broad heads of male flowers, and few-flowered, slightly larger clusters of female flowers. Male and female flowers are nearly always borne on separate trees. In rare instances, some black-gums bear flowers that possess both male and female parts; such bisexual flowers are termed perfect. The flowers, greenish white, are less colorful than the bright red buds from which the young leaves unfurl. Insects, including honeybees, pollinate the female flowers; the tree is a major honey source, especially in the South, where black-gum is common and often grows to a large size.

Over summer, the female flowers develop into fruits, called drupes, that stand in twos and threes at the ends of long stems. The drupes are blue-black, oval, and pea-size, consisting of a thin pulp surrounding a slightly ridged stone. When I first tasted a black-gum fruit many years ago, I spat out the bitter thing immediately; yet many birds and some mammals relish them. In *Shake Them 'Simmons Down,* Janet Lembke reports on a large black-gum, growing near her home along the Neuse River in coastal North Carolina, whose fruit attracted mockingbirds, blue jays, brown thrashers, robins, cardinals, summer and scarlet tanagers, grackles, four species of woodpeckers, starlings, rose-breasted grosbeaks, Baltimore orioles, and veeries. Warblers and vireos flitted among the tree's boughs, taking flying insects attracted by the ripe and overripe drupes.

Black-gum fruits have a fat content of more than 14 percent, according to one study, comparable to the fat-rich fruits of flowering dogwood (16.7 percent) and cucumber-tree (22 percent). Fall fruits of other trees are lower in fats and are less attractive to migratory birds: American holly (8 percent), mountain-ash (4.6 percent), and hackberry (4.4 percent). Fats provide almost twice as much energy as carbohydrates, making them ideal for birds that must burn huge amounts of energy but cannot afford to load themselves down by gorging on bulky foodstuffs. The payoff to the plant comes after the seeds pass through the birds' digestive tracts and are defecated onto the ground, often hundreds of yards or even several miles away from their place of origin.

On bitter winter days, I have watched as small flocks of eastern bluebirds descended on our black-gums and cleaned up all the shriveled fruits remaining on the twig tips. Pileated woodpeckers swing up and down on the supple branches, snapping up black-gum drupes with their big bills. Ruffed grouse, ring-necked pheasants, wild turkeys, gray squirrels, red and gray foxes, opossums, and raccoons also consume the fruits. At Bear Meadows Natural Area, on state forest land in southern Centre County, many tall, sturdy black-gums grow in saturated soil at the edge of a bog; black bears climb high into the trees and gorge on the fruit, whose seeds are packed by the hundreds in the bruins' droppings. White-tailed deer browse the twigs and foliage of black-gum, especially young sprouts.

Seeds that overwinter on cool, damp soil usually germinate the following spring. Seedlings and young trees grow best in nearly full sunlight but can survive overtopping by other trees. In our woods is a small black-gum only 6 feet tall; its crown spreads out over 15 feet, with all of the twigs and leaves in a single plane, like the palm of a hand, directed upward to catch any sunlight filtering through the crowns of taller oaks and maples. Black-gum usually grows in mixed stands, where it is often a medium-size tree, taller than the dogwoods, which are even more shade tolerant, but not as lofty as the shade-intolerant species, such as hickories and most oaks. As oaks become fewer in the eastern woods, on account of the devastation wrought by the gypsy moth, the numbers of several other trees, including black-gum, are rising. The current decline of flowering dogwood may also be contributing to the increase in black-gums.

In *Terrestrial and Palustrine Plant Communities of Pennsylvania,* a publication of the Pennsylvania Natural Diversity Inventory, ecologist Jean Fike recognizes two major forest types in which black-gum is a major constituent. In the "Black-Gum Ridgetop Forest," *Nyssa sylvatica* is the dominant species, growing with black birch, sassafras, red maple, chestnut oak, black oak, and northern red oak. The leaf canopy is fairly open on the dry ridgetop sites, which sometimes are swept by wildfires. Trees grow slowly in such an impoverished setting, where the trunks of mature black-gums may be only forearm-thick. In the "Red Maple/Black-Gum Palustrine Forest," associated trees include yellow birch, eastern white pine, eastern hemlock, swamp white oak, and pin oak, with alders and dogwoods in the understory. "Palustrine" means wetlands; black-gums can tolerate brief springtime flooding, and they tend to grow quite large on such damp sites.

Old black-gums usually die from the top down, so the trees become shorter as they age. Wounds caused by fires or broken branches let wood decay fungi enter the trunk. Trees 2

Mature black-gums often become hollow, providing nesting and escape habitats for wildlife.

or more feet in diameter are often hollow, their trunks still alive, even though their walls are only a few inches thick. Woodpeckers, wood ducks, hooded mergansers, squirrels, and raccoons nest in hollow black-gums. Owls roost in them by day. Black bears hibernate in them during winter. Loggers generally leave black-gums standing, a practice that often preserves cavities in stands where heavy cutting removes most of the larger, and potentially cavity-containing, trees.

Settlers sawed hollow black-gum trunks into various lengths and used them as hives for honeybees (hence the old term "bee-gum"), storage bins ("corn-gums"), and box traps ("rabbit gums"). They rejected the wood for fencing, since it refused to split and rotted quickly in contact with the soil.

Its moderate weight, about 38 pounds per cubic foot when dry, and inter-locking grain made it excellent for wheel hubs.

The heartwood is yellowish white, and the thick sapwood is the color of old ivory. Because of its enduring strength, black-gum has been fashioned into maul heads, rollers for cables in mine shafts, scaffolding, tool handles, pallets, boxes, ironing boards, rolling pins, chopping blocks, and flooring for factories. If air-dried, the wood shrinks and warps wildly; lumbermen used to say that a freshly sawn black-gum board, when the sun shone on it, would curl up and crawl out of a lumberyard as fast as a black snake. Kiln-dried, the wood is more stable. It has an attractive ribbon figure when quarter-sawn; it is sometimes sliced as a veneer and stained dark to imitate mahogany. I cut up a bunch of black-gum when clearing a horse pasture, smallish trees that I didn't have to split. They made second-rate firewood, with much leftover ash.

Black-gum is also known as sour-gum because of its bad-tasting fruit. Some call it pepperidge, an obscure name that may derive from an Old English word for the shrub we now know as barberry. In the South, it is tupelo, from a Creek Indian name, *ito opilwa,* meaning swamp tree. It's hard to figure out how it came to be called a gum, because, as the writer Donald Peattie observes in *A Natural History of Trees,* "Nowhere on the American continent has anyone ever expressed from this dry and disobliging vegetable one fluid ounce of any sort of gum." The taxonomic name is both descriptive and poetic: *Nyssa* denotes a water nymph in classical Greek mythology, and *sylvatica* means "of the forest."

FLOWERING DOGWOOD

After buying our wooded land in the late 1970s, I would hike there with particular delight in early May. I'd watch migrating warblers and thrushes as they hunted for insects among the new leaves, the foliage unfurling in many pale shades of pink, gold, and green—above all green—the luminous quality of the forest enhanced by the creamy white blossoms of dogwood trees. Flowering dogwood *(Cornus florida)* was an agreeably common species in our woods, standing above the mountain laurel and witch hazel shrubs and below the tops of the maples, hickories, and oaks.

Today I can count on the fingers of both hands the number of dogwoods surviving on our thirty acres. Two of the trees, on the edge of our house clearing, appear healthy: 15 feet tall, their crowns flush with leaves that, in springtime, become spangled with the large, distinctive blossoms. The few other dogwoods still hanging on in our woods are deformed, their lower branches dead, sparse foliage in their crowns, putting out but few flowers in spring. And many are the lifeless snags of dogwoods, grim reminders of an epidemic that swept through the Appalachians in the 1980s.

Flowering dogwood is a small to medium-size tree adapted to live in partial shade. Mature dogwoods stand 10 to 40 feet tall and can have a trunk diameter of 12 to 18 inches. The trunk is short, quickly dividing into boughs that are generally horizontal and sometimes turned up at the tips. The species ranges from New England and New York west across lower Ontario to Michigan, and south to central Florida and Texas. In much of the South, *Cornus florida* is—or was—the most abundant species of the forest understory. In Pennsylvania, dogwood is present in the southern and eastern counties, but absent from parts of the northern tier.

Flowering dogwood inhabits moist-to-dry woods, old fields, fencerows, and roadsides. It grows best in rich, well-drained soil and does not thrive in damp, mucky ground, terrain that is flooded frequently, or sandy soils that drain rapidly. A dogwood's roots are extensive but shallow. If the tree's trunk and crown are badly damaged or killed by logging or fire, the root system will send up shoots. Dogwood grows slowly, increasing the circumference of its trunk by adding annual rings no more than $1/16$ to $1/8$ inch wide. Individual trees may live for 125 years.

Dogwood leaves conduct photosynthesis most efficiently in open shade where the light intensity is slightly less than one-third that of full sunlight. Where the shade is too deep, they either do not become established or they die out. *Cornus florida* seldom, if ever, grows in pure stands. In the Northeast, dogwoods are common in oak-hickory and in beech-birch-maple forests; they are uncommon in or absent from coniferous woods. In the South, dogwoods grow abundantly in mixed oak and pine stands.

The leaves are egg-shaped, 2 to 5 inches long by about half as wide, and marked by a prominent central vein with five or six curving lateral veins on each side roughly paralleling the leaf margin. Often they have wavy edges. They are a bright dark green above, paler green and covered with fine hairs beneath, and grow opposite each other on the twigs. The bark perhaps does not contribute to the tree's overall impression of gracefulness, but it is decidedly interesting to touch: rough, scaly, and broken up into little squarish plates like alligator hide.

Dogwood flowers suggested "white butterflies" to the naturalist and author Hal Borland. The four white "petals," opening to form a cross 2 to

The four, white "petals" of flowering dogwood are actually bracts, coverings that protected the developing flowers, located where the bracts intersect.

4 inches wide, are in fact bracts, coverings that protected the incipient, dormant flowers over winter. Most dogwoods have white bracts, although a few have pale salmon or pink ones. The bright colors attract insects, which pollinate the small, green florets clustered where the bracts intersect. The florets are the actual flowers; each cluster has twenty to thirty of them. Dogwoods begin flowering at around age six and produce abundant seed crops about every other year.

Generally one to five of the central florets complete their development into fruit. The elliptical fruits are brilliant red, 1/2 inch long by 1/4 inch wide, and borne at the ends of long stalks. The pulp is thin and mealy; some sources say it is poisonous to humans, and in any case, it is too bitter to be eaten. Hidden in the pulp is a hard, two-chambered, usually two-seeded stone. As the fruits ripen in September and October, the leaves of dogwoods become wine red, the undersides a paler pink. Those bright colors catch the eyes of birds, which land and eat the fruits. Later, perhaps far from the parent tree, the birds void the seeds in their droppings. Dogwood seeds usually germinate in the spring after they have fallen.

More than thirty-six species of birds eat dogwood fruits: local residents, such as ruffed grouse, wild turkeys, and woodpeckers; short-range migrants, including wood ducks, yellow-shafted flickers, crows, cedar waxwings, robins, cardinals, and catbirds; and birds that travel long distances, including pine and evening grosbeaks, as well as Neotropical migrants such as red-eyed vireos and Swainson's and wood thrushes. The fruits, about 17 percent crude fat, by weight, are loaded with energy, which the birds need for the rigors of migrating.

The ecological value of dogwoods extends beyond feeding birds. The leaves of *Cornus florida* decompose quickly, freeing minerals for use by other plants. Dogwood leaves break down three times faster than hickory leaves; four times faster than those of tuliptree, eastern red-cedar, and white ash; and ten times faster than sycamore and oak leaves. They enrich the top layers of the soil with calcium, fluorine, potassium, phosphorus, magnesium, and other elements.

Native Americans made a scarlet dye from dogwood roots and treated diarrhea and fevers with a preparation made by boiling the inner bark. The pinkish wood is hard and quite heavy, at 51 pounds per cubic foot. Fine-textured and homogeneous, it withstands abrasion and wears smooth under friction. People have used it for chisel handles, pulleys, knitting needles, sledge runners, hay forks, wheel hubs, rake teeth, splitting wedges, and the heads of mallets and golf clubs. In the nineteenth century, great quantities of the wood went into the shuttles used in the textile industry in the United States and Europe; today plastic shuttles have replaced the wooden variety in weaving machinery.

I have often wondered if the name dogwood has a true canine connection. There is that old and apt mnemonic: "How can you tell a dogwood? By its bark." Most sources link it to the Germanic word *dag,* meaning a skewer to hold meat together for cooking—and likely this hard wood would be up to the task. In *The Book of Forest and Thicket,* John Eastman suggests another explanation, based on his experiences cutting dogwood to clear survey lines: the name may come from the fetid smell of the freshly cut wood, which, Eastman contends, resembles the odor of dog feces.

In the 1970s, dogwoods in the Pacific Northwest began dying from a mysterious disease. Soon eastern dogwoods started showing the same symptoms: tan leaf spots that developed into large, purple-bordered blotches. Often the infection spread to twigs, branches, and trunk, with cankers girdling the main stem and killing the tree. The pathogen causing the epidemic turned out to be a fungus never before identified; it may have entered the continent on infected nursery stock, perhaps of *Cornus kousa,* an Asian dogwood that seems relatively resistant to the disease. Within a few years, the fungus, named *Discula destructiva,* spread throughout the East, affecting seedling and adult trees and wild and ornamental specimens. Scientists speculate that birds feeding on dogwood fruits may carry fungal spores, spreading the infection.

Catoctin Mountain Park, in Maryland, lost 88 percent of its dogwoods between 1984 and 1988. On Pennsylvania's Allegheny Plateau, near the northern edge of the species' natural range, all of the dogwoods that researchers examined between 1995 and 1998 had either died of dogwood anthracnose, as the disease came to be known, or were infected with it. Some studies suggest that acid rain increases the incidence and severity of the plague. In Pennsylvania as a whole, forest pathologists estimate that 75 percent of all dogwoods have died, either killed outright by the fungus or weakened so that drought or wood-boring insects caused their death.

In May 2001, while driving through Lancaster County, I rejoiced to see many dogwoods blooming on the edges of woodlots, in roadside thickets, and on lawns. The trees that seem to be surviving the disease are those growing away from damp habitats, in places where air circulation dries out the leaf surfaces and prevents the fungus from taking hold. It seems likely that not all dogwoods will perish—as forest pathologists once feared—but that the species will never again be as numerous as it once was.

The loss of so many dogwoods has changed the face and the ecology of the eastern woods, particularly in the South. Without dogwood leaves continually restoring calcium to forest soils—many of which are calcium-poor in the first place—acid rain may leach the usable calcium out of the system. Soil invertebrates such as insects and arthropods need calcium for their exoskeletons; birds prey heavily on those invertebrates. Some scientists fear that the destruction of dogwoods has contributed to the decline in forest-nesting birds, which require calcium for their eggshells. Other animals that eat invertebrates, including salamanders and toads, may also be affected.

Studies in Tennessee suggest that as dogwoods dwindle, two other bird-dispersed plants increase: black-gum, *Nyssa sylvatica,* and spicebush, *Lindera benzoin,* both of which offer high-fat fruits in late summer and autumn.

PERSIMMON

The common persimmon *(Diospyros virginiana)* is a member of Ebenaceae, the ebonies, a family of trees and shrubs with dense, hard, heavy wood that is often black in color. The vast majority of ebonies grow in the tropics, including India and Africa; only one other member of the group occurs in North America: the Texas persimmon, *Diospyros texana,* of

Texas and Mexico. In Pennsylvania, the common persimmon nears the northern limit of its range. Persimmons are found in the lower Connecticut River Valley; on Long Island, New York; and in northern New Jersey. The species extends across the southern half of Pennsylvania, west to southeastern Iowa and eastern Kansas, and south to Florida and Texas.

The name persimmon comes from an Algonquian Indian word. Other names for the tree include date plum, possum wood, and the abbreviated 'simmon. *Diospyros,* the species name, means "fruit of the gods."

Adaptable trees, persimmons sprout in dry, sandy soil of uplands; they also survive on wet lowland sites, including sloughs and swamp margins that flood for part of each year. In Illinois, they have sprouted on coal-mined lands stripped of topsoil. Persimmons grow in old fields and fencerows, and along woods edges and ditch banks. In the past, farmers clearing off the original forest often left persimmons remaining in fields so that they could partake of the trees' fruits; for the same reason, people planted persimmons in farmyards. In forests of the Northeast, persimmons grow in company with sassafras, elms, hickories, sugar and red maples, tuliptree, box-elder, and oaks. Persimmons occur as single trees or in small groups mixed in with other species; they do not form pure stands.

In Pennsylvania, most persimmons are 25 to 50 feet tall at maturity, with a trunk about 1 foot in diameter. In summer 2001, I looked at some persimmons in a mature forest on the south side of Conococheague Mountain in western Perry County, on resettlement lands—impoverished farms from which the federal government had relocated people during the Depression era of the 1930s, lands that today form part of Pennsylvania's state forest system. Knowing the history of the area, I presumed that the trees in those woods were not much more than seventy years old. The persimmons stood as straight as ramrods, their trunks 15 inches in diameter at breast height, their crowns merging 50 to 60 feet up with those of red maples, red oaks, and Table Mountain and Virginia pines. Although large and robust, those persimmons were nothing like the old-growth specimens logged in southern forests in the last century: trees 100 and even 130 feet tall. Today five national cochampions—as recognized by the American Forestry Association—have been found in Missouri, Arkansas, Georgia, and South Carolina, which boasts two cochampions. The tallest of those trees is 132 feet; the thickest has a trunk 136 inches in circumference.

Persimmon is renowned for its straight, vertical trunk. The dark brown or blackish bark is thick and broken up into many small, squarish, scaly blocks, a texture and pattern that resembles the "alligator bark" of black-gum, *Nyssa sylvatica*. Some people also see a resemblance to the barks of flowering dogwood and blackhaw viburnum, a common shrub. In the persimmon, the tree's inner bark often shows through the outer layer as cinnamon red streaks in the deep furrows between the fractured blocks. From the upright trunk, branches extend outward in a crooked or zigzag pattern— "like mad snakes," according to Rutherford Platt in *Discover American Trees*. The dense crown is usually rounded or cylindrical.

The egg-shaped leaves are 3 to 6 inches long by 2 to 3 inches wide. They are simple, not compound, and they alternate along the stems. Persimmon leaves, borne on 1/2-inch to 1-inch leafstalks, are thicker than the leaves of many other trees. Their margins lack teeth. The top surfaces are dark green and shiny, and have a tropical look to them; the whitish green undersurfaces may be furred with small hairs, or they may be hairless. The foliage turns yellow before releasing from the twigs in autumn.

In May or June, persimmons put out white or yellowish, bell-shaped, four-lobed flowers, whose fragrance attracts pollinating insects, including bees. Some trees send forth female flowers, about 5/8 inch long, while other trees produce male flowers, about 3/8 inch in length. The female flowers are solitary; the males blossom in pairs or trios. The female flowers develop into the fruits known as persimmons. Botanically speaking, the fruits are berries. They become as large as Ping-Pong balls. Persimmons bear good fruit crops about every second year. Some trees start producing persimmons as early as age ten; the optimum fruit-bearing age is between twenty-five and fifty years.

Persimmon has thick dark brown or blackish bark that fractures into many squarish, scaly blocks.

Until they ripen, persimmons are loaded with tannins, mouth-puckering compounds that deter some fruit-eating animals, the same substances that make acorns bitter. Capt. John Smith, founder of the Jamestown settlement in colonial Virginia, wrote a

Generall Historie of Virginia, New-England, and the Summer Isles, published in 1624, in which he described the flavor of the persimmon (*putchamin,* he called it, phonetically rendering the local Indian word): "If it be not ripe, it will draw a man's mouth awry, with much torment, but when it is ripe, it is as delicious as an apricot."

Time, warmth, and sunlight—not frosts, as some people believe—bring persimmons to perfection. The fruits mature in autumn and may hang on the branches into winter. Ripe persimmons are orange-colored, often with a reddish blush, their skins wrinkled and sagging. The soft, juicy flesh feeds songbirds, including catbirds, robins, and cedar waxwings; wild turkeys and bobwhite quail; and mammals such as squirrels, red and gray foxes, opossums, raccoons, skunks, mice, deer, and bears.

Indians baked the sweet pulp into corn-based breads and dried persimmons whole for winter use. Modern foragers use them in cakes, pies, cookies, puddings, and jams. The flavor resembles that of a date. Euell Gibbons, a Pennsylvania author, labeled *Diospyros virginiana* "the sugar-plum tree" in his book on foraging, *Stalking the Wild Asparagus.* He presented recipes for molasses, beer, and vinegar made from persimmons, which, he said, are best harvested by shaking the tree so that the ripe fruits come tumbling down. Gibbons reported eating persimmons straight off the tree as late as mid-January. He noted that a tea rich in vitamin C can be brewed from the dried summertime leaves.

Most of the persimmons Gibbons obtained from Pennsylvania trees had no seeds. The naturalist and wildlife artist Ned Smith, also a Pennsylvania resident, noted the same phenomenon in *Gone for the Day:* seven out of ten persimmons he picked on a ridge near Millersburg, in Dauphin County, contained no seeds whatsoever, while three others had a single seed. A typical persimmon has four to eight seeds, which are oblong, flattened, and about 1/2 inch long. Birds and mammals spread the seeds in their droppings.

Seedlings are shade-tolerant and will sprout in the forest understory, although their growth there is slow. In addition to seeding itself naturally, persimmon sends up suckers from its roots, particularly on nutrient-poor sites, yielding thickets of stunted, shrubby trees. When sawed down or scourged by fire, persimmons sprout from the base of the stump.

The wood consists largely of sapwood having a pale brown color. The heartwood—tissues at the center of the trunk, no longer involved in transferring water and nutrients, but functioning as a columnar support for the tree—may not develop until a persimmon is a century old. The tree's membership in the ebony family is confirmed by the heartwood's color: dark brown to jet black. The sapwood, too, sometimes becomes streaked with black or dark gray.

Persimmon wood is harder than oak and denser and heavier than some of the hickories. A cubic foot of it can weigh 52 pounds, dry weight— almost as heavy as black locust. Persimmons from northern regions grow more slowly and accumulate denser wood than do trees in the South, where warmer temperatures spur faster growth. Persimmon wood shrinks considerably and may crack, or check, if the ends of logs are not sealed with paraffin to slow the drying process. Because few trees grow large, the wood is fashioned mainly into small items—golf club heads, billiard cues, mallets, shoe lasts, shuttles for the textile industry, and brush backs—although today some of those products are made out of plastic or metal. The dark heart-wood has been used for inlays in cabinetry; the sapwood, sawed into thin panels and stained dark, imitates black walnut as a veneer for covering fur-niture. The wood is uniform in texture and takes a bright polish.

ASHES

B otanists recognize between sixty and seventy species of ash trees across the Northern Hemisphere. Sixteen species occur in North America, including three in Pennsylvania. The ashes belong to the family Oleaceae, the olives, and are closely related to three well-known shrubs: privet, for-sythia, and lilac.

The largest and most abundant ash species in Penn's Woods, and the most valuable for lumber, is white ash *(Fraxinus americana)*. Black ash *(Fraxinus nigra)* is also statewide in Pennsylvania, an occasional denizen in swamps and bottomlands. Red ash *(Fraxinus pennsylvanica)*, sometimes called green ash, is also widespread in the state.

Ash trees have strong links to legend and mythology. Germanic peoples believed that a giant ash, Yggdrasil, supported the universe. One of the tree's roots extended into the underworld, another into the land of the giants, and a third into the home of the gods; dew that dripped from the tree's leaves made flowers spring up all over the earth. Scholars suggest that this "world tree" concept is reflected in today's maypole and Christmas tree traditions. American settlers brought with them a sense of awe regarding the ash, and in the New World they found ash trees very similar to the ones in Europe. To some immigrants, a door framed with ash was a "witch door"

that warded off evil spirits. Others placed ash leaves in their boots and leg-
gings, believing that no snake would ever cross such a barrier. If bitten, they
treated snakebite with preparations made from the buds and bark of ash.

White Ash *(Fraxinus americana)*. White ash is a medium to large tree that
grows in forests and open habitats from Nova Scotia west across southern
Canada to Michigan and Minnesota, and south to Florida and Texas. At
one time, taxonomists recognized a separate species, Biltmore ash, whose
twigs are velvety and hairier than those of white ash; today Biltmore ash is
considered a variety of white ash. Two other common names for *Fraxinus
americana* are Canadian ash and American ash.

A mature specimen will stand 70 to 80 feet tall, with a trunk 2 to 3 feet
in diameter; old-growth trees can reach 120 feet, with a trunk diameter of 6
feet. The trunk of white ash tends to be quite straight and, on a forest-grown
tree, clear of branches and branch scars for a considerable distance from the
ground up. The rounded or conical crown bears compound leaves with large,
distinct leaflets; glimpsed high in the tree, the leaflets may not appear to be
parts of a compound structure, but rather a collection of individual leaves.

The compound leaves stand opposite each other on the stout, round,
gray-brown twigs. A single leaf is 8 to 12 inches long and consists of five to
nine leaflets. Each leaflet measures 3 to 5 inches long by about $1^1/2$ inches
wide and stands off from the main stem on a short stalk. Leaflets can be
slightly toothed along their margins or not toothed at all. Lance-shaped and
tapering to a point, the leaflets are a lustrous dark green above and silver-
white below. In general, the foliage is thicker on the outer fringes of the
tree, and an observer leaning against the trunk usually can look up and see
the sky through the rather sparse crown.

The columnar trunk of the white ash is clad with distinctive bark:
divided by diamond-shaped fissures that are long and narrow, running with
the length of the trunk. Fine, tight, slightly flat-topped ridges intersect with
one another and stand between the diamond fissures. The pattern has
always suggested to me the reticulated skin of a snake. Most sources judge
the bark of the white ash dark, but many of the ashes I see have medium
gray or pale gray-brown bark. It is believed that the tree's common name
comes from the bark's color, which resembles wood ash (this ancient name
presumably first described the European ash, *Fraxinus excelsior*).

White ash is the most common ash species across the Northeast. Joseph
Illick, in the 1928 edition of *Pennsylvania Trees,* pronounced white ash gen-

White ash bark is broken into diamond-shaped fissures. The tree's compound leaf is made up of five to nine leaflets.

eral throughout the state: "common in the eastern, southern, central, and western parts," sparse in the mountains "except in moist valleys and rich bottomlands," and locally rare in northern Pennsylvania. The range map for white ash in *The Vascular Flora of Pennsylvania,* by Ann Rhoads and William Klein, published in 1993, supports Illick's observations. White ash is more common in oak-hickory woods than in beech-birch-maple forests. It rarely grows in swamps. The tree does best in rich, moist, well-drained soil, particularly along streams and lakes. In my neck of the woods, ashes grow singly or in small clusters, generally (but not always) within a few to 50 feet of some spring-fed rivulet trickling down off the mountain.

Ash trees are either male or female. Trees of both sexes send out flowers just before they leaf out or while they are putting forth their leaves, around May in Pennsylvania. Usually more male than female trees flower. The male flowers hang in dense, reddish purple clusters; the female flowers are also clustered but are airier and not crowded together as tightly. The wind carries pollen from the male to the female blossoms. Over summer, the female reproductive structures grow and mature into samaras, or keys. An ash samara is 1 to 2 inches long and consists of a seed encased in a thin husk, with a papery wing. Its overall shape and rounded tip resemble the blade of a canoe paddle; it is more symmetrical than a maple samara. Ash samaras dangle in drooping clusters of a dozen or more seeds; they are not paired like maple samaras. They may hang on the twigs all winter. Seeds can lie dormant in the forest litter for up to seven years.

Mature trees produce good seed crops about every third year. The wind blows the samaras off the tree and may carry them 400 feet or farther. Naturalists have spotted wood ducks, bobwhite quail, purple finches, pine grosbeaks, and fox squirrels eating white ash seeds; no doubt other wild animals also feed on them. Rabbits, beavers, and porcupines eat the bark of young trees, and deer browse ash seedlings.

Early in its life, white ash is remarkably tolerant of shade. A seedling in deep shade may grow only a foot in fifteen years. However, its well-developed root system will let it respond quickly if a neighboring tree dies or falls, opening up a gap in the canopy toward which the ash lifts its crown. Young trees have few branches; to minimize snow and ice loading, they reach upward in a candelabra shape. As trees grow older, they become less shade-tolerant and structurally sturdier. White ash generally forms a taproot that splits into several downward-growing roots, with side roots branching off at intervals. White ash is vulnerable to drought, especially in spring and early summer. Stumps cut low to the ground freely send up shoots and sprouts that may develop into new trees.

In autumn, white ash begins to change its leaf color earlier than almost any other tree. In a dry year, the foliage may simply turn a dull bronze and fall off. Other years, the leaves become a beautiful purplish blue or burgundy. In *A Natural History of Trees,* Donald Culross Peattie nominated ash as "the most versatile colorist of all our woods," supplying, as it does, "the bronze and mauve tints that are the rarest in our autumn displays." After the leaves fall and fade, they enrich the soil with high levels of sugars and nitrogen.

Ash has some of the toughest wood, pound for pound, of American trees. It weighs a little over 40 pounds per cubic foot, which is lighter than white oak and sugar maple, about the same as red oak, and heavier than red maple. Ash wood is strong and flexible, able to withstand sudden shocks. Native Americans used it for snowshoe frames, canoe paddles, and sleds—products that are still made from ash. Settlers built wagon frames from ash; they also fashioned butter tubs from it, since the wood is flavorless and odorless as well as strong. Today ash gets turned into tool handles (especially long tools, such as shovels and hoes), oars, skis, porch swings, polo mallets, hockey sticks, and baseball bats. The noted Louisville Slugger, used by most major league ballplayers, comes from white ash cut in northern Pennsylvania and southern New York. Buyers select young, smallish trees, 16 to 18 inches in trunk diameter; larger than that, the wood becomes "brash," lacking in resilience. White ash is an excellent firewood that splits easily and can be burned even in a green or unseasoned condition. Some authorities credit this property to flammable sap; in fact, white ash simply has a lower natural moisture content than most other woods. An old English poem goes: "Ash wet or ash dry/A king will warm his slippers by." A friend who burns wood to heat his house reports that white ash yields more ash than any other type of wood he burns.

Joseph Illick, state forester for Pennsylvania in the early twentieth century, ranked white ash among the commonwealth's premier timber trees, in part because of its "immunity from the attack of fungous diseases and insects." Unfortunately, ashes are nowhere near so healthy today. A generalized malady known as ash decline or ash die-back appeared in the Northeast in the 1980s and has stricken many trees in the region. Scientists are unsure of the cause or causes, but believe that drought, fungi, air pollution, and viruses may play a role. A microbe classified as a mycoplasmalike organism, or MLO, has been isolated from the phloem or food-conducting tissue of ash trees afflicted with ash yellows, a possibly related disease. Sick trees grow slowly, have patchy foliage and stunted leaves, and turn colors prematurely in autumn. Branches die back, cracks appear in the trunk, spindly shoots arise from the trunk's base, and some ashes eventually die from the condition.

What has changed between Illick's era and today? An increase in air pollution has resulted in acid rain and snow; it would not surprise me if such ongoing environmental degradation lay behind the decline of this beautiful, useful tree.

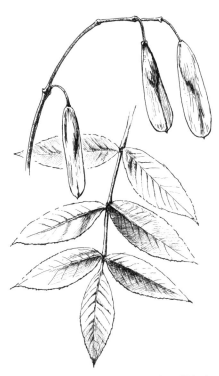

The samaras, or winged seeds, of black ash have blunt or slightly notched ends. The leaflets attach directly to the compound leaf's central stem.

Black Ash *(Fraxinus nigra).* Black ash is a smaller, slenderer tree than white ash. A mature black ash is 60 to 80 feet, with a trunk diameter of 1 to 2 feet. The trunk is often crooked or leaning, and the branches extend strongly upward. Distinguish black ash from white by the former's leaflets, which attach directly to the compound leaf's central stem rather than standing off on short stalks. The northernmost of the ashes, *Fraxinus nigra* prefers cool, damp habitats and often grows in swamps and floodplains. It ranges from Atlantic Canada west to Manitoba and south to Delaware, Virginia, and Kentucky.

Black ash samaras have blunt rather than rounded ends. Their seeds may lie dormant on the ground for two to eight or more years before germinating. In autumn, the leaves turn rusty brown, with no particular color variation.

Two other names for the tree are hoop ash and basket ash. Craft workers will season a black ash billet—a log a foot or so long—and then pound it on the end grain, causing the wood to split into sheets along the annual growth rings. Cut into thin strips, or splints, and soaked in water for added pliancy, the splints can be woven into baskets. People also use this tough wood for barrel hoops, oars, and furniture. Black ash gets its name from its dark heartwood.

Red Ash *(Fraxinus pennsylvanica).* Red ash and green ash once were considered separate species (the former has hairy twigs; the latter doesn't), but now taxonomists merge the two under the generally accepted name of red ash. This hardy lowland tree grows to a maximum height of around 75 feet in wet habitats such as bottomland woods, stream banks, and moist fields. The roots are shallow and wide-spreading. Red ash is not a common species, and it is more plentiful in southern than in northern Pennsylvania. On a continental scale, *Fraxinus pennsylvanica* grows from Atlantic Canada west to the Rocky Mountain states and south to Florida and Texas—the largest range of any North American ash.

The wood is heavy, at 44 pounds per cubic foot, hard, and strong. Generally mills do not distinguish it from white ash. Red ash has been widely planted as a street tree and an ornamental, especially in the western states.

ODD OTHERS

The following are uncommon or rare trees, or borderline specimens that are more like shrubs but are given official tree status in "Checklist of Pennsylvania Native Trees," published by the University of Pennsylvania's Morris Arboretum, the official arboretum of the commonwealth of Pennsylvania.

Balsam Poplar *(Populus balsamifera)*. Balsam poplar grows up to 80 feet tall. It is closely related to the similar eastern cottonwood but is much less common in Pennsylvania. Found in scattered locations statewide, balsam poplar thrives in cool, damp, seasonally flooded soils along the edges of rivers and bogs. It needs full sunlight and develops a shallow root system. The leaves are 6 to 10 inches long, fine-toothed, and narrowly heart-shaped.

Balsam poplar is a northern species that comes as far south as Pennsylvania, Ohio, and West Virginia. Its range extends far into Canada and Alaska, where it is an important source for paper pulp. Some botanists consider balsam poplar the northernmost broad-leaved tree in North America. Its name comes from the pleasing fragrance of the resin coating its buds; another name is tacamahac.

Allegheny Chinkapin *(Castanea pumila)*. Pennsylvania is the northern range limit of Allegheny chinkapin, a diminutive relative of American chestnut, *Castanea dentata*. Allegheny chinkapin—also called American, common, or tree chinkapin, alternately spelled chinquapin—grows mainly in dry oak-hickory woodlands in Pennsylvania; its range carries south to Florida and west to Arkansas and Texas. In the North, it is usually a multistemmed shrub 5 to 10 feet tall, and occasionally an understory tree climbing to 20 feet. In the South and west of the Mississippi River, it becomes more treelike, sometimes achieving a height of 50 feet and a trunk diameter of 2 to 3 feet. In the Keystone State, it has been found in the southeast, south-central, and southwest regions.

The leaf is 3 to 5 inches long and looks much like that of American chestnut: lanceolate, with a pointed tip and prominent marginal teeth ending in bristle tips. Downy, white hairs cloak the leaf's underside. The leaves turn yellow in autumn. In autumn also, the spiny husk parts to reveal a single egg-shaped nut smaller than the American chestnut. Capt. John Smith first reported chinkapin nuts from the New World, in 1612, noting that Indians in Virginia harvested the sweet kernels for food. Squirrels, chipmunks, rabbits, mice, and eastern woodrats are some of the wild animals reported to eat the nuts. Thickets of Allegheny chinkapin provide food and cover for deer, ruffed grouse, wild turkeys, bobwhite quail, and other wildlife. People have used the wood for fuel, charcoal, fence posts, and railroad ties.

The imported chestnut blight fungus that nearly wiped out the American chestnut during the twentieth century is also deadly to Allegheny chinkapin.

Sweetbay Magnolia *(Magnolia virginiana).* Also known as laurel magnolia, this species ranges from New Jersey and southeastern Pennsylvania to Florida and Texas. Seldom topping a height of 25 feet in the North, it grows taller in the South, particularly Florida, where it can be 70 feet tall, with a trunk 3 feet in diameter. Sweetbay magnolia inhabits swamps and moist woods. Its leathery leaves are 3 to 6 inches long, the smallest among our native magnolias. When crushed, foliage and twigs emit a spicy, aromatic scent. The leaves usually fall off in autumn in the North and persist as evergreen foliage in the South. According to Joseph Illick in *Pennsylvania Trees,* leaves on some specimens found in Franklin County, Pennsylvania, hang on the twigs through winter and into spring.

Umbrella Magnolia *(Magnolia tripetala).* Huge, pale green leaves, 10 to 24 inches long and 5 to 10 inches broad, distinguish this small, often straggling tree that can reach 30 feet tall and 1 foot in trunk diameter, but is usually smaller. The leaves, on abbreviated stalks at the ends of the branches, arc outward like the ribs or panels of an umbrella. Umbrella magnolia grows in scattered stands across the South. It achieves its maximum size along streams in the Great Smoky Mountains, where it can be abundant.

According to Joseph Illick in the 1928 edition of *Pennsylvania Trees,* umbrella magnolia is native only to the Susquehanna River valley in York and Lancaster counties in Pennsylvania. Introduced elsewhere in the state, it has become naturalized and is spreading rapidly in some locales, particularly in disturbed forests. I have encountered it at Goat Hill Serpentine Barrens Natural Area, on state forest land in southern Chester County, just north of the Mason-Dixon line. (Other intriguing trees at Goat Hill include blackjack oak, post oak, and southern red oak, found only in Pennsylvania's southeastern corner.)

The solitary flowers of umbrella magnolia are typical for the magnolia family: creamy white and 7 to 10 inches long. Their odor, although disagreeable to humans, attracts insect pollinators. The pollinated flowers develop into rose-colored, cone-shaped fruit heads containing numerous red, flattish seeds.

Wild Plum *(Prunus americana)*. This small tree, also known as American plum, reaches a height of 9 to 30 feet and has a trunk 6 to 12 inches in diameter. The short trunk branches quickly into many wide-spreading boughs. The sharp-pointed leaves are 1½ to 4 inches long, their margins sharply and often doubly saw-toothed. The short, stiff thorns that armor the tree are mainly bud-bearing spur branches.

Prunus americana ranges from New England south to Florida and west to the Great Plains. It grows throughout Pennsylvania, except for the northern counties. It does best on rich, moist soil and often forms thickets in hedgerows and along roadsides.

Wild plum is sometimes called red plum, as its fruits, about an inch in diameter, are often red in color, although they can also be yellow. The plums have a thick, tough skin. They are eaten by many animals, and they make excellent preserves and jellies. Taxonomists recognize numerous varieties, some of which are cultivated.

Allegheny Plum *(Prunus alleghaniensis)*. Allegheny plum is a thicket-forming shrub or a small tree whose spotty, interrupted range extends from Connecticut through Pennsylvania to Tennessee. In the Keystone State, it grows mainly in the western sections, on stony bluffs, roadsides, floodplains, and shale barrens. The height is no more than 20 feet, and the trunk diameter is about 6 inches. The leaves are 2 to 4 inches long, elliptical to lance-shaped, with prominently saw-toothed margins. *Prunus alleghaniensis* rarely has the spine-tipped twigs possessed by the more common wild plum. Profuse springtime blossoms develop into small plums, about ½ inch in diameter, which ripen in August. The reddish purple fruit often has a whitish bloom like that of blueberries and grapes. The sour, yellow flesh encloses a large stone. Bears, songbirds, and other wildlife—as well as human foragers—eat the fruit.

Taxonomists place the plums in the same genus as the cherries. The telltale bitter-almond odor of the broken twigs is present in the plums but is less intense than in cherries.

Kentucky Coffee-Tree *(Gymnocladus dioica)*. This native species is sometimes planted as an ornamental. Kentucky coffee-tree is found throughout Pennsylvania, with a concentration of specimens reported from the southern counties and particularly from the Philadelphia area. This 40- to 70-foot tree favors rich, moist soil of bottomlands. The species' range centers on the Midwest, including western Ohio, Indiana, Illinois, and Missouri, and extends into parts of its namesake state and several others. The genus name, *Gymnocladus,* means "naked branch" and refers to the fact that coffee-trees leaf out late in the spring and shed their foliage early in autumn, their branches remaining naked for more than half the year. Huge compound leaves, 1 to 3 feet long, alternate along the stems. The leaves are bipinnate, or twice-compound: the main stem of the leaf sends out multiple side stems, each bearing six to ten or more oval, 2-inch-long leaflets; thus the entire leaf may be composed of dozens of leaflets. This filigreed foliage yields a pleasant dappled shade, leading landscape designers and arborists to include *Gymnocladus dioica* in their plantings.

In autumn, from the naked limbs dangle broad, flat, leathery seedpods. The pods are 4 to 10 inches long and 1 to 2 inches wide; they contain six to nine large seeds in a sweetish pulp. The pods fall to the ground unopened. The raw seeds and the pulp are toxic. It is reported that high temperatures destroy the toxin, and the roasted seeds can be eaten or ground into a coffee substitute. The reddish wood is sometimes used for cabinetry.

Poison Sumac *(Toxicodendron vernix).* Usually 5 to 10 feet high, poison sumac sometimes becomes 20 feet tall, with an 8-inch trunk diameter. It generally branches near the ground into several stems. The compound leaves, 7 to 14 inches long, are made up of seven to thirteen oval, smooth-edged leaflets that are dark green and shiny above and paler on their undersides. All parts of this relatively uncommon plant contain a toxin that causes a skin rash and intense itching in humans; poison sumac, also known as poison oak, is said to be more virulent than its common relative poison ivy, *Toxicodendron radicans.*

Poison sumac grows in moist soil of floodplains, river islands, swamps, fens, and marshes, mainly east of the Mississippi River. It occurs throughout Pennsylvania.

Poison sumac flowers in June. The flowers develop into drooping clusters of white berries, each berry about 1/4 inch in diameter. The fruits ripen around August. Many species of birds eat the berries, particularly in winter when other foods are scarce.

Staghorn Sumac *(Rhus typhina).* Staghorn sumac ranges from Nova Scotia to Minnesota, and south to North Carolina and Tennessee. It often forms thickets in old fields, along roadsides and fencerows, and on stone piles. At maturity, it may stand 30 feet tall, with a trunk 8 inches in diameter; the largest specimens approach 40 feet and 15 inches in diameter. The

Staghorn sumac forms thickets in old fields, along roadsides and fencerows, and on stone piles. Female plants produce the cone-shaped, fuzzy fruiting heads.

plant comes by its name because its stout, widely forking twigs are cloaked with fuzzy hair, which makes them look like deer antlers in velvet; this trait is exhibited by one- to three-year-old twigs and is seen most easily when the leaves are off the plant in winter. The leaves are 16 to 24 inches long and compounded of eleven to thirty-one leaflets. Each leaflet is 2 to 5 inches in length, with toothed margins and a pointed tip. In summer, the leaves are a smooth, dark green, with silvery undersides. They turn a fiery orange-red in autumn.

The flowers appear in May or June: erect, greenish yellow cones 5 to 12 inches high, made up of multiple blossoms. Male and female flowers are separate, and only plants with female flowers produce fruit. The fruiting head, sometimes called a bob, is a furry cone. It is made up of hundreds of berries covered with sticky, scarlet hairs; each berry, or drupe, contains a small, hard seed. People have observed nearly a hundred species of birds eating the seeds. Some of the more prominent feeders are ruffed grouse, wild turkeys, bobwhite quail, crows, bluebirds, robins, catbirds, brown thrashers, and cardinals. Deer browse the stems and foliage, and cottontail rabbits eat sumac bark, especially in winter. If a rabbit girdles a stem, it may die, stimulating the plant's root system to send up new sprouts. During the Civil War, when the Federal navy's blockade of secessionist ports prevented the importation of foodstuffs, including citrus fruits, Southerners dipped red-colored sumac bobs in water and created a new drink: pink lemonade.

Smooth sumac *(Rhus glabra)* is much like staghorn sumac, except that its twigs and leafstalks lack hairs. It usually does not grow as large as staghorn sumac.

Mountain Maple *(Acer spicatum)*. Mountain maple grows in moist, rocky woods, often near mountain streams. Even more of a shrub than its close relative the striped maple, it usually arises as a clump of stems from a single root system. Mountain maple sometimes reaches a height of 35 feet, with a trunk 11 inches in diameter. It ranges from Newfoundland to Manitoba and south to Georgia in the Appalachians. *Acer spicatum* is found mainly in the mountainous parts of Pennsylvania and is rare or absent in the southeastern and northwestern counties.

The bark is dark or slightly greenish, and it lacks the vertical white markings of striped maple. The leaves have either three or five lobes, with coarse teeth around their edges. The Latin species name refers to the plant's spiky flower clusters. The fertilized flowers develop into paired, long-winged samaras typical for the maples. In the wild, deer and beavers browse the bark, and ruffed grouse eat the buds. In the far north, moose eat the bark; there the tree is known as moose maple. The leaves in autumn turn brilliant orange and scarlet. Arborists sometimes plant mountain maple on damp, shady sites.

Devil's-Walking-Stick *(Aralia spinosa)*. Also known as Hercules'-club, this shrub or small tree usually stands about 10 feet tall; rarely does it reach 20 feet. Its name derives from sharp-pointed prickles that liberally stud the twigs and trunk. The species occurs from southern New York to Florida, and west to Missouri and eastern Texas. It is scattered through much of Pennsylvania, with specimens recorded most frequently from the Allegheny Plateau in the western part of the state. The twice-compound or thrice-compound leaves are often 3 feet long and 2 feet wide: the largest leaves of any of our native trees. They are composed of numerous ovate leaflets 2 to 3 inches long, with saw-toothed margins. After leaf-fall, the stalks, or rachises, of the leaves litter the ground below.

Large clusters of creamy white flowers develop into oval black berries about 1/4 inch long; the thin-fleshed fruits hang on the limbs from fall into winter. Each fruit has one seed. Sparrows, thrushes, other birds, and some mammals are reported to eat the berries.

The preferred habitat for devil's-walking-stick is moist soil near streams in the understory of hardwood forests. I have found it growing on the edges of clear-cuts and in stands of gypsy-moth-killed oaks in dry, stony woods on central Pennsylvania mountains. In colonial times, people used the inner bark as a poultice to ease toothaches. During the Victorian period, in the mid to late 1800s, wealthy Americans planted *Aralia spinosa* to ornament the grounds around their rococo mansions—"the acme of ostentatious ugliness," opined Donald Culross Peattie in *A Natural History of Trees.*

Alternate-Leaved Dogwood *(Cornus alternifolia).* Alternate-leaved dogwood is the only type of dogwood to have an alternating, rather than opposing, placement of leaves on the twigs. Alternate-leaved dogwood is also called pigeonberry, blue dogwood, or pagoda dogwood. This shrubby tree—at most 30 feet tall, and usually much shorter—favors damp habitats such as wooded lowlands and shady ravines. Its small, cream-colored flowers bloom in clusters in late May and early June. By late summer, the flowers have developed into blue-black fruits eaten by many birds.

Cornus alternifolia ranges from Newfoundland to Alabama and west to Minnesota and Arkansas. Although statewide in Pennsylvania, alternate-leaved dogwood is not nearly as common as flowering dogwood. So far, it has shown good resistance to the fungal disease known as dogwood anthracnose.

Sourwood *(Oxydendrum arboreum).* The foliage of this primarily southern tree is acidic and sour-tasting. The mature tree may become 50 to 60 feet tall and have a trunk 20 inches in diameter, but a more usual size is 25 feet with a trunk about 8 inches across. On older trees, the brown or gray bark is deeply fissured into narrow, scaly ridges. The oval leaves are a glossy yellow-green and 4 to 7 inches in length; they have finely toothed edges and resemble peach leaves. In summer, white, bell-shaped flowers stand upright on stalks; the flowers look like those of the ground-dwelling plant lily-of-the-valley. They develop into seed-filled capsules.

A small area in the southwest corner of Pennsylvania represents the northernmost extension of the sourwood's range. The tree grows on moist soils of valleys and uplands. It is esteemed as an ornamental because of its late flowering (July and August in Pennsylvania), its conical or rounded crown, and its foliage, which turns scarlet, orange, or crimson in autumn. Honeybees make honey from the nectar of sourwood flowers; its taste is celebrated in the South. According to Joseph Illick in *Pennsylvania Trees,* the hard, heavy wood was once fashioned into tool handles and the runners of sleds used for hauling bark employed in the leather-tanning industry.

Fringetree *(Chionanthus virginicus).* With a range centered on the southern coastal states, fringetree just reaches north into southern Pennsylvania, New Jersey, West Virginia, and Ohio. It grows in moist soils along streams and lakes and in valleys and floodplains, sometimes reaching a height of 40 feet. In Pennsylvania, 20 feet is usually the maximum height for this rare species. The trunk diameter is 6 to 8 inches; the brown bark is clad with reddish-tinged scales. The leaves stand in pairs, opposite each other on the twigs, as do maples' leaves. They are 4 to 8 inches long and 1 to 4 inches wide, with untoothed edges. Drooping, white flowers appear in May; in their great abundance, they resemble fringe, earning the tree its name, as well as another moniker, old-man's-beard. The flowers develop into dark blue or blackish fruits that hang, grapelike, clustered at the ends of long stems. Fringetree is sometimes planted as an ornamental.

COMMON
INTRODUCED
TREES

The following trees are not native to Pennsylvania and the Northeast but have been planted widely in the state and region. Some are North American in origin; others were brought in from as far away as China. Individuals of most species have escaped from cultivation and become mingled with the native trees of our farmland and forests.

Blue Spruce *(Picea pungens).* It is ironic that *Picea pungens,* also called Colorado blue spruce, is more familiar to most Pennsylvanians than our two native spruces, black spruce and red spruce. Even the popular booklet *Common Trees of Pennsylvania,* distributed by the state Bureau of Forestry, has listings for Colorado blue spruce and Norway spruce but none for the native species.

Blue spruce, a native of the Rocky Mountains, is a slow-growing tree widely planted in yards, campuses, towns, and cemeteries. You can also find blue spruce on commercial Christmas tree farms and in groves on watershed holdings and public lands such as state game and state forest lands. Blue spruce is pyramidal in form, with stout, horizontal branches cloaking the tree from ground level to the topmost growing whorl. The tree's stiff, spiny needles are about 1 1/4 inch long. They range in color from a frosty blue-green to a pale yellowish green and persist on the twigs for as many as ten years. The 4-inch chestnut brown cones are larger than those of our native spruces. Mature blue spruces typically reach 50 to 80 feet in height, with some soaring to 150 feet.

On our thirty acres, blue spruce is the only conifer I have planted that the deer haven't browsed back to oblivion; maybe they avoid the prickly needles. The trees provide nesting habitat for songbirds, especially chipping sparrows. Many other birds roost and find winter shelter in the dense foliage.

Norway Spruce *(Picea abies).* With its branches ending in long, pendulous branchlets cloaked with soft-looking needles, this tall tree looks like it is wearing a thick, green robe. Norway spruce grows 50 to 80 feet tall, with a trunk 2 feet in diameter. Very old trees can reach 125 feet in height and 3 feet in diameter. A native of northern Europe, *Picea abies* is an important tree in the forests of Germany, Switzerland, Austria, and Russia. People have planted it as an ornamental and a forest tree throughout the northeastern United States.

You can find Norway spruce anywhere from the deep woods to the "his and her" trees traditionally planted on either side of a farmhouse entry, and ultimately dwarfing the dwelling. By 1925, as part of the effort to reforest Pennsylvania following extensive logging in the nineteenth and early twen-

tieth centuries, the Department of
Forests and Waters, the predeces-
sor of the Bureau of Forestry, had
planted more than five million Norway spruce seedlings on state land.
Many of those trees still stand.

   The trunk of Norway spruce
is straight; the tree has a pyramidal
form. The evergreen needles are 1/2
to 1 inch long, stiff, and a shiny, dark
green. The tree produces 4- to 6-
inch cones, the largest of any spruce.
Lower branches sweep down to near
the ground. The central Pennsylvania
naturalist Marcia Bonta planted two
thousand Norway spruce on her

*Black-capped chickadees and other birds
feed on Norway spruce seeds, which are
borne in large, dangling cones.*

Blair County farm in the mid-1970s. She has recorded scores of native birds
using the groves for nesting, feeding, and sheltering from harsh winter
weather. They include mourning doves, crows, blue jays, tufted titmice, dark-
eyed juncos, ruffed grouse, northern goshawks, and barred and long-eared
owls. In winter, red and white-winged crossbills extract and eat seeds from
Norway spruce cones. Porcupines feed on the bark and needles.

White Spruce *(Picea glauca).* The huge natural range of white spruce spans
Canada, from Newfoundland to the Yukon; it dips into the United States
in northern New England and the Great Lakes and Northern Plains states;
white spruce is also common across Alaska. Along with black spruce and
tamarack, white spruce marches to the northern limit of tree growth on the
continent. In Pennsylvania, state agencies have planted *Picea glauca* in scattered upland sites as a wood-producing forest species and to provide food
and cover for wildlife.

   Unlike the branchlets of Norway spruce, those of white spruce do not
droop; the tree's many tiers of horizontal branches ascend to a conical
crown, where shorter branches angle upward. Mature trees are 50 to 60 feet
tall. The blue-green needles of this evergreen are 3/8 to 3/4 inch long; they
release a skunklike odor when crushed. The cylindrical cones are 1 to 2
inches long, tan, and shiny; they drop soon after ripening and releasing
seeds. The brown seeds are paired and have long wings. Various species of
birds eat the seeds. Deer, snowshoe hares, and grouse feed on the foliage.

Native Americans used the pliable rootlets of white spruce to make baskets and sew together the skins of bark canoes. Today white spruce is Canada's most valuable lumber tree. It is logged extensively for pulpwood and general construction lumber. The highly resonant wood is used for piano sounding-boards, violins, and other musical instruments.

Austrian Pine *(Pinus nigra).* Austrian pine carries its stiff, 3- to 6-inch-long needles in bundles of two. The tree develops a straight trunk; dense, dark green foliage; and a conical shape. The bark is dark gray to yellowish, rough, and broken into irregular scaly plates. At maturity, the tree reaches 50 to 100 feet tall. The egg-shaped cones are yellow-brown and 2 to 3 inches long. A fast-growing species, Austrian pine tolerates pollution and drought. People have planted it in cities, in shelterbelts, and to form dense visual screens. It occurs naturally in Europe, Asia Minor, and northern Africa.

Scots Pine *(Pinus sylvestris).* A native of Eurasia, including the Highlands of Scotland, *Pinus sylvestris* has been planted widely in northeastern North America by state forestry and game commissions, Christmas tree growers, farmers, city parks, and water companies and other entities wanting to reforest watersheds or restore mined lands. If Scots pine gets the ample sunlight it requires, it will grow in a wide range of soil and moisture conditions. Trees can reach 70 feet or higher, but most, especially on poorer sites, become about 50 feet tall. The hard wood is used for lumber and paper pulp. Botanists believe Scots pine is the most widely spread pine species in the world.

The evergreen needles are 2 to 3 inches long, stout, sharp-pointed, and twisted. They come two to a bundle. From a distance, Scots pine can look like pitch pine; a good way to identify *Pinus sylvestris* is from its upper trunk and adjoining branches, whose smooth bark is an eye-catching orange color. Also, pitch pine needles are bundled in threes.

The egg-shaped cones of Scots pine are $1^1/4$ to $2^1/2$ inches long. The $1/4$-inch seeds come attached to a broad, $1/2$-inch wing. A neighbor of mine had a Christmas tree plantation with many Scots pines. After they were cut, most of the trees resprouted from lower whorls of branches left on the stump, creating thick winter cover for deer and wild turkeys; ice storms and heavy, wet snow broke the tops and limbs out of many of the regrown specimens.

Weeping Willow *(Salix babylonica).* Despite its Latin species name, China is the country of origin for *Salix babylonica;* when taxonomists first classified it, they confused this tree with a poplar from the Euphrates River region in the Middle East. Today the species ranges from southern Canada south to Georgia, and west to Missouri. In Pennsylvania, weeping willow is found mainly in the southern part of the state.

The trunk is short, dividing into many branches that arch upward, then cascade gracefully down; overall, the tree is about 70 feet tall. The finely saw-toothed, blade-shaped leaves are 2 to 5 inches long and 1/4 to 1/2 inch broad. They attach to thin, flexible, yellowish or brown branches and twigs that, drooping, seem to "weep" toward the ground. Weeping willow is one of the first deciduous trees to put out foliage in spring and one of the last to shed its leaves in autumn. Greenish female flowers light up the tree in early spring. People have planted weeping willows on farmsteads; in meadows, cemeteries, and parks; and on the banks of lakes and ponds.

Other naturalized willows include white willow *(Salix alba)* a wetlands species from Europe brought to North America as early as the colonial era; and crack willow *(Salix fragilis)* so named because its brittle twigs break off easily at the base. Settlers introduced crack willow to produce charcoal for the manufacturing of gunpowder; it escaped from cultivation and is now common along streams in parts of the Northeast.

European Alder *(Alnus glutinosa)*. The European or black alder is a native of Europe, North Africa, and Asia that has been planted widely in Canada and the northeastern United States. The Latin species name refers to the glutinous, or gummy, feel of the young twigs. European alders thrive along streams and in wetlands. *Alnus glutinosa* is more upright and treelike than our two native alder species, growing to 30 feet tall. The serrated, usually double-toothed leaves are blunt-ended, and the female cones are 5/8 to 7/8 inch long, twice as large as those of our native alders. People have planted European alder as a shade tree and an ornamental since colonial times.

A shrub, common winterberry holly *(Ilex verticillata),* is sometimes called black alder; it is unrelated to European alder and our native *Alnus* species.

White Mulberry *(Morus alba)*. White mulberry is a Chinese tree originally imported to provide food for silkworms. The silk industry never got off the ground in the United States, but white mulberry escaped cultivation and is now a fairly common tree, growing in fencerows and disturbed areas, more abundant in many places than the native red mulberry, *Morus rubra.*

White mulberry is a slightly smaller tree than red mulberry and has yellow-brown bark, as opposed to the red-tinged brownish bark of *Morus rubra.* Its toothed leaves are hairless and smooth, not sandpapery; like those of red mulberry, they are variable in shape. The fruits of the Asian import—whitish to pink, and occasionally purple—ripen in June. They make good preserves and are excellent dried and added to breads and muffins. Like red mulberries, they also feed many wild birds and mammals. Despite such excellent qualities, I have heard more people complain about mulberries than extol them, since the fallen fruits stain sidewalks, clothing, and cars.

Osage-Orange *(Maclura pomifera)*. From a limited range in Texas, Oklahoma, and Arkansas, this small to medium-size tree has been transplanted throughout North America east of the Rocky Mountains. Its name stems from its place of origin, the area where the Osage Indians dwelt, and from its fruit, a yellow-green sphere like a lumpy, oversize orange. The tree usually becomes about 30 feet tall, with a trunk 1 to 2 feet in diameter. It thrives in fertile soil along streams but will also grow on drier upland sites. The leaves are around 4 inches long, oval, and have a pointed tip. Their upper surfaces are glossy green. In the past, farmers planted osage-orange trees to create hedgerows: inch-long thorns on the plants helped make barriers to keep animals in fields. Some authorities estimate that more than a quarter million miles of osage-orange hedgerows were planted in the 1800s, before the invention of barbed wire fencing.

The surface of an osage-orange fruit is made up of many small drupes, each containing a seed. The fruit can be 5 inches in diameter.

Trees are either male or female. Inconspicuous greenish flowers blossom around June. The wind-pollinated female flowers become the wrinkly oranges, 4 or 5 inches in diameter and with a faint citrus smell. The hard, stippled surface of an osage-orange is made up of many small drupes (a drupe is any fruit with a fleshy part surrounding a single seed) compacted together. Too heavy to be wind-blown, and not especially attractive as wildlife food, the seeds are probably scattered by periodic flooding of the rivers along which the trees grow in their native habitat. Old osage-orange hedgerows offer escape cover to many birds and mammals.

The yellow to orangish wood is hard and dense and a good stove fuel. Because it is flexible as well as strong, Native Americans used osage-orange wood for making bows and war clubs. People have fashioned it into fence posts and railroad ties, duck and goose calls, harps, policemen's nightsticks, and wagon wheels. Osage-orange grows readily from seeds and root cuttings. Look for it in abandoned farmland and along roadsides.

Apple *(Malus sylvestris)*. I know of many old apple trees, survivors of orchards on the brushy, deserted farms scattered through the valley where I live. I visit them in May in search of morels, delicious mushrooms that often spring up near the trunks of the trees: the fungi producing the mushrooms form a symbiotic relationship with the roots of apple trees. In autumn, I hunt for ruffed grouse that feed on fallen apples dotting the ground beneath the trees; sometimes I find a worm-free apple and eat it myself, and marvel at the tang of some long-forgotten variety grafted onto the tree by a farmer in his grave these many years. In winter, I like the silhouettes of apple trees, bent and crooked, with hulking trunks, their crowns dense with branches and twigs offering resting and hiding places to birds.

Malus sylvestris has a short, rugged trunk covered with scaly, gray bark; the trunk divides into many stout branches that hold up a rounded crown. The oval leaves are 2 to 3 1/2 inches long, their wavy edges saw-toothed. The pretty, pink-white flowers have five rounded petals; they blossom in May, perfuming the air and attracting nectar-gathering bees that effect pollination. The familiar fruits, usually red or yellow, ripen in late summer and early fall. The fruits are plentiful in some years, scarce or absent in others. Deer, bears, coyotes, foxes, raccoons, opossums, porcupines, woodchucks, ring-necked pheasants, crows, woodpeckers, blue jays, finches, sapsuckers, robins, thrushes—it is almost easier to list the wild creatures that do not eat apples than the ones that do eat them. Ruffed grouse nip off the energy-packed buds, and cottontail rabbits gnaw the bark; deer browse twigs and foliage. In spring and summer, many songbirds nest in the boughs. If you own land with apple trees, consider cutting down any taller trees nearby that cast shade on, and suppress, the apples.

Malus sylvestris is a European import. Apple trees came across the Atlantic with the first settlers and followed them west across North America. In some states, it was necessary for a settler to plant a certain number of apple trees before he could gain title to his land. John Chapman, known as Johnny Appleseed, was an itinerant preacher in the early 1800s who gave

*Old apple trees often break down and fall apart; where their branches touch
the ground, they may send down roots that give rise to new trees.*

out apple seeds to souls he met in the frontier states of Ohio, Illinois, and
Indiana. He also planted many seeds himself, creating small orchards wherever he went.

Apple wood makes an excellent fuel; it burns hot and gives off colorful
flames and a sweet smell. People have used the tough wood for tool handles, spoons, early machine parts (cogs, wheels, and gears), and paneling.
Old apple trees sometimes resurrect themselves: the trunk, which can be up
to 3 feet thick on a venerable tree, splits apart, and the broken tree falls to
the ground—only to have its living branches, in contact with the soil, send
down roots and produce a new trunk.

Sweet Cherry *(Prunus avium)*. The domestic sweet cherry is native to Eurasia. It grows in forests, woods edges, and fencerows in Pennsylvania, mainly
east of the Allegheny Mountains. The species name, *avium*, means "of
birds" and reflects the fruit's importance as a food for wildlife. Many sweet
cherries have been planted through the agency of bird droppings. The
mature tree can become 70 feet tall, with a wide-spreading crown of gray
branches. The leaves are 3 to 6 inches long, oval, and end in a pointed tip;
coarse teeth line their margins. The red to purplish cherries are 3/4 to 1
inch in diameter, or about twice the size of the native black cherry.

The prettiest paneling I've ever seen—a rich, fiery red, with orange and
mahogany highlights and a swirling grain pattern—came from a sweet
cherry tree.

Ailanthus *(Ailanthus altissima)*. People have planted ailanthus as an ornamental, a shelterbelt tree, and a source for paper pulp. Considered the starling of introduced trees, this fast-growing Asian import has crowded out many native plants. Also known as tree of heaven, although some dub it "tree from hell," ailanthus can reach a height of 80 feet; more often, it is a short, low-forking, several-stemmed tree with an open, rounded crown. Its form resembles that of staghorn and smooth sumac. Storms often break the brittle branches. The branches are few, since the tree relies on large, compound leaves for spreading out its light-gathering foliage. They are 1 to 2 feet long and composed of a central stem with thirteen to twenty-five or more leaflets proceeding in pairs down the stem, with a single leaflet at the tip. Each leaflet is lance-shaped, with a few large teeth toward the base. The crushed foliage and the male flowers emit a funky, disagreeable smell.

Ailanthus produces copious winged seeds that the wind blows about. The plant colonizes many habitats: old fields, forest clearings, roadsides, abandoned factory lots, railroad yards. A seed can send down roots through a crack in a concrete sidewalk or asphalt parking lot, or a fracture in the rock face of a highway roadcut. Individual trees also spread by sending up shoots from the root system. In cities and suburbs, the roots clog drains and get into wells. Botanists strongly discourage the planting of this species; in some places, workers have begun cutting down ailanthus and applying herbicide to the stumps in an effort to stop the spread of this undesirable alien.

Norway Maple *(Acer platanoides)*. In Europe, *Acer platanoides* ranges from Norway to northern Turkey. Introduced to America as a shade tree, Norway maple has spread far and wide, its winged seeds carried by the wind. Mature trees are 50 to 60 feet tall, with a 2-foot-diameter trunk. The leaves are big and broad, up to 8 inches across. They have the classic maple shape, with five coarsely toothed lobes, and turn bright yellow in autumn. The leafstalks, when broken, exude a milky sap. Because it tolerates pollution better than sugar maple does, Norway maple has been planted extensively along city streets and in urban parks. In the wild, look for it along roadsides and in disturbed woods. Norway maple leaves cast a full, deep shade that inhibits native plant regeneration.

Horse-Chestnut *(Aesculus hippocastanum)*. The Eurasian horse-chestnut has been planted as a shade tree in the northeastern United States for many years. Henry Wadsworth Longfellow was probably referring to this tree, and not the American chestnut, *Castanea dentata,* a native forest species, when he wrote in his oft-quoted poem, "Under the spreading chestnut tree, the village smithy stands." It is said that horsemen in Turkey used the seeds of this plant to brew a remedy given to horses afflicted with coughing, a practice commemorated in the tree's common name and the Latin species name.

According to Ann Fowler Rhoads and Timothy Block, in *The Plants of Pennsylvania,* horse-chestnut is "cultivated and occasionally escaped to railroad banks or waste ground." Easily propagated from seeds, it tolerates polluted city conditions. As a boy, I found horse-chestnut seeds beneath trees on Penn State University's golf course. The smooth, mahogany brown kernels were somewhat irregular in shape, with an intriguing tan eyespot; they became ever more polished riding around in my pants pockets.

Horse-chestnut trees grow 60 to 75 feet tall. Each large, compound leaf is made up of a whorl of seven to nine broad, wedge-shaped leaflets. White flowers appear in late May, weeks after those of the closely related Ohio buckeye and yellow buckeye, which are Pennsylvania natives. Horse-chestnut flowers are grouped in showy, candelabralike clusters 6 to 12 inches long. The seeds develop inside leathery, thorn-studded, walnut-size husks. I remember my botanist father informing me that those handsome seeds that I carried around, and rubbed and polished so assiduously, were poisonous. Symptoms include depression, vomiting, weakness, stupor, and paralysis. The nuts have killed children who have eaten them. All parts of the plant are toxic.

Catalpas (*Catalpa* species). Last summer, I spent several puzzled minutes looking at a tree in the woods at Pine Ridge Natural Area, Bedford County. It had heart-shaped leaves almost as big as my hand; a broad, spreading crown; and scaly, brown bark. On the ground, I spotted a last year's fruit: a long, brown pod, cylindrical and tapering to a point at both ends. I knew then that the tree was not a native species, but a catalpa, probably planted seventy or more years earlier, when Pine Ridge was farming country, before the Depression years when the federal government bought the impoverished farms and relocated the families on better land elsewhere.

Southern catalpa *(Catalpa bignonoides)* has a small natural range centered on Mississippi, Alabama, Georgia, and northern Florida. Widely planted as an ornamental, it is hardy enough to survive as far north as New England. Catalpa grows fast. The tree does best on shady sites with moist, fertile soil. In summer, the big leaves—5 to 7 inches long and 4 to 7 inches wide—cast a deep, cooling shade. In June, catalpas put out 10-inch mounds of white flowers with frilly, outspread petals. Pollinated flowers become the dangling, spindle-shaped pods, 6 to 20 inches long. The pods open in autumn, releasing flat, winged seeds; empty, the husks remain attached to the tree, rustling in the winter wind.

Catalpa wood weighs only 26 pounds per cubic foot, dry weight. Although extremely light, it is durable in contact with the soil and has been used for fence posts, telegraph poles, and railroad ties. The name catalpa comes from the Creek Indian language and means "head with wings"; it describes the flower petals with their ruffled lobes.

A second catalpa species, northern catalpa *(Catalpa speciosa),* occurs in and near the Mississippi River valley from Illinois to Arkansas. It, too, has been widely planted outside of its original range.

BIBLIOGRAPHY

Bolgiano, Chris. *The Appalachian Forest.* Mechanicsburg, PA: Stackpole Books, 1998.

Borland, Hal. *A Countryman's Woods.* New York: Alfred A. Knopf, 1986.

Burns, Russell M. and Barbara H. Honkala, coordinators. *Silvics of North America.* Washington, D.C.: U.S. Department of Agriculture, Forest Service, 1990.

Davis, Mary Bird, ed. *Eastern Old-Growth Forests.* Washington, D.C.: Island Press, 1996.

Eastman, John. *The Book of Forest and Thicket.* Mechanicsburg, PA: Stackpole Books, 1992.

―――. *The Book of Swamp and Bog.* Mechanicsburg, PA: Stackpole Books, 1995.

Fergus, Charles. *Natural Pennsylvania: Exploring the State Forest Natural Areas.* Mechanicsburg, PA: Stackpole Books, 2002.

Fike, Jean. *Terrestrial and Palustrine Plant Communities of Pennsylvania.* Harrisburg, PA: Pennsylvania Department of Conservation and Natural Resources, 1999.

Forestry Branch, Canada Department of Northern Affairs and National Resources. *Native Trees of Canada.* Ottawa: Forestry Branch, Canada Department of Northern Affairs and National Resources, 1956.

Fox, William F. *The Adirondack Black Spruce.* Albany, NY: New York State Forest Commission, 1895.

Gibbons, Euell. *Stalking the Wild Asparagus.* New York: David McKay, 1971.

Heinrich, Bernd. *The Trees in My Forest.* New York: Cliff Street Books, 1997.

Illick, Joseph S. *Pennsylvania Trees.* Harrisburg, PA: Pennsylvania Department of Forests and Waters, 1928.

Kricher, John C. *A Field Guide to Eastern Forests of North America.* Boston: Houghton Mifflin, 1998.

Lembke, Janet. *Shake Them 'Simmons Down*. New York: Lyons & Burford, 1996.

Li, Hui-lin. *Trees of Pennsylvania, the Atlantic States and the Lakes States*. Philadelphia: University of Pennsylvania Press, 1972.

Lillard, Richard G. *The Great Forest*. New York: Alfred A. Knopf, 1947.

Little, Charles E. *The Dying of the Trees*. New York: Viking Penguin, 1995.

Little, Elbert L. Jr. *Atlas of United States Trees*. Washington, D.C.: U.S. Department of Agriculture, 1971.

―――. *The Audubon Field Guide to North American Trees (Eastern Region)*. New York: Alfred A. Knopf, 1980.

McPhee, John. *Survival of the Bark Canoe*. New York: Farrar, Straus & Giroux, 1975.

Peattie, Donald Culross. *A Natural History of Trees of Eastern and Central North America*. Boston: Houghton Mifflin, 1966.

Petrides, George A. *A Field Guide to Eastern Trees*. Boston: Houghton Mifflin, 1998.

Platt, Rutherford H. *Discover American Trees*. New York: Dodd Mead, 1968.

Rhoads, Ann Fowler and Timothy A. Block. *The Plants of Pennsylvania*. Philadelphia: University of Pennsylvania Press, 2000.

Rhoads, Ann Fowler and William McKinley Klein Jr. *The Vascular Flora of Pennsylvania*. Philadelphia: American Philosophical Society, 1993.

Sloane, Eric. *A Reverence for Wood*. New York: Funk and Wagnalls, 1965.

Smith, Ned. *Gone for the Day*. Harrisburg, PA: Pennsylvania Game Commission, 1971.

Weidensaul, Scott. *Mountains of the Heart: A Natural History of the Appalachians*. Golden, CO: Fulcrum Publishing, 1994.

Wertz, Halfred W. and M. Joy Callender. *Penn's Woods*. Wayne, PA: Haverford House, 1981.

White, J. H. *Forest Trees of Ontario*. Toronto: Ontario Department of Lands and Forests, 1925.

Yahner, Richard H. *Eastern Deciduous Forest*. Minneapolis: University of Minnesota Press, 2000.

Request the free sixty-six page booklet *Common Trees of Pennsylvania* from the Bureau of Forestry, Pennsylvania Department of Conservation and Natural Resources, P.O. Box 8552, Harrisburg, PA 17105-8552.

GLOSSARY

Achene. A small, hard, dry, often seedlike fruit.

Bisexual. A flower that has both male and female sexual organs; also referred to as perfect.

Blade. The green, light-gathering portion of a leaf, apart from the stalk.

Bract. A leaflike structure located just below a flower, fruit, or stalk.

Bud. A small bump on a stem or branch, usually covered with protective scales and containing an undeveloped leaf or flower, or both.

Cambium. A layer of tissue, one cell thick, between the bark and the wood; through cell division, it produces phloem to the outside and xylem to the inside, increasing the diameter of a tree's trunk.

Catkin. A spike-shaped reproductive structure supporting flowers which are all of the same sex.

Compound leaf. A leaf made up of two or more similar leaflets attached to a stalk.

Crown. The upper mass of limbs and branches in a tree.

Deciduous. Falling off, usually at the close of a season.

Drupe. A fruit whose flesh covers a hard pit or stone, which in turn houses a seed.

Habitat. The home of an animal or plant.

Heartwood. Woody tissue of the interior of the trunk, dead and no longer involved in transferring water; it is usually darker than the sapwood.

Lanceolate. Shaped like the head of a lance, tapering from a rounded base toward the tip.

Leaflet. One of the small blades that makes up a compound leaf.

Lenticel. A pore in the bark of trunk or limb that allows an exchange of gases between interior wood tissues and the atmosphere.

Lobe. A segment of a leaf separated from other similar parts by a notch or cleft.

Midrib. The central, main rib or vein of a leaf or leaflet.

Nut. A hard, dry, single-seeded fruit with a stiff, sometimes thick covering.

Ovate. Egg-shaped.

Panicle. A compound flower cluster.

Petiole. The leafstalk.

Phloem. Food-conducting tissue; carries sugars throughout the tree. As it ages, it becomes part of the bark.

Pith. The soft, spongy tissue inside a twig.

Pollen. Dustlike substance released by a male flower, carrying genetic material and capable of fertilizing a female flower.

Pome. A fleshy fruit with an inner, seed-bearing core; for example, an apple.

Raceme. A collection of stalked flowers arranged singly on a stem.

Rachis. The elongated central stem of a compound leaf.

Radicle. The part of a plant embryo that develops into a root.

Samara. A winged fruit; also called a key.

Sapwood. The newly formed, light-colored wood lying outside the heartwood; it carries water up from the roots to the leaves. Also called xylem.

Simple leaf. A leaf that is not compound and has a central midrib attached to the blade.

Sinus. The cleft or notch between two lobes of a leaf.

Stamen. The pollen-bearing part of a flower.

Sterigmata. Projections from twigs that bear the leaves or needles.

Strobile. A fruit sheathed with overlapping scales, such as the cones and conelets borne by pines, hemlocks, birches, and other trees.

Taproot. A strong, vertical, central root that anchors the tree in the ground.

Umbel. A flower cluster in which all the stalks arise from the same point.

Xylem. Sapwood.

INDEX OF
SCIENTIFIC NAMES

INDEX OF
COMMON NAMES